SERGIO ARAGONES

MAD

AS USUAL!

D1552936

WARNER BOOKS

A Warner Communications Company

WARNER BOOKS EDITION

For information address:
E.C. Publications, Inc.
485 Madison Avenue
New York, NY 10022

This Warner Books Edition is published by
arrangement with E.C. Publications, Inc.

Warner Books, Inc.
666 Fifth Avenue
New York, NY 10103

A Warner Communications Company

Printed in the United States of America

First Printing: May, 1990

10 9 8 7 6 5 4 3 2 1

TO THE USUAL GANG OF IDIOTS!

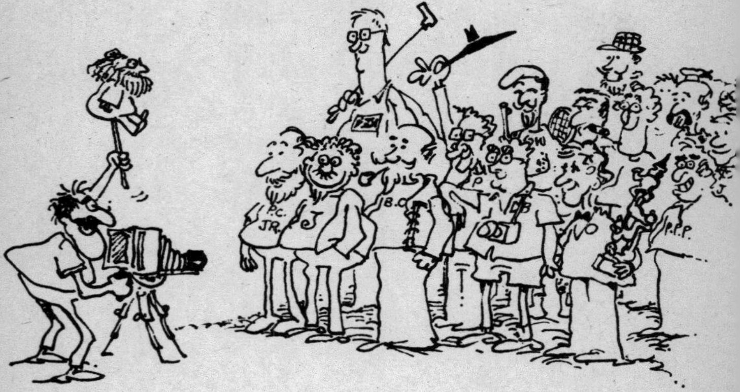
P.C.
JR.
J
P.P.P.

1

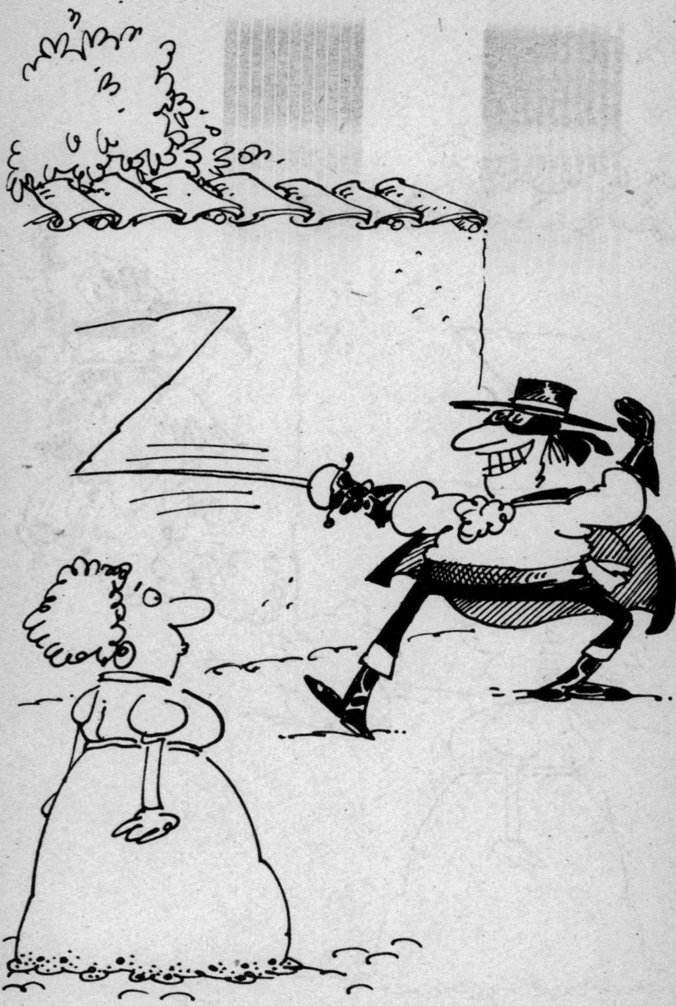

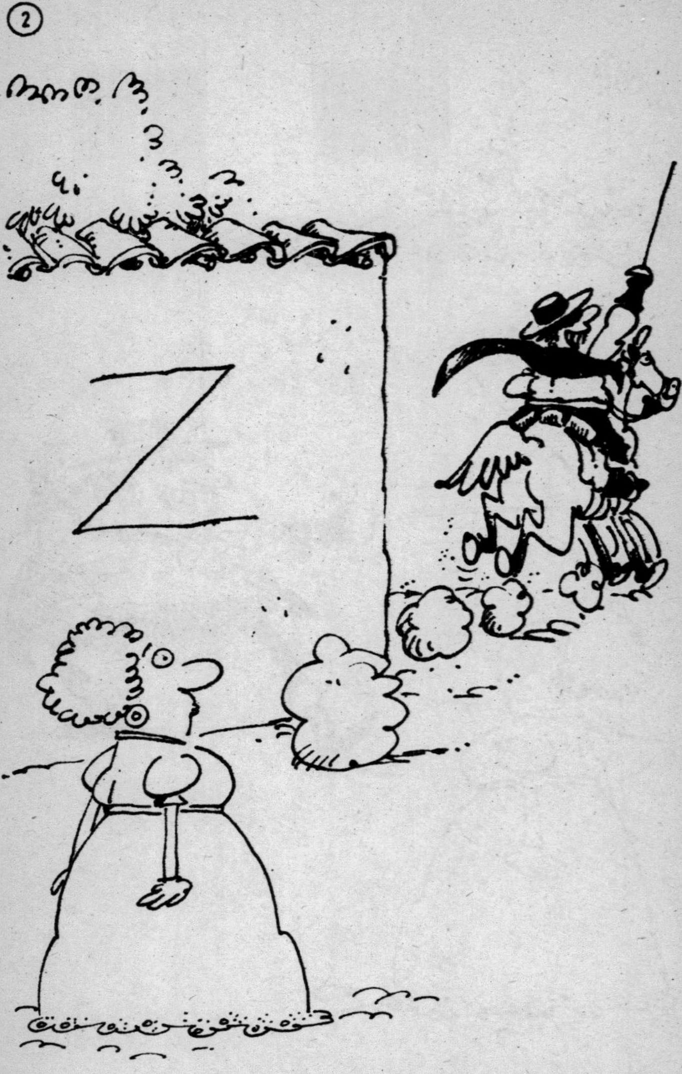
Z

3

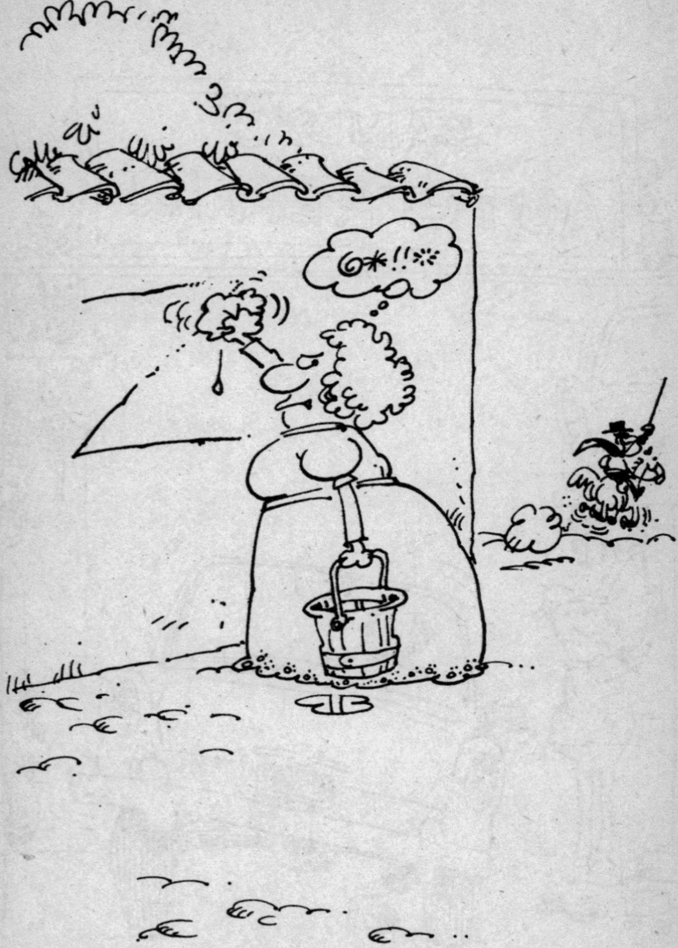

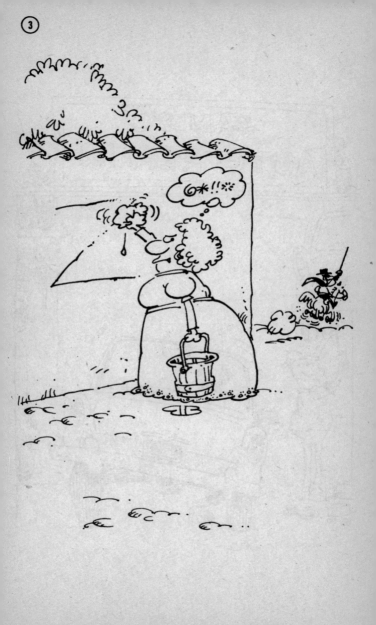

①

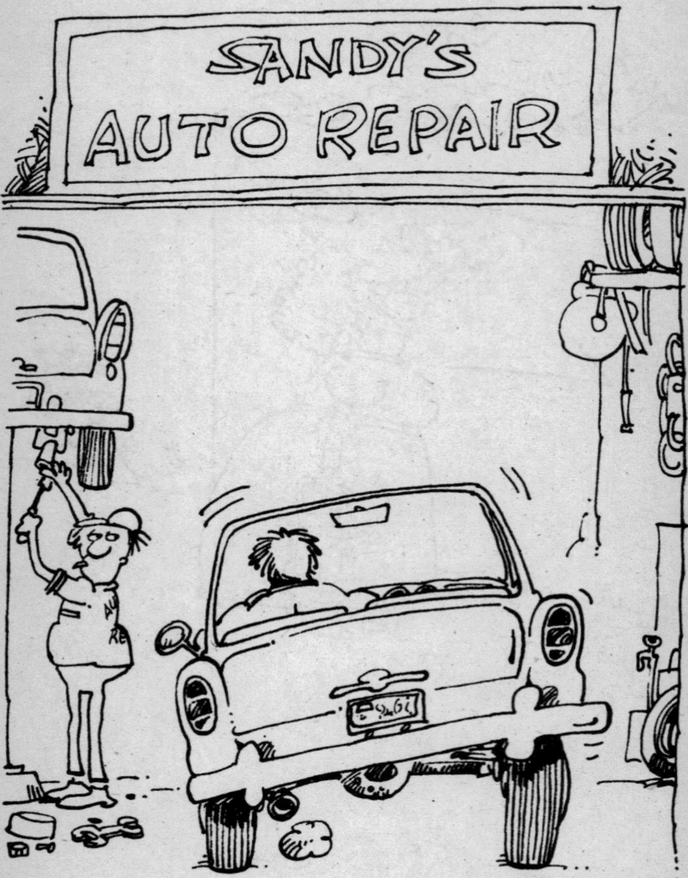
SANDY'S
AUTO REPAIR

2

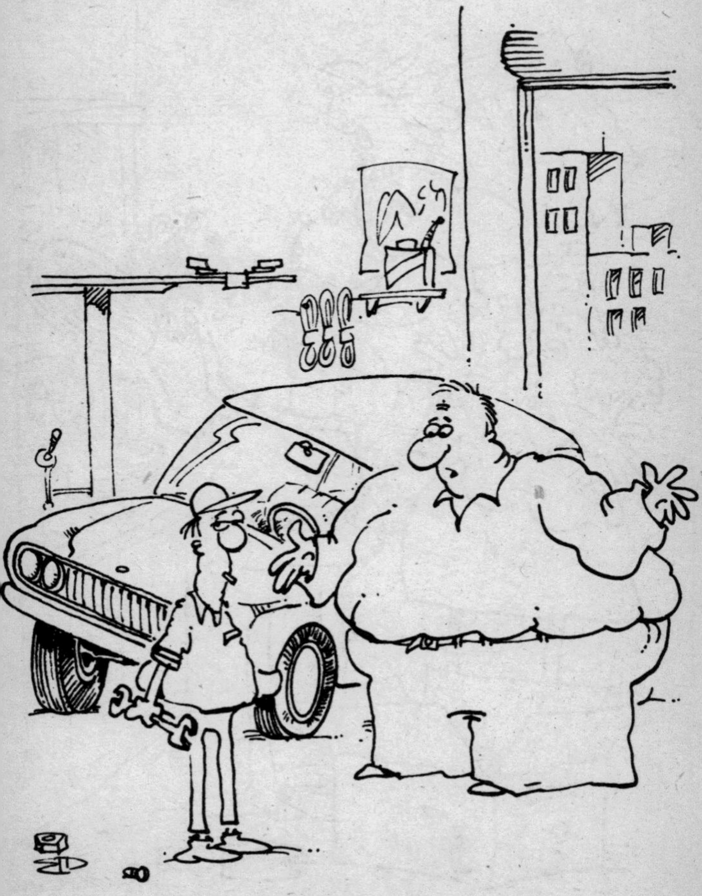

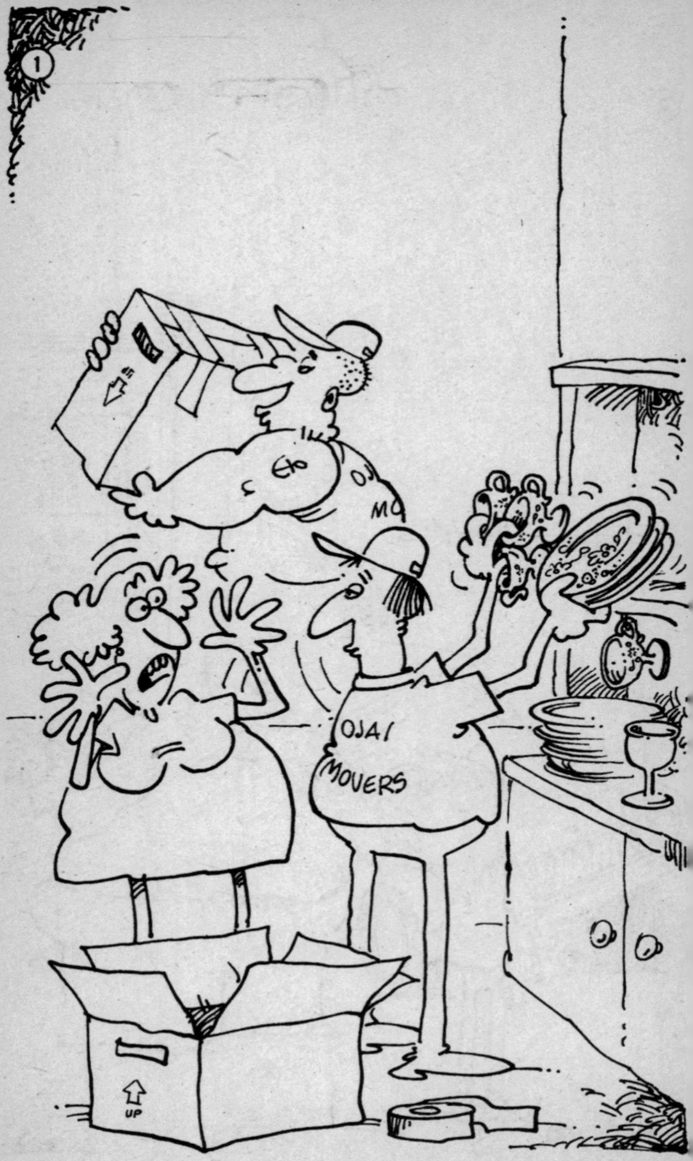
1
OJAI
MOVERS
UP

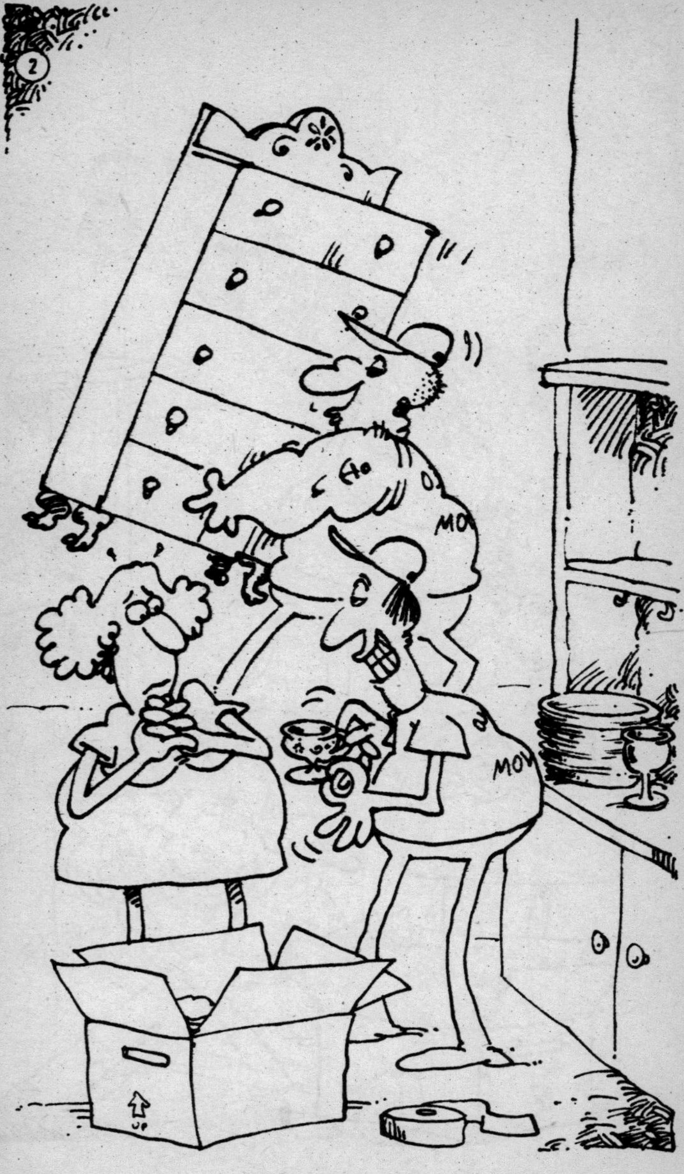
2
MOV
MOV

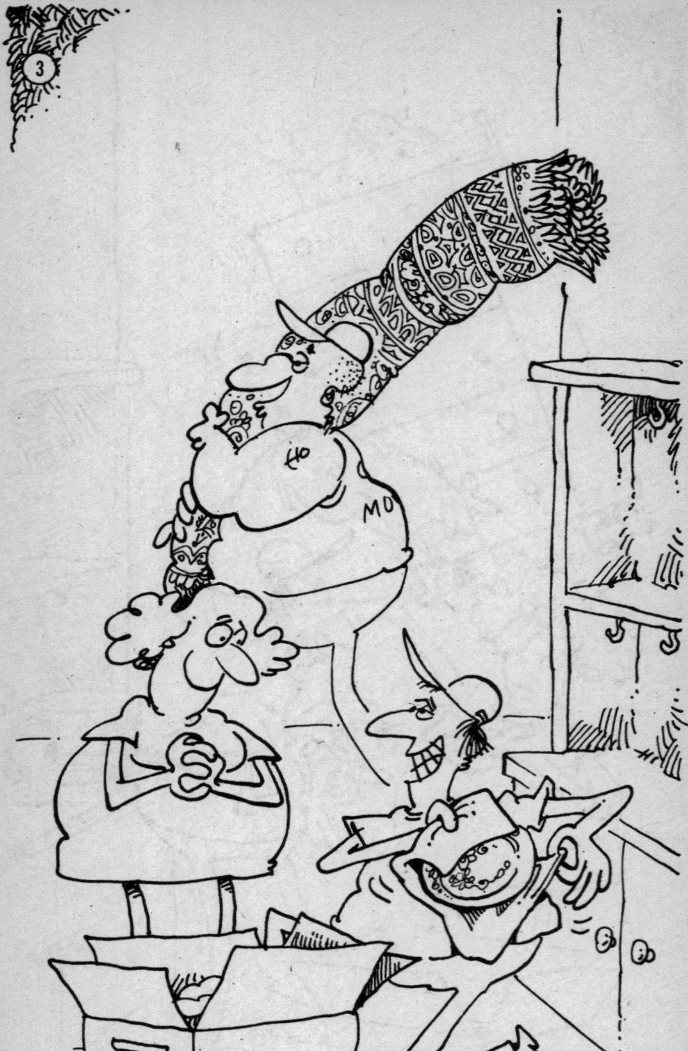
MO

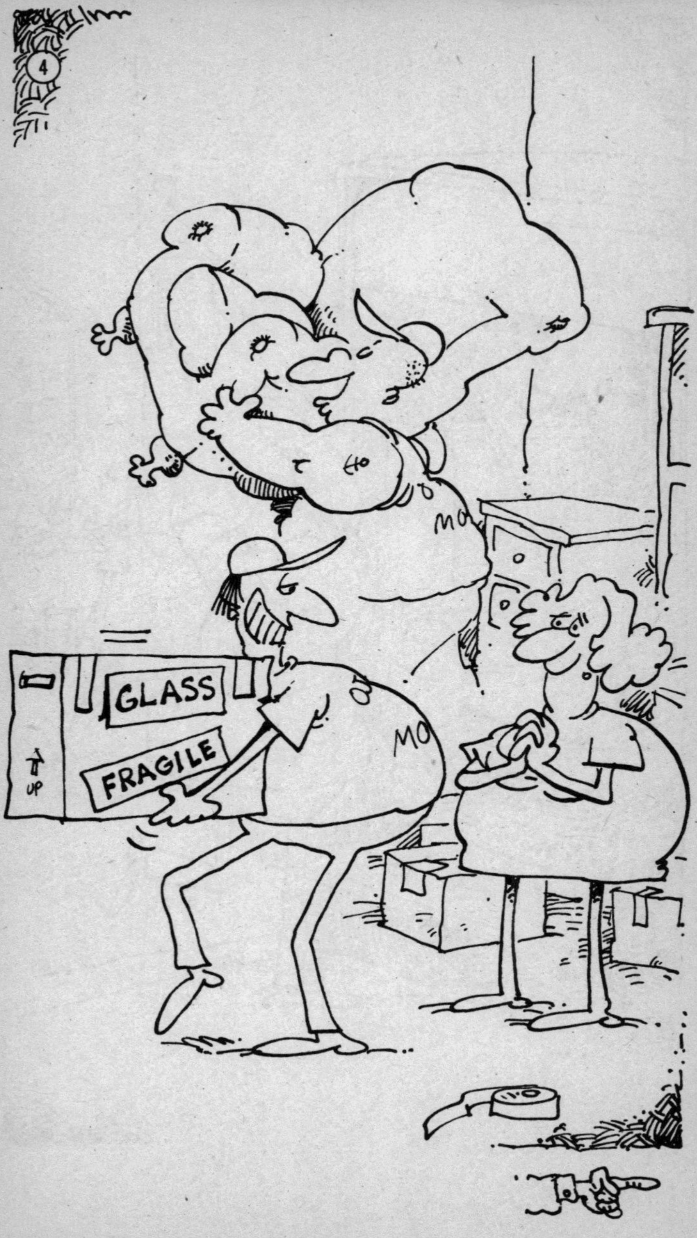

GLASS
FRAGILE
UP

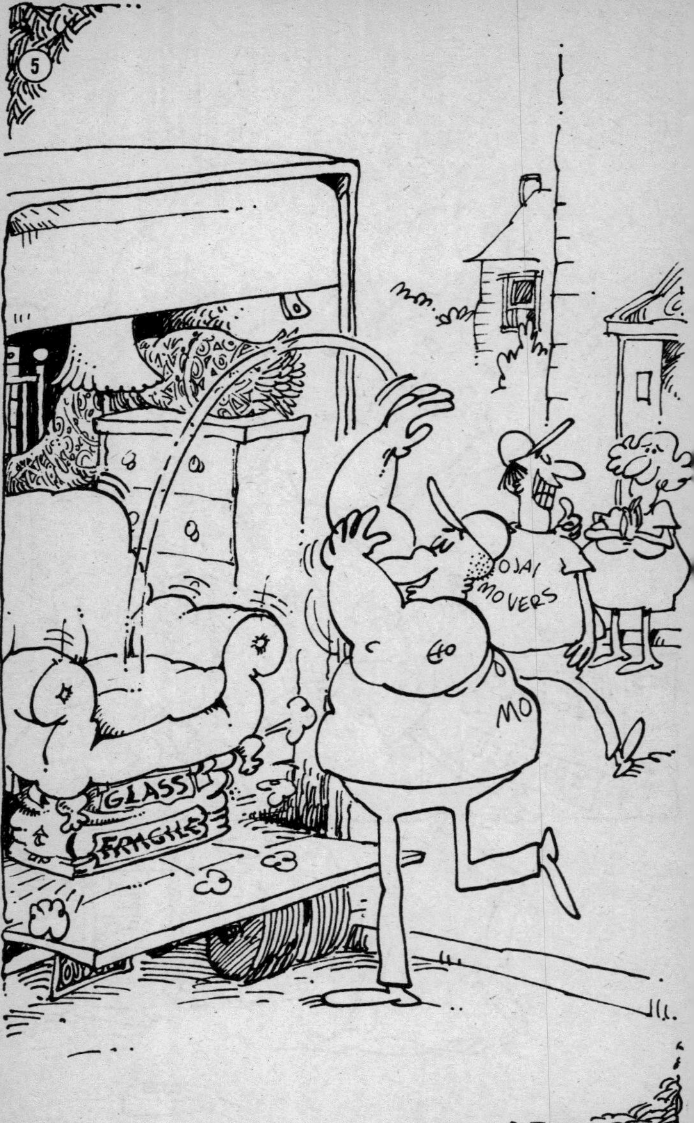
5
OJAI MOVERS
MO
GLASS
FRAGILE

1

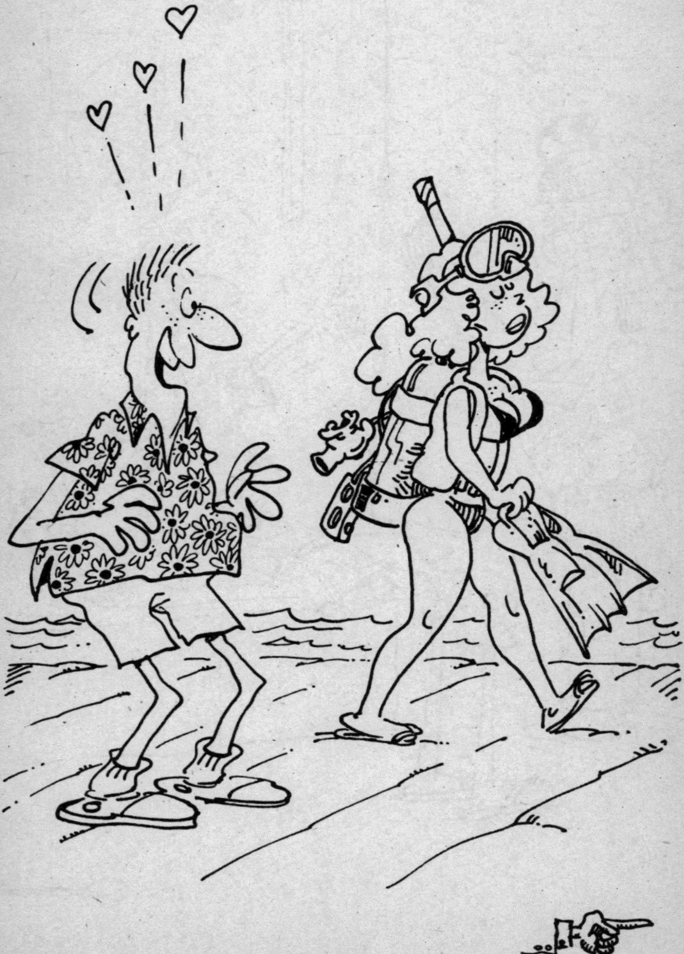

2

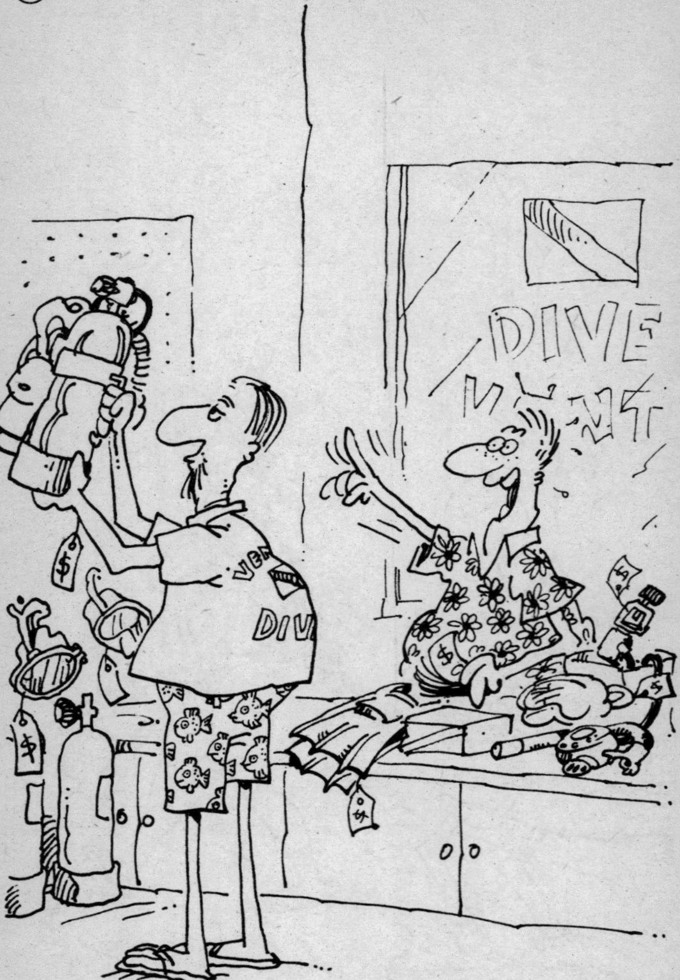
DIVE

①

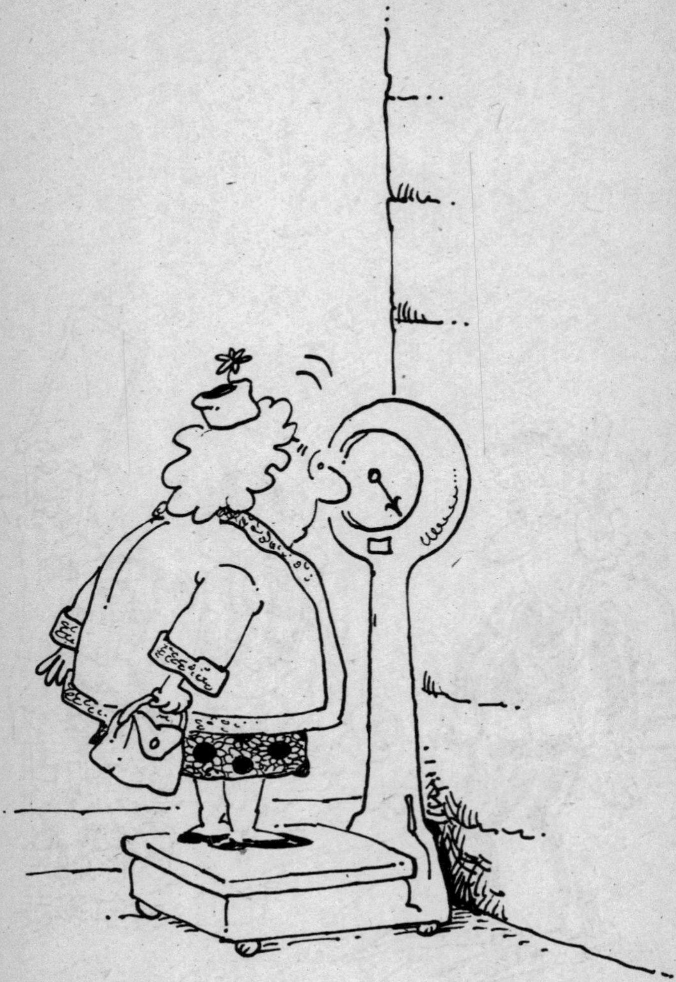

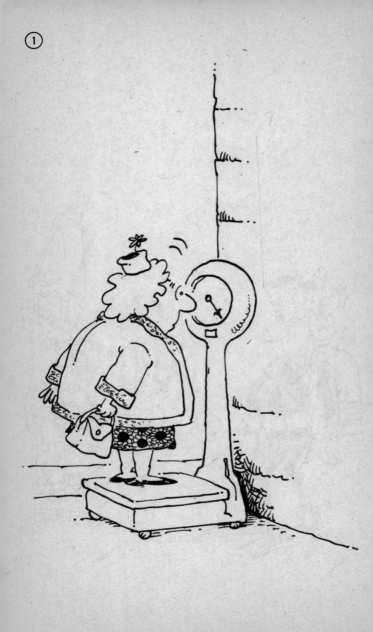

2

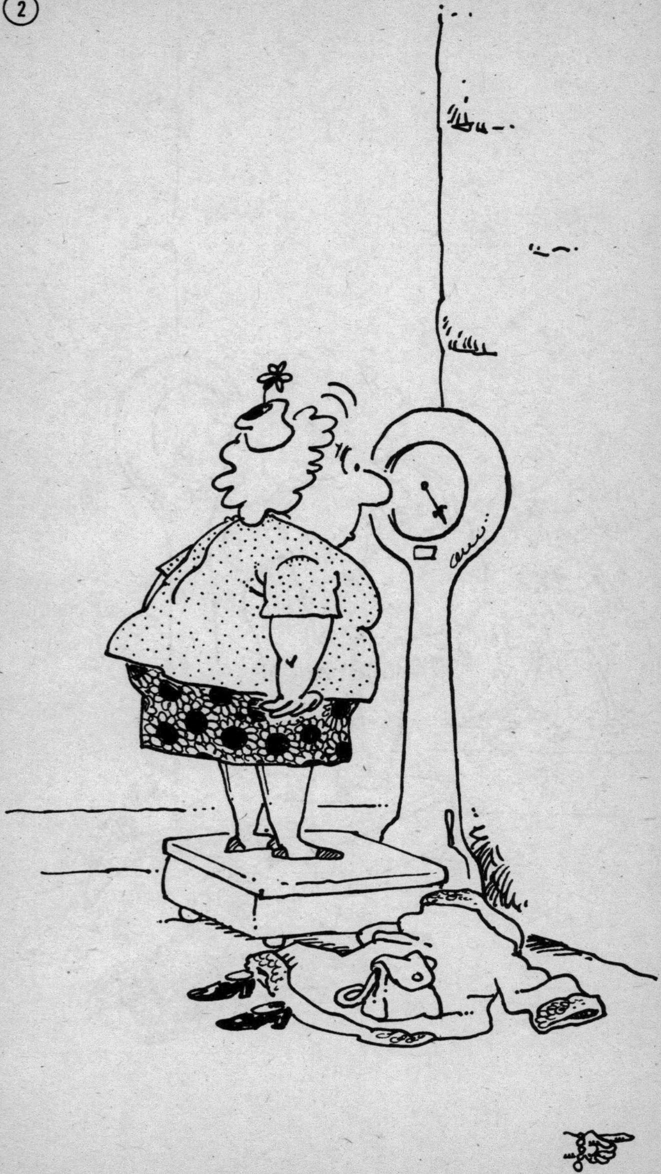

3

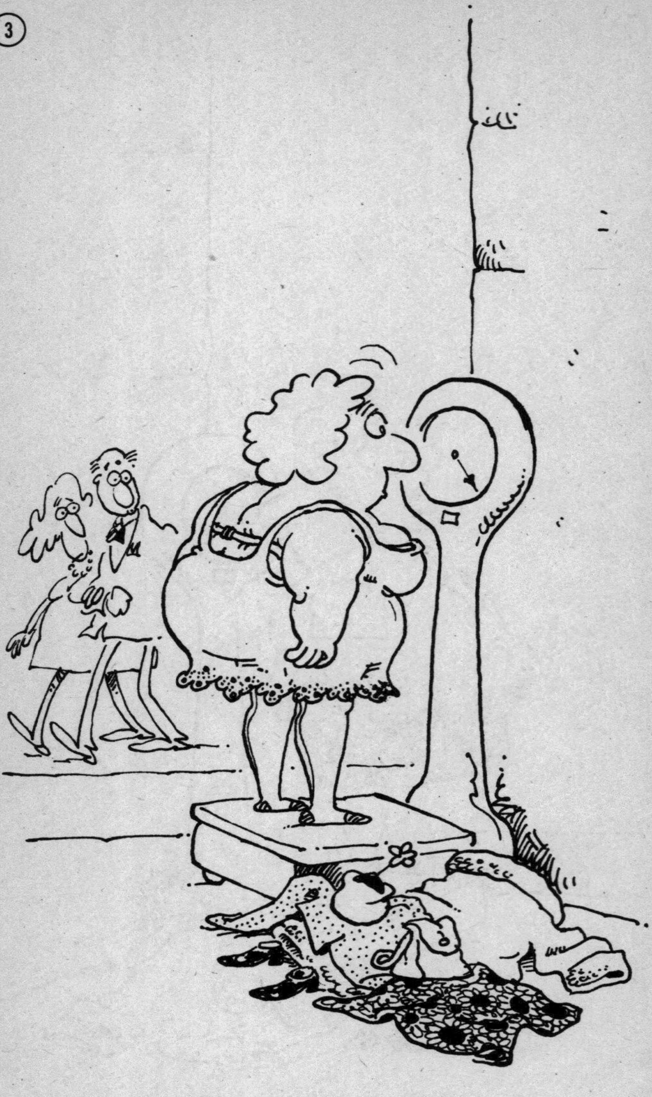

4

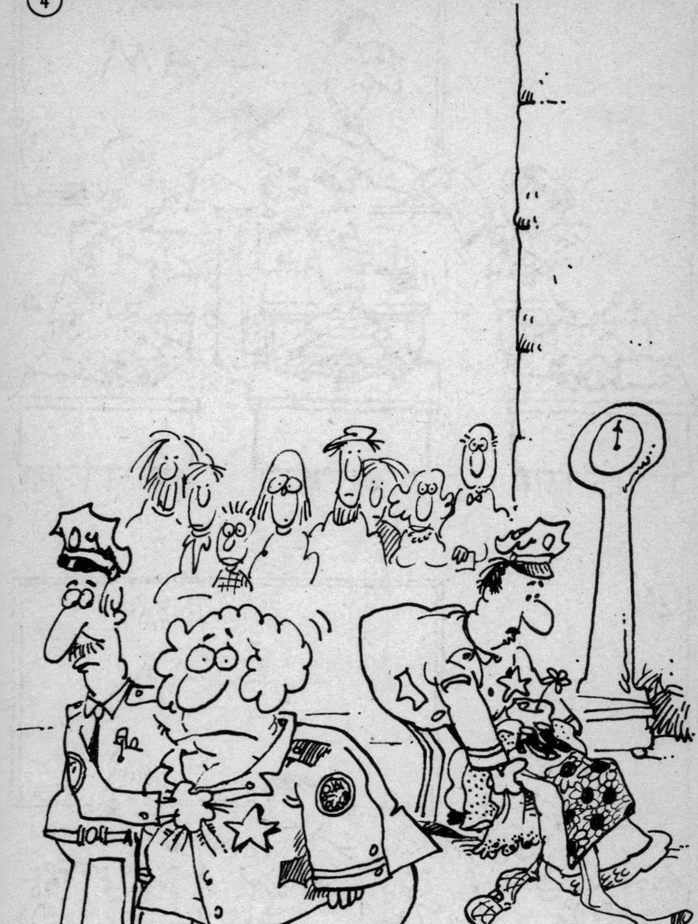

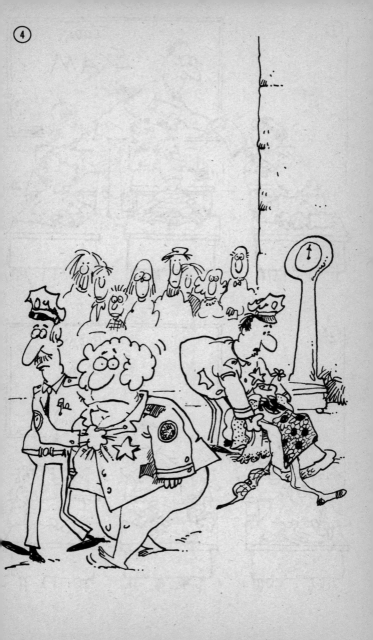

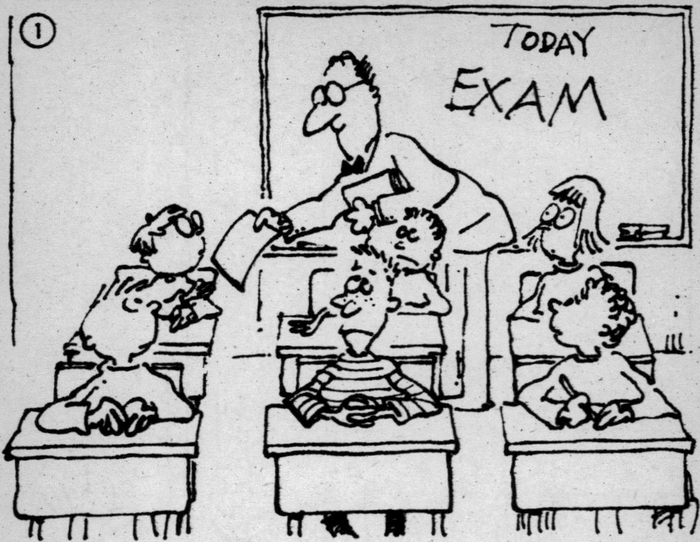
1
TODAY
EXAM

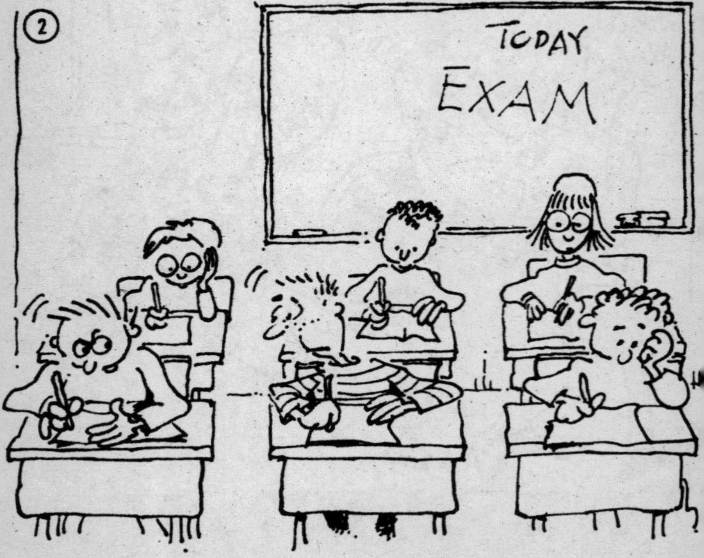
2
TODAY
EXAM

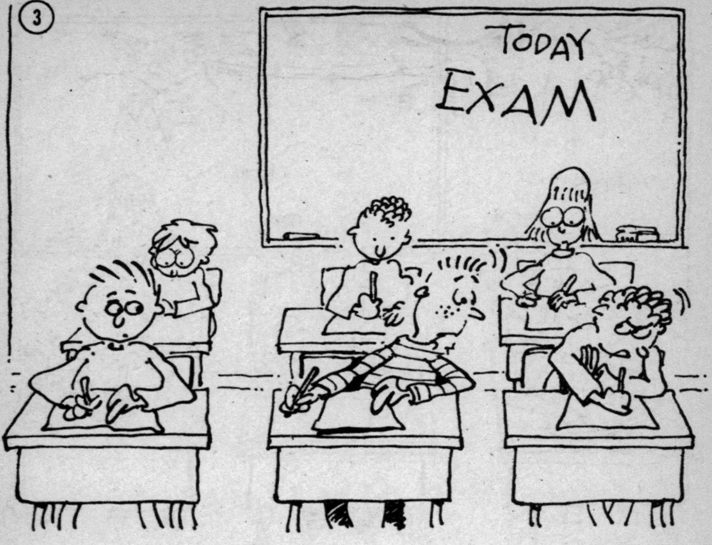
3
TODAY
EXAM

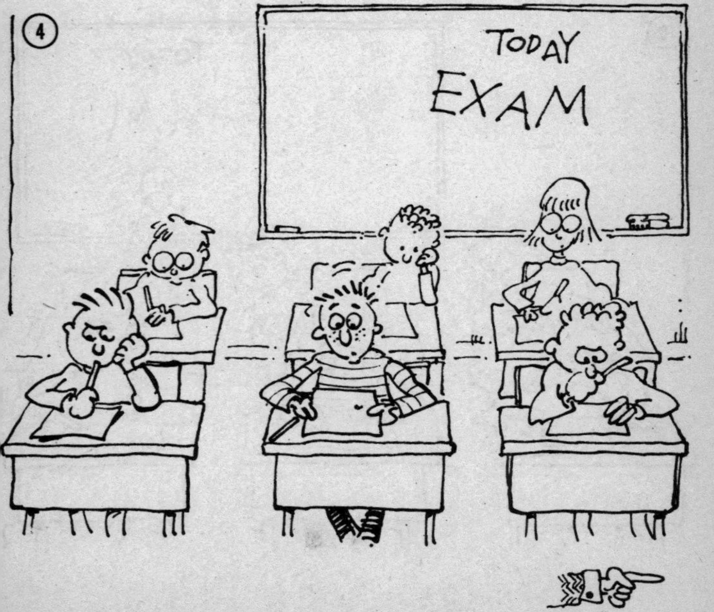
4
TODAY
EXAM

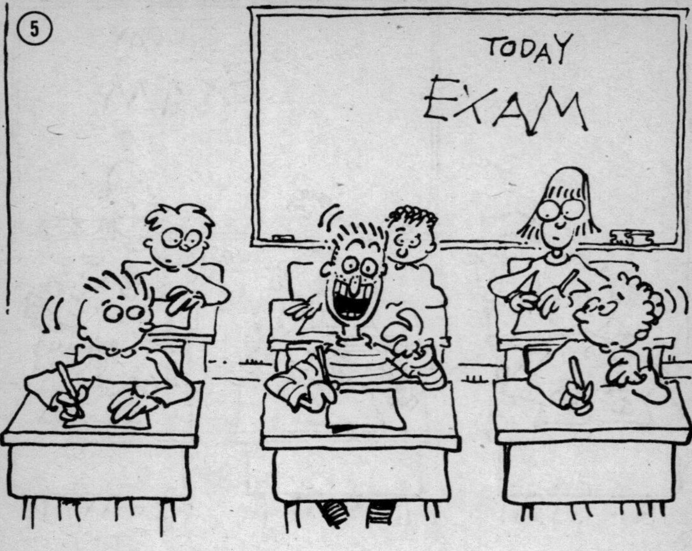
5
TODAY
EXAM

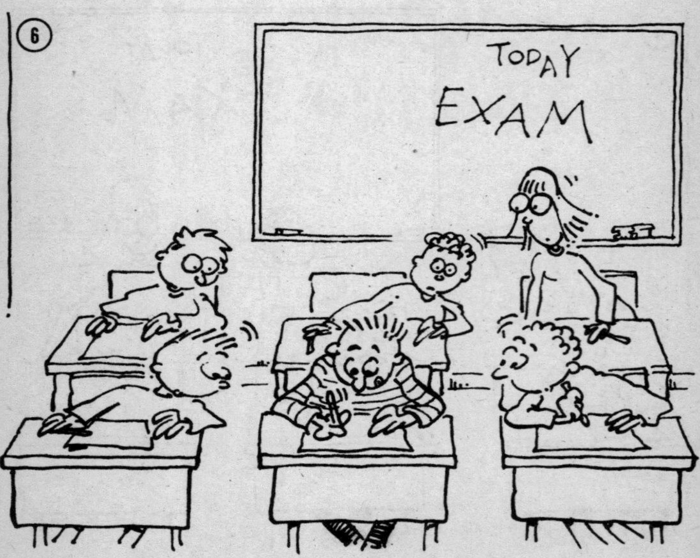
6
TODAY
EXAM

1

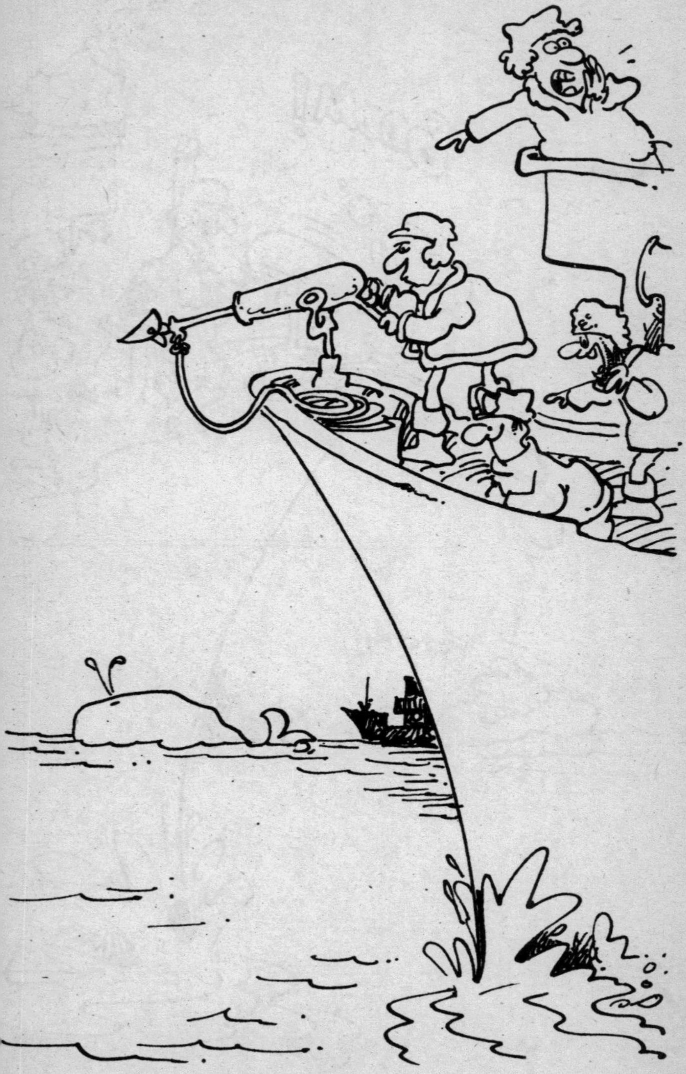

②

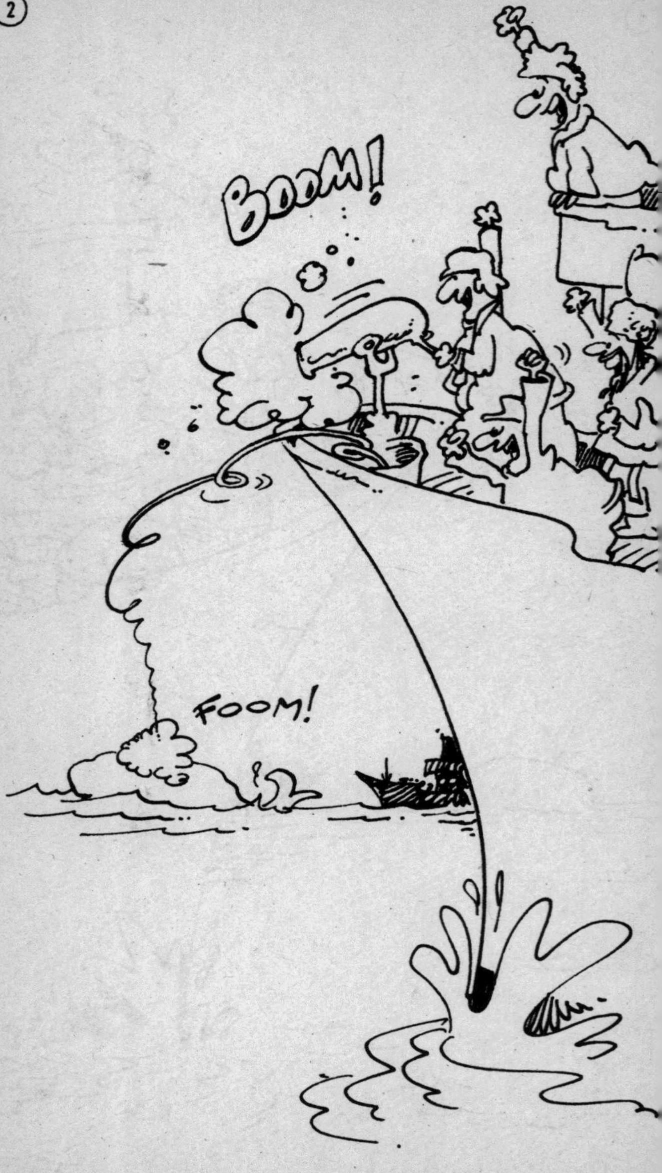
BOOM!
FOOM!

3

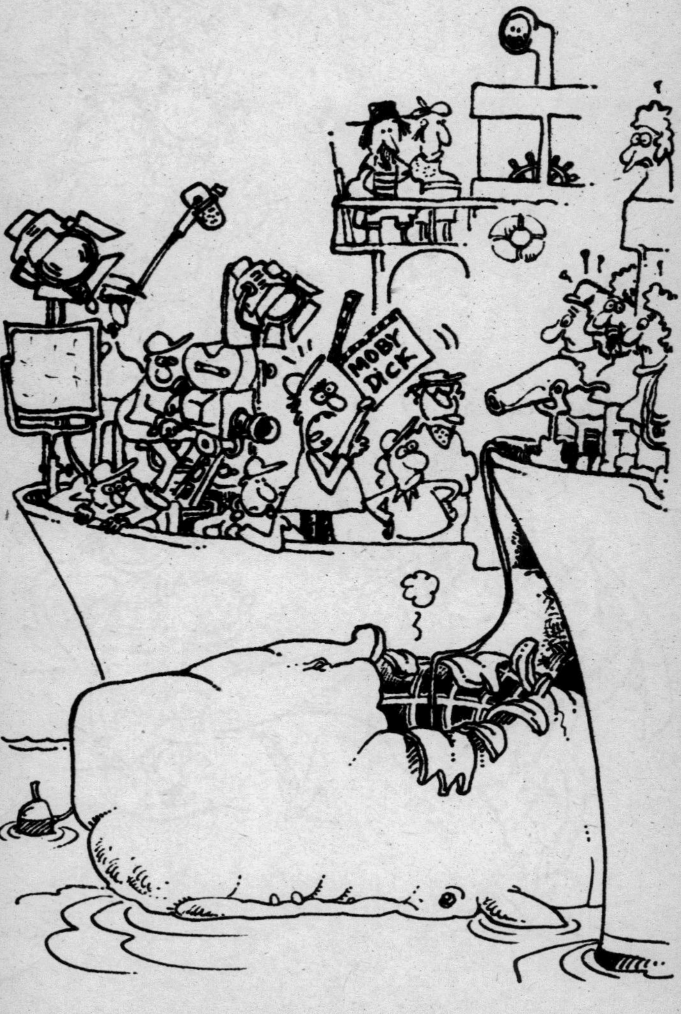
MOBY DICK

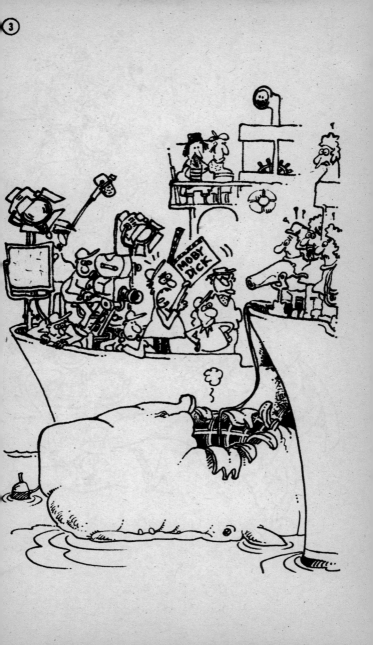

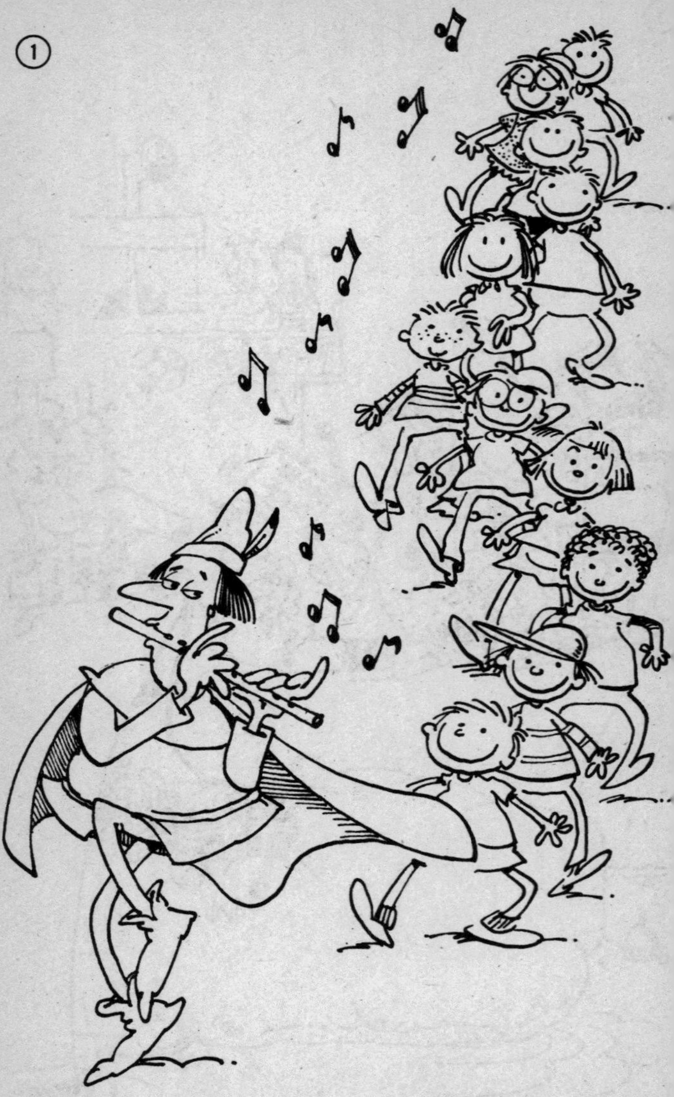

(2)

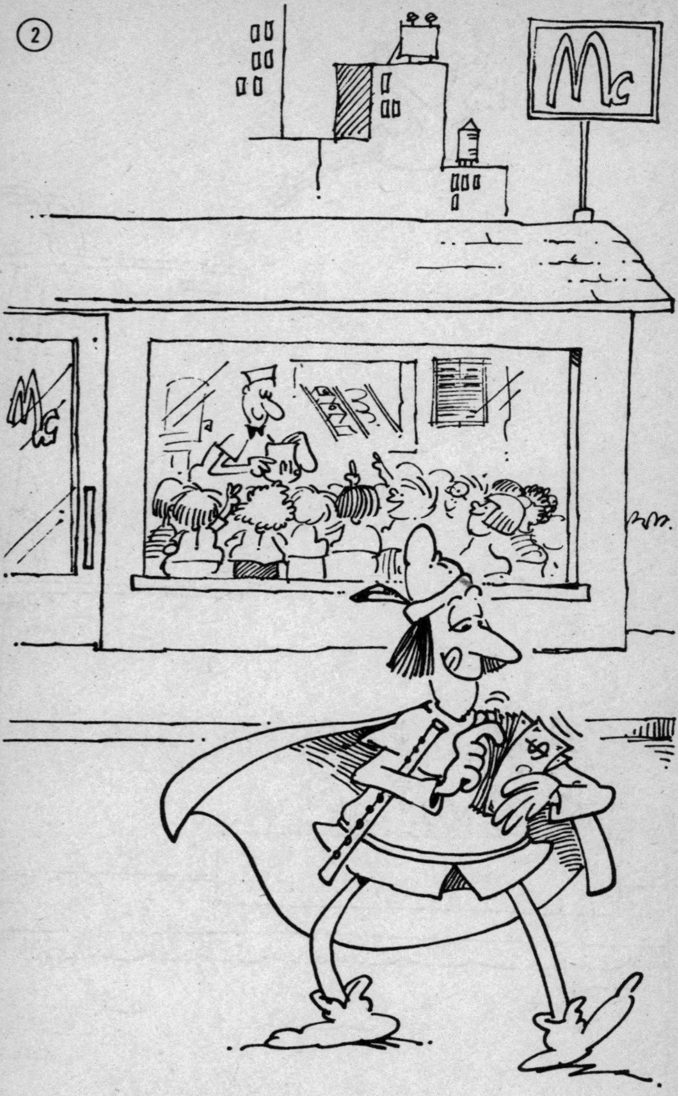
Mc

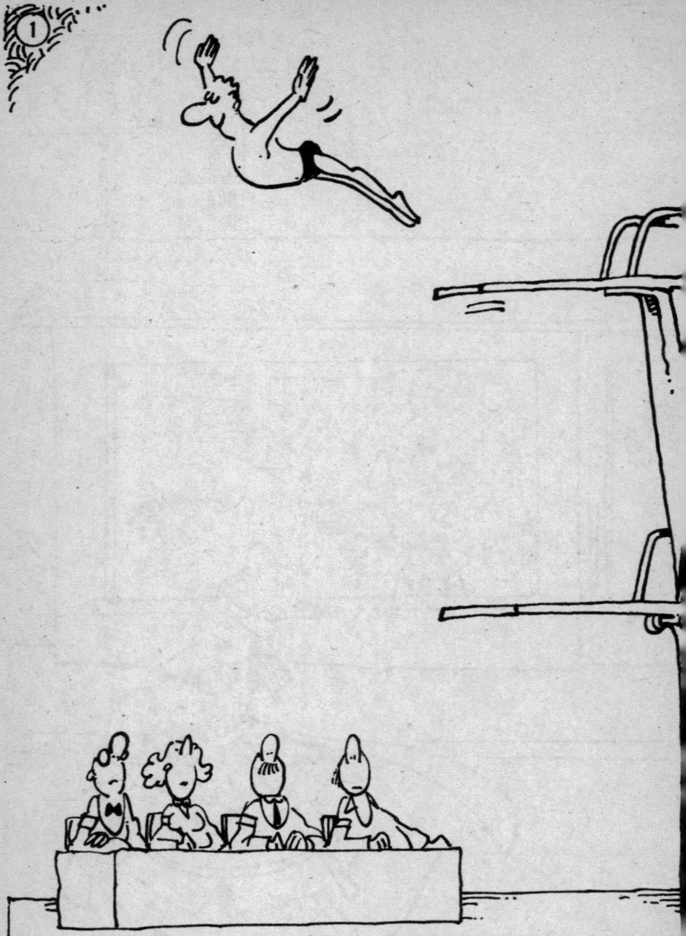
1

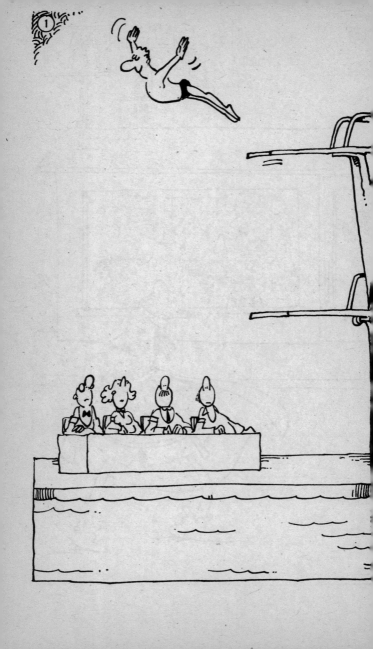

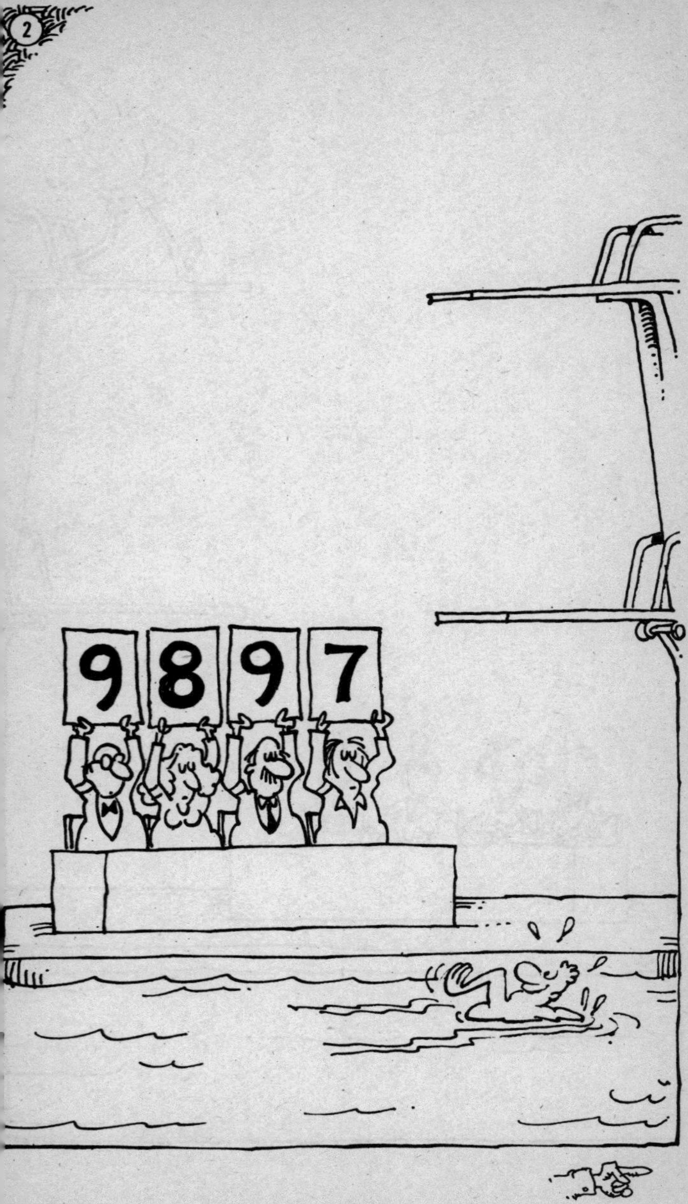
2
9
8
9
7

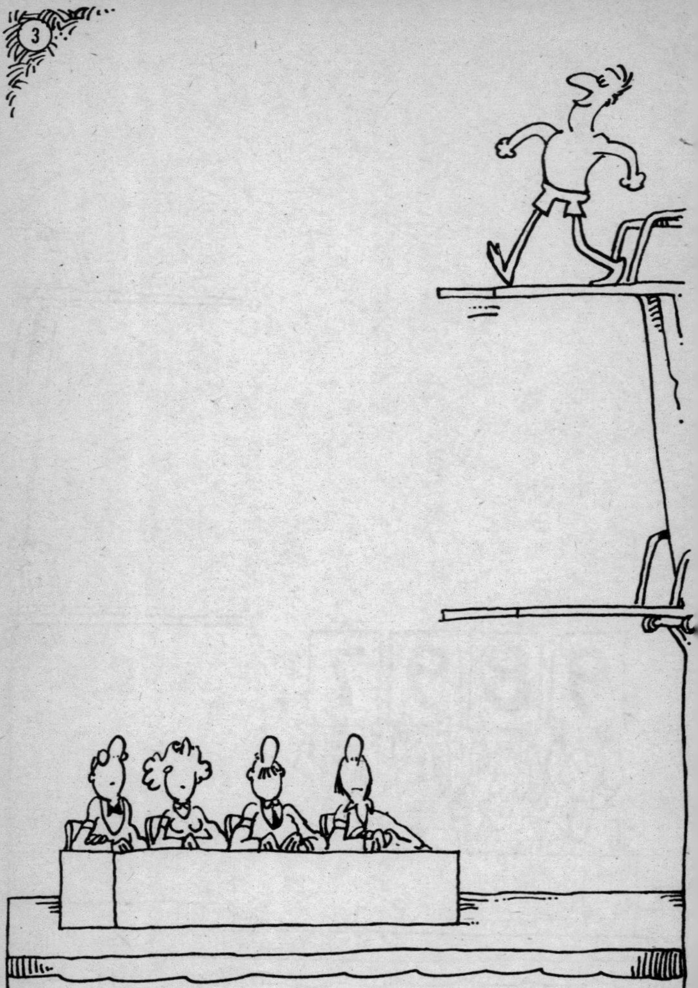
3

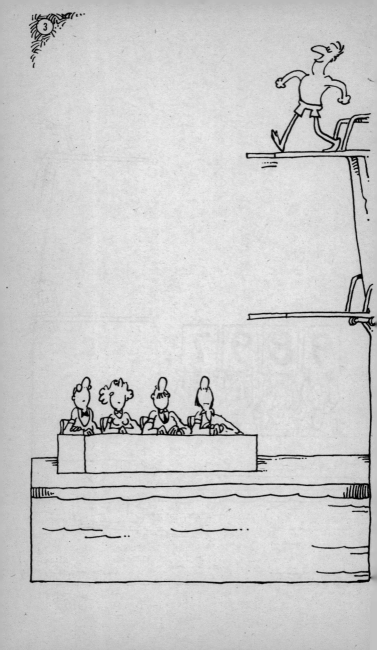

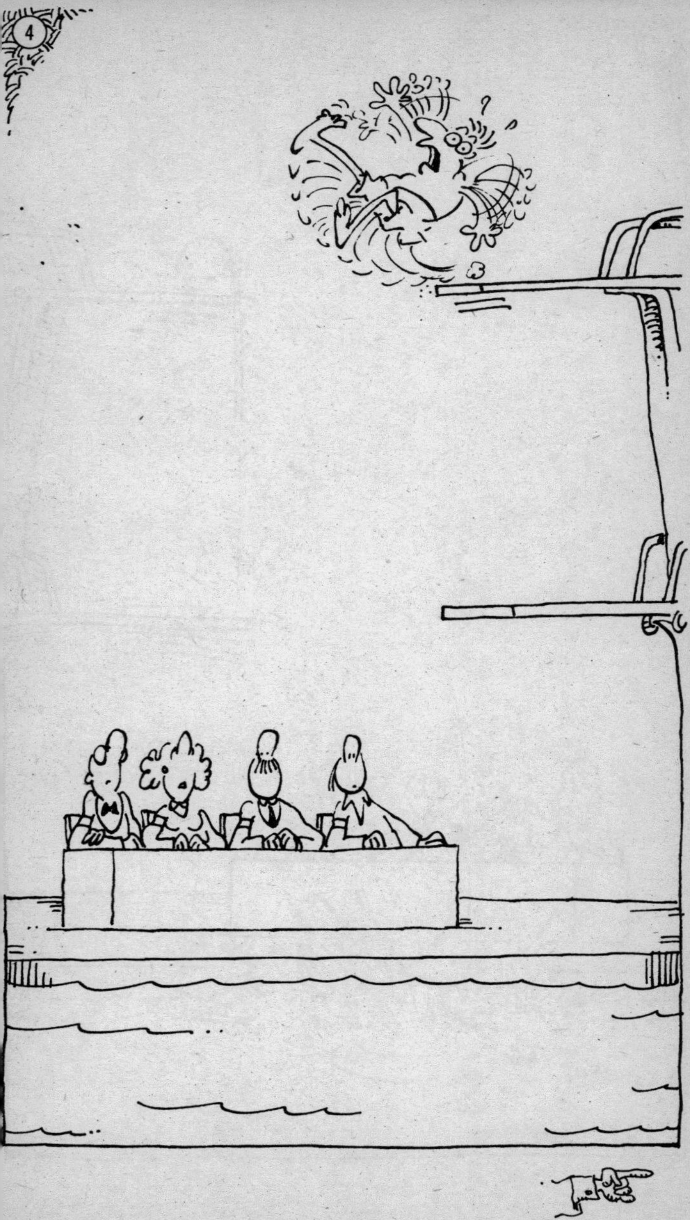
4

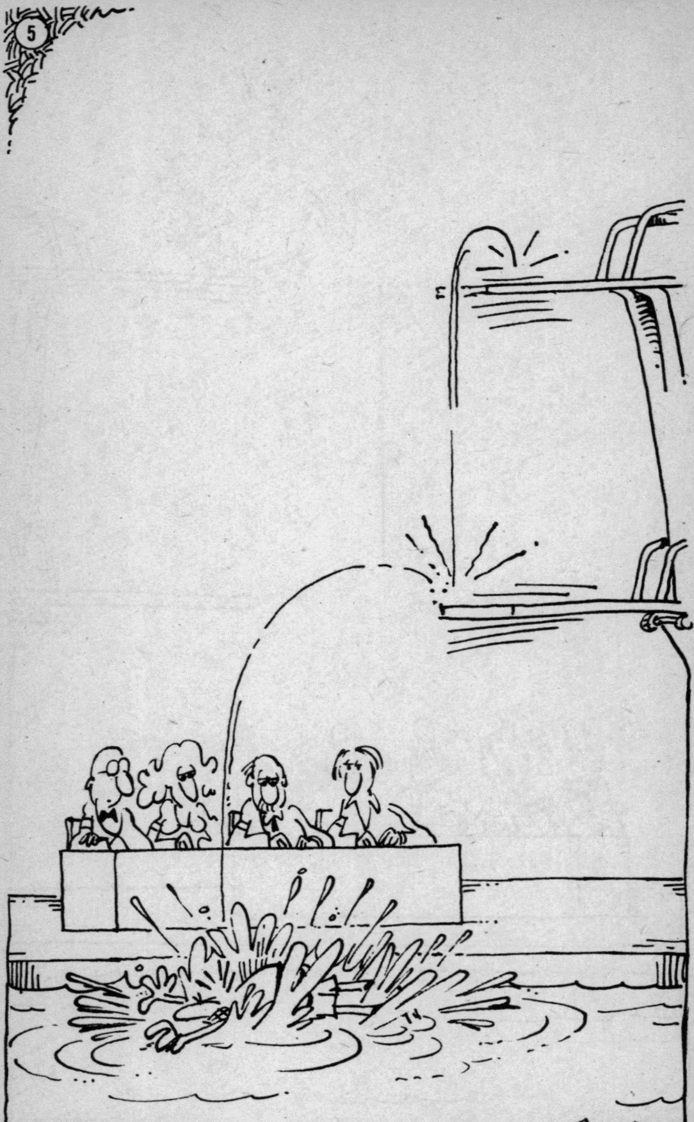
5

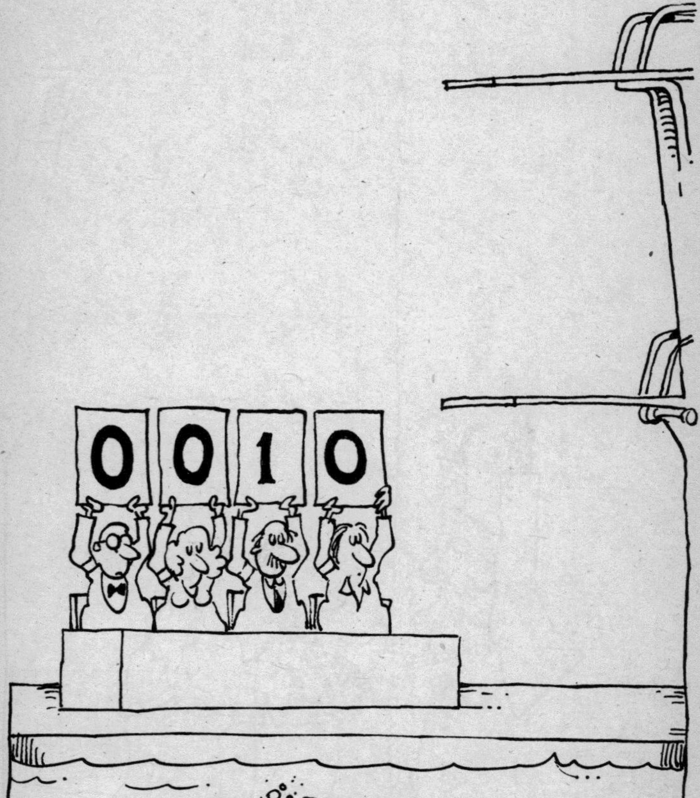
0
0
1
0

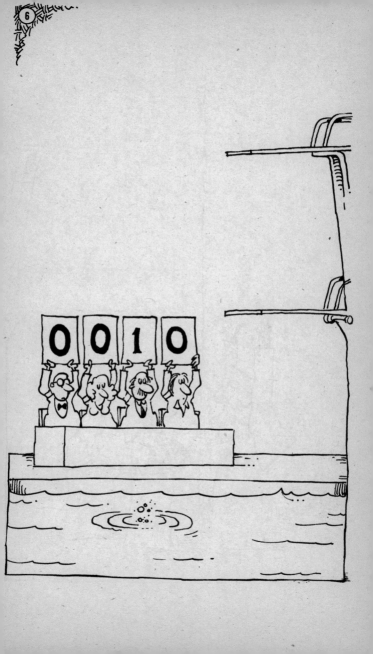

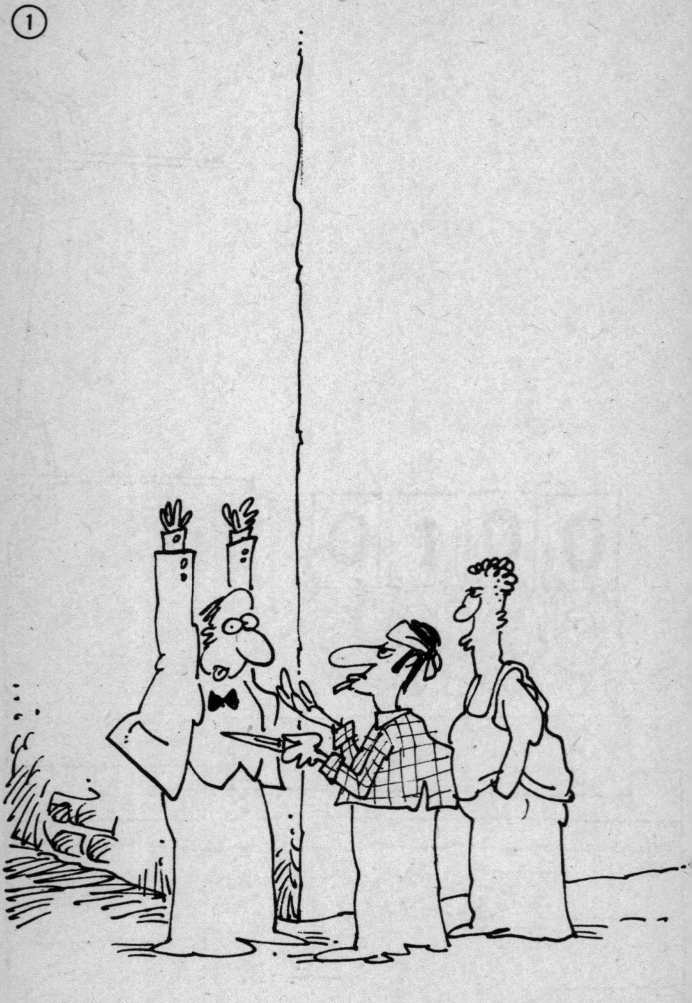
1

2

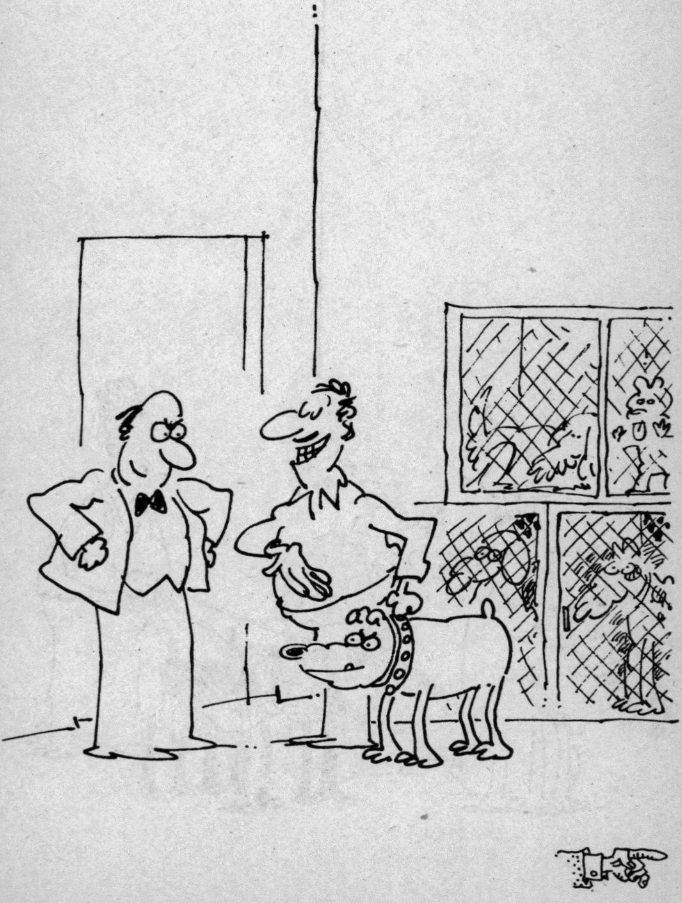

③

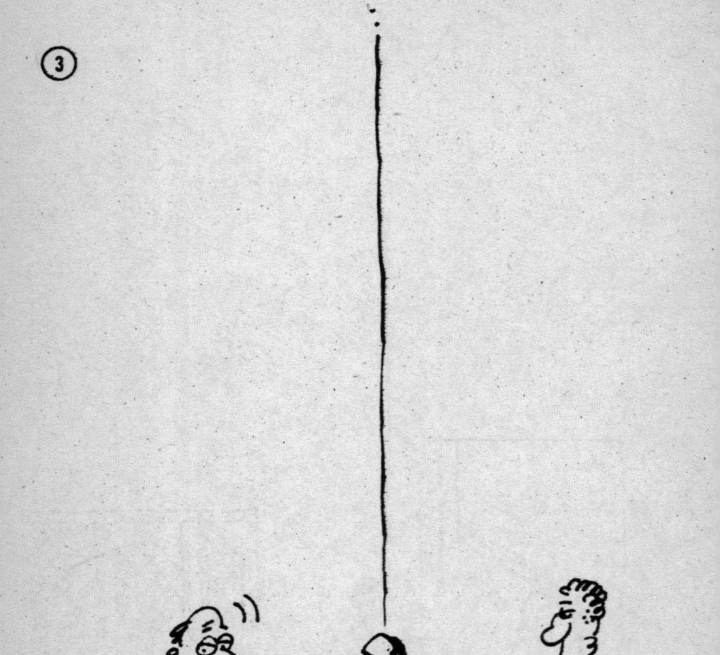

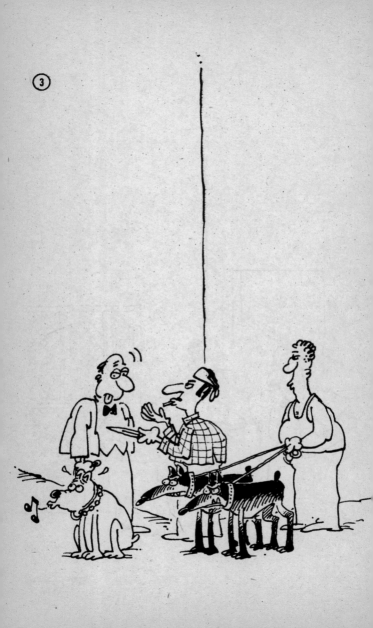

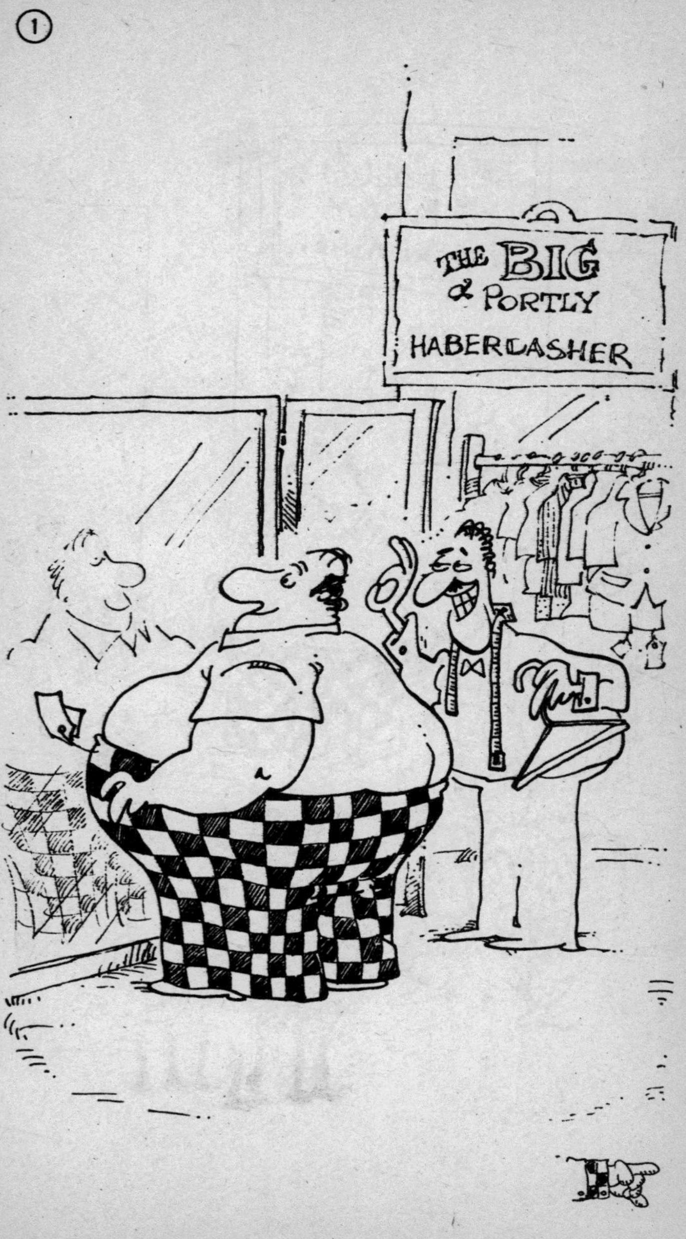
1
THE BIG & PORTLY
HABERDASHER

②

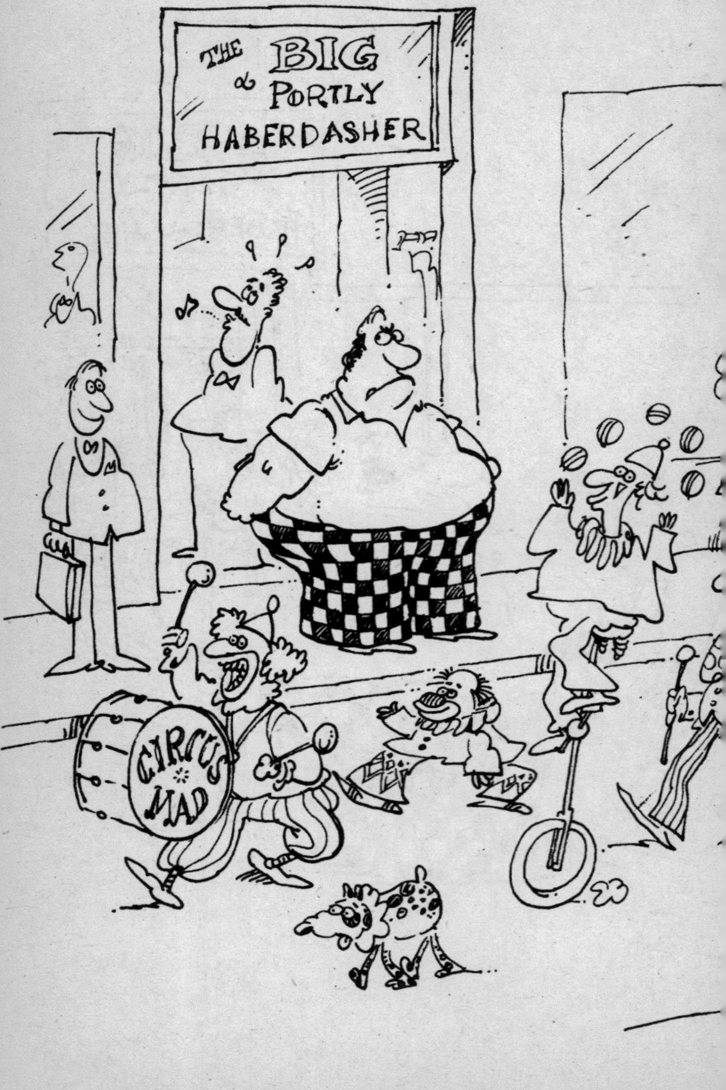
THE BIG & PORTLY
HABERDASHER
CIRCUS MAD

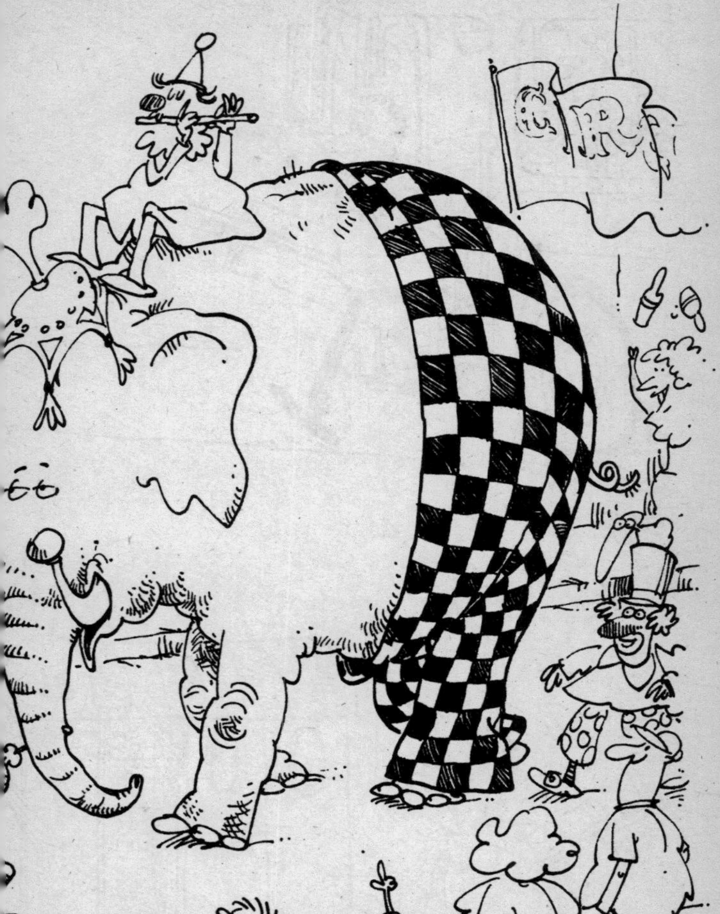

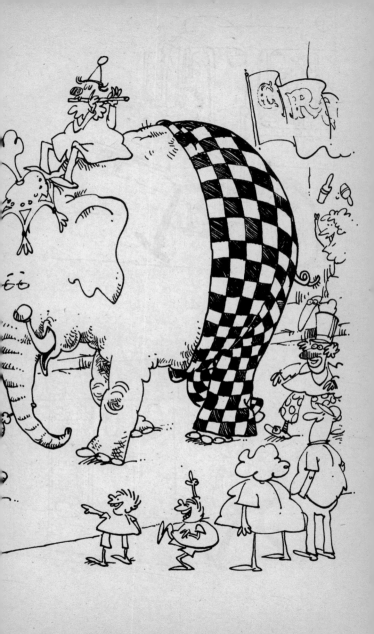

1

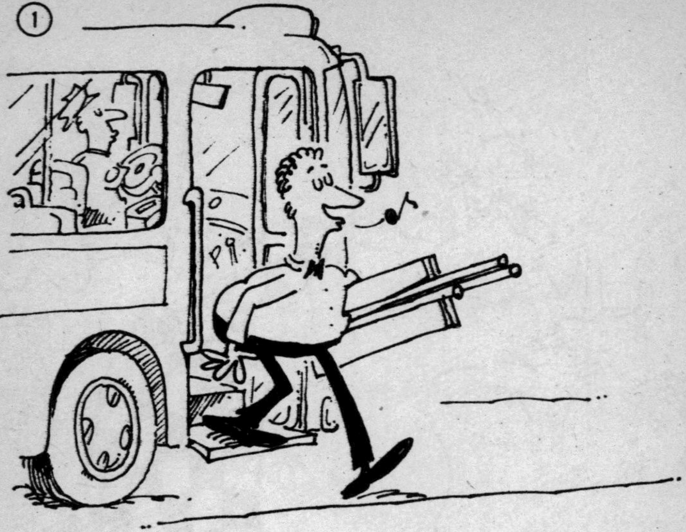

2

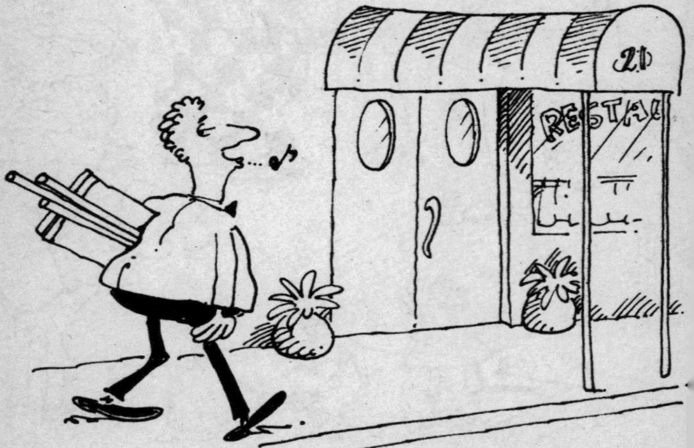
21

3

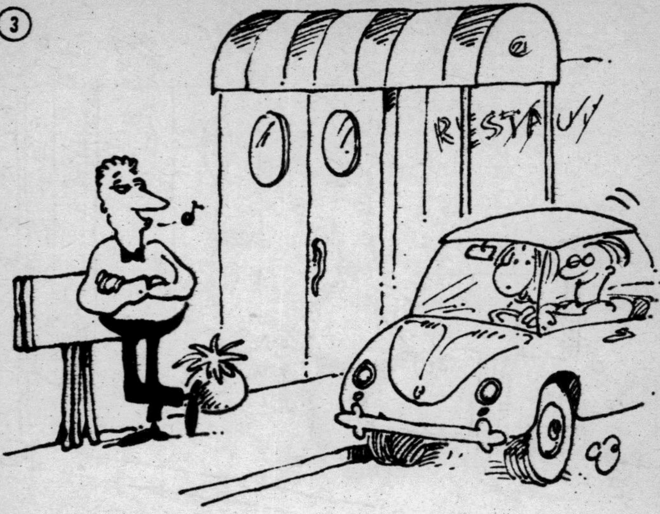

4

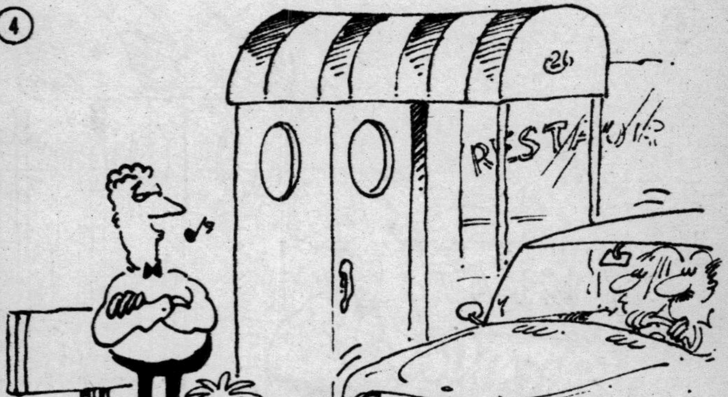

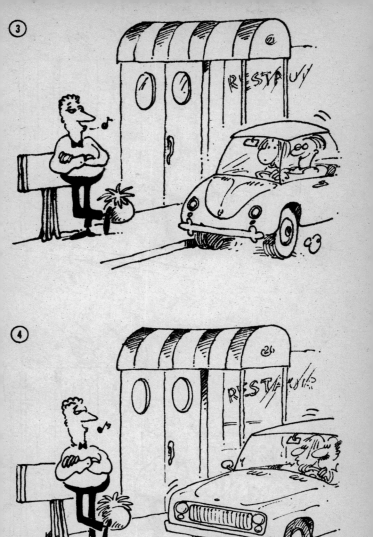

5

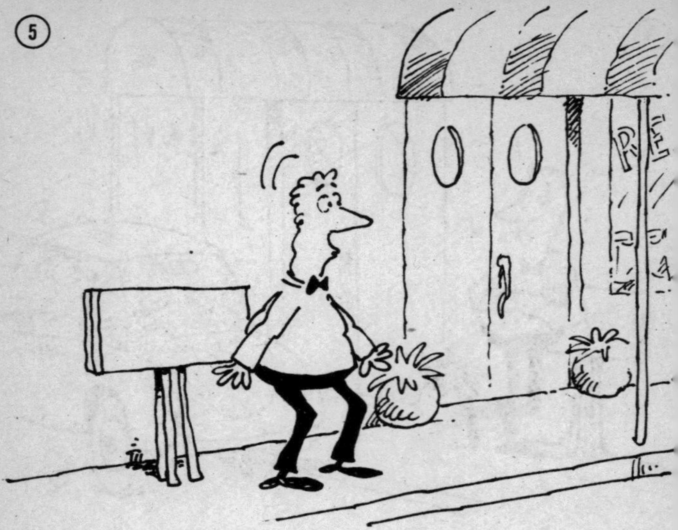

6

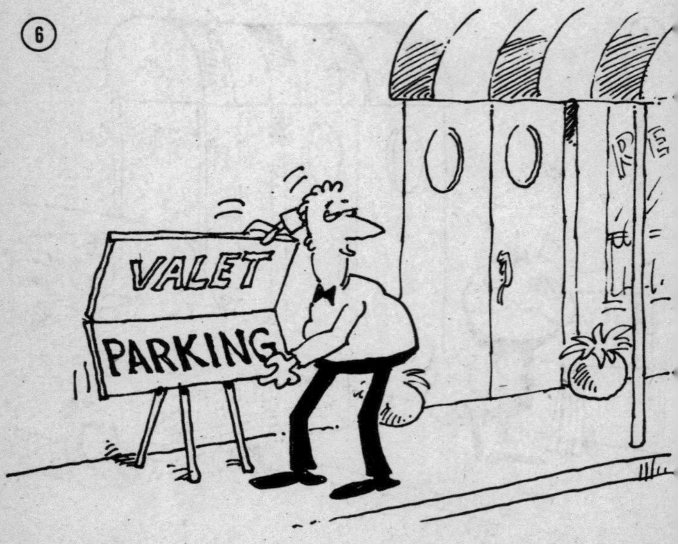
VALET
PARKING

7

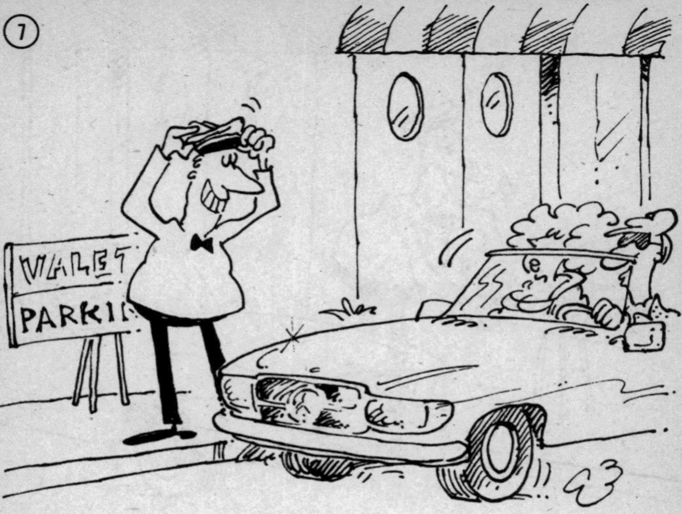
VALET
PARKI

8

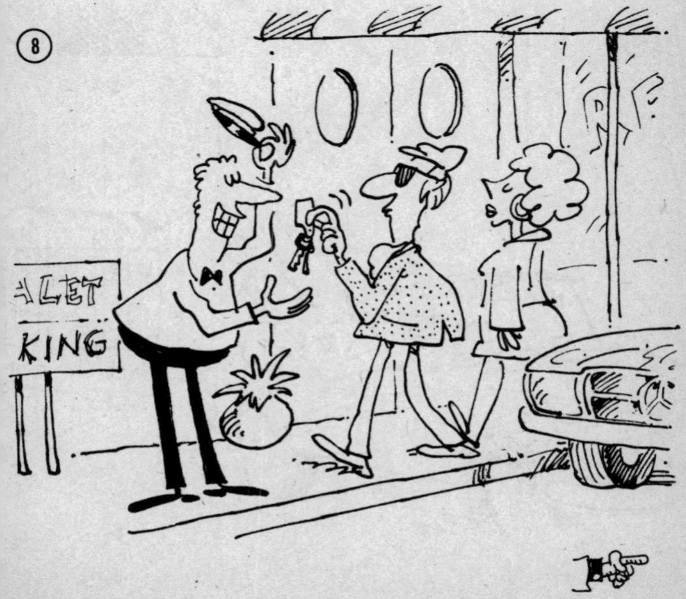
ALET
KING

9

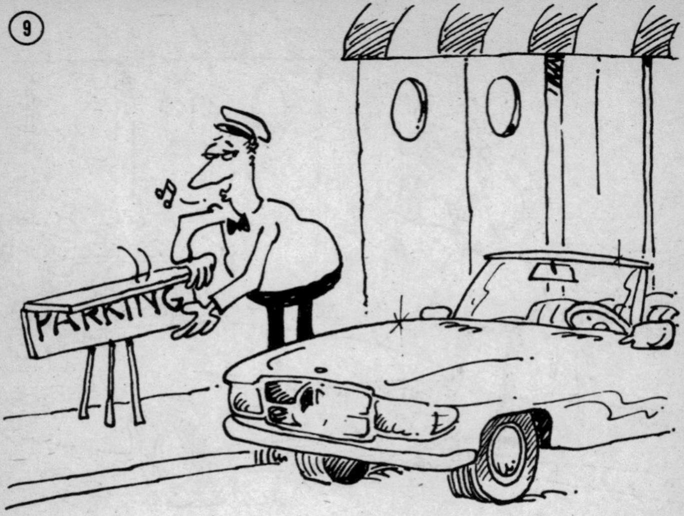
PARKING

10

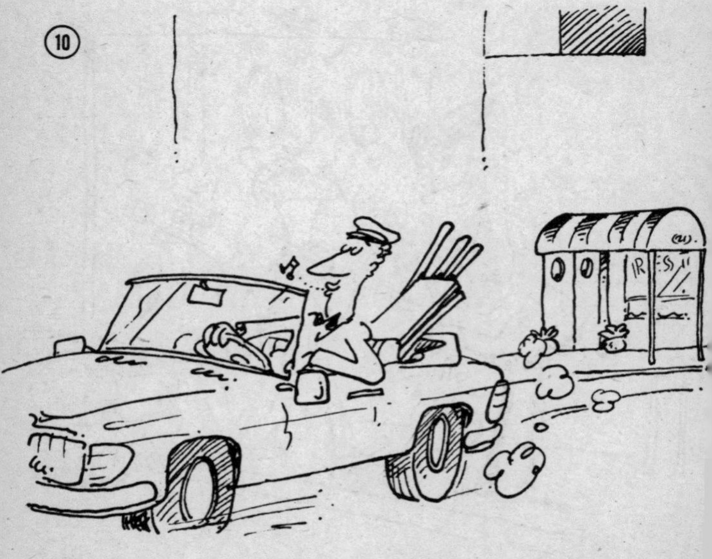

(1)

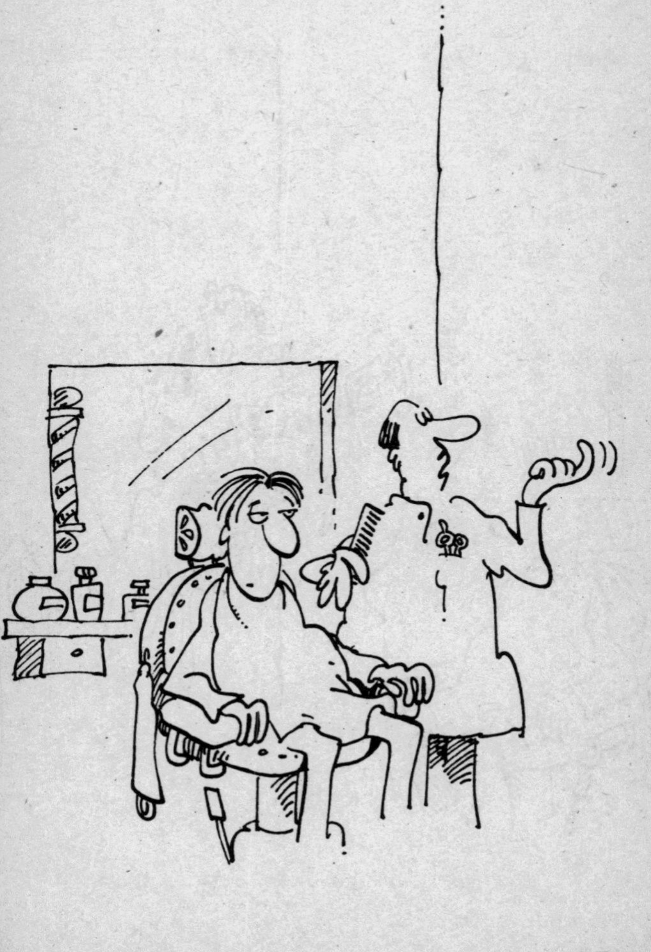

(2)

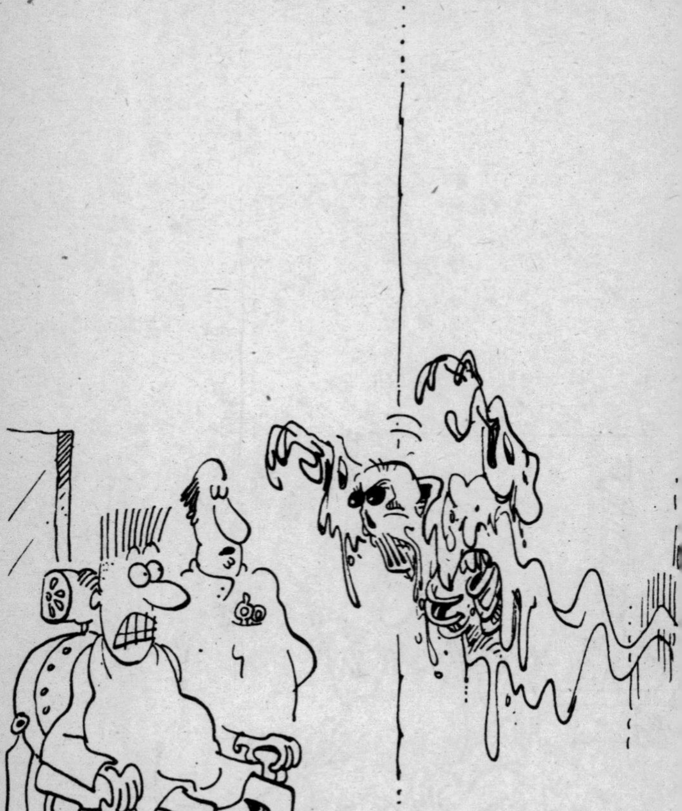

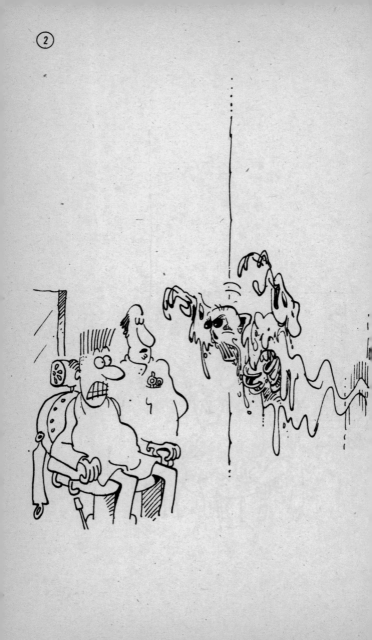

3

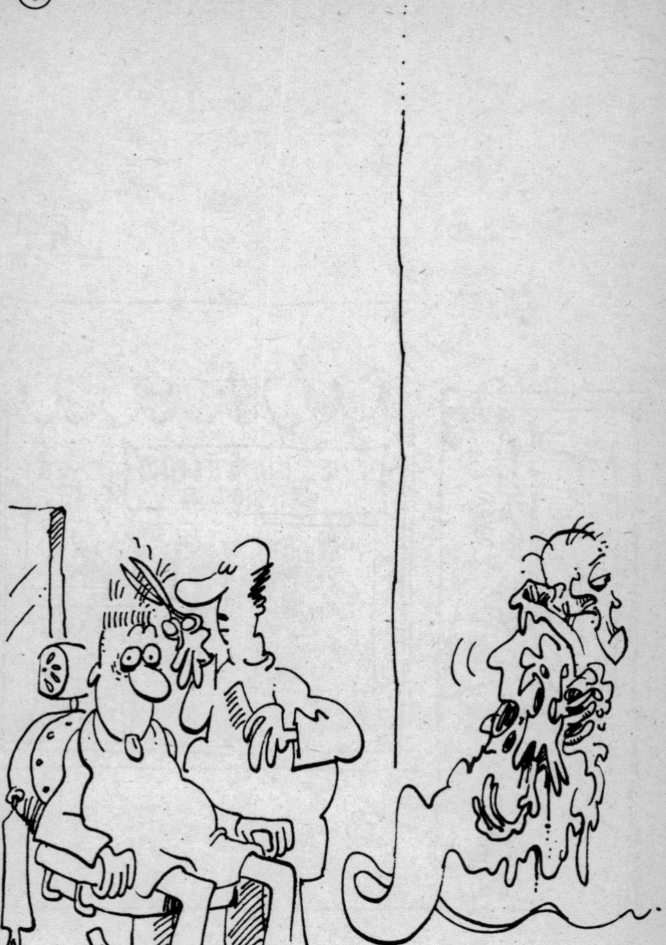

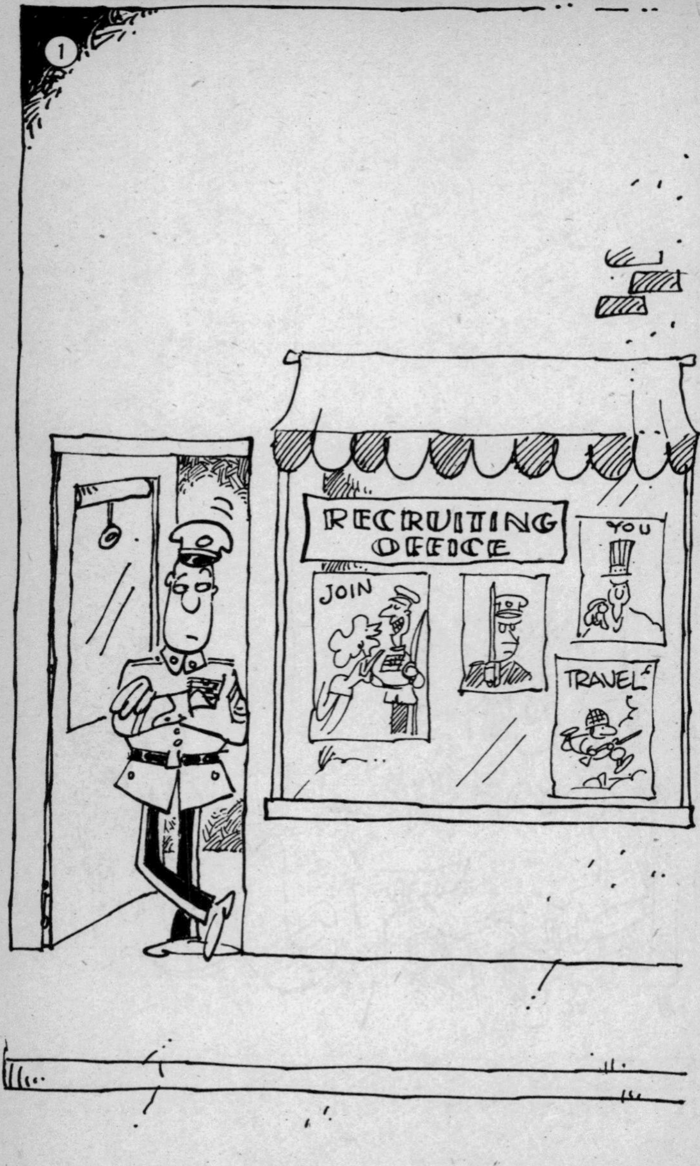
1
RECRUITING OFFICE
JOIN
YOU
TRAVEL

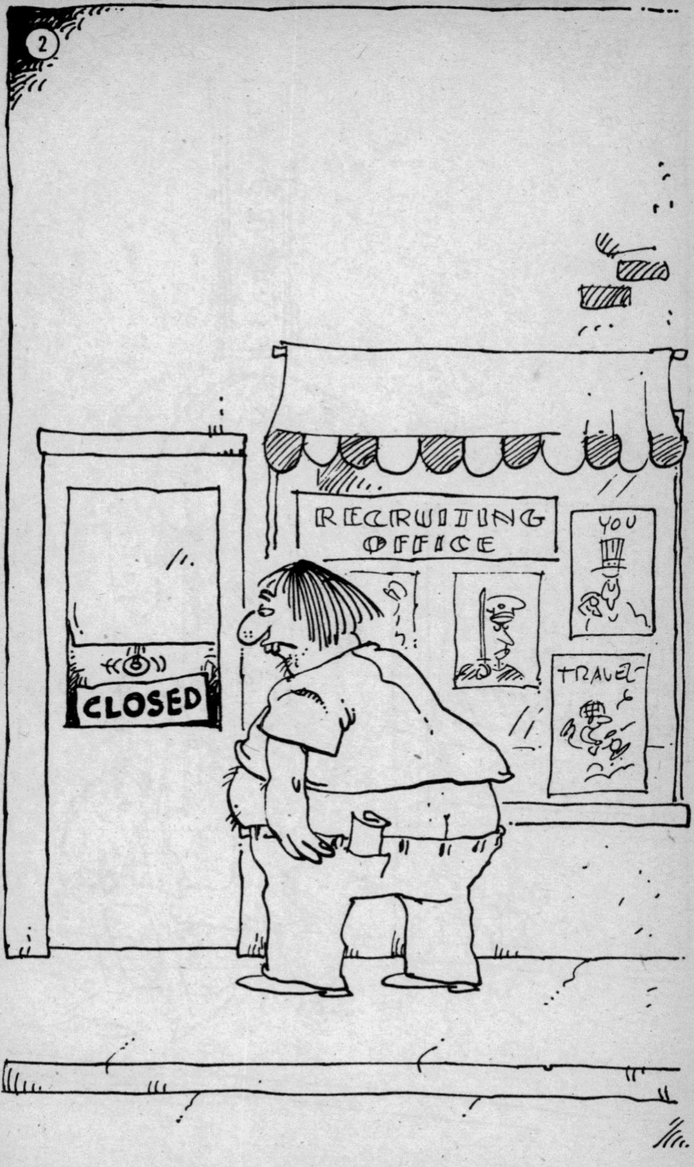
2
CLOSED
RECRUITING
OFFICE
YOU
TRAVEL

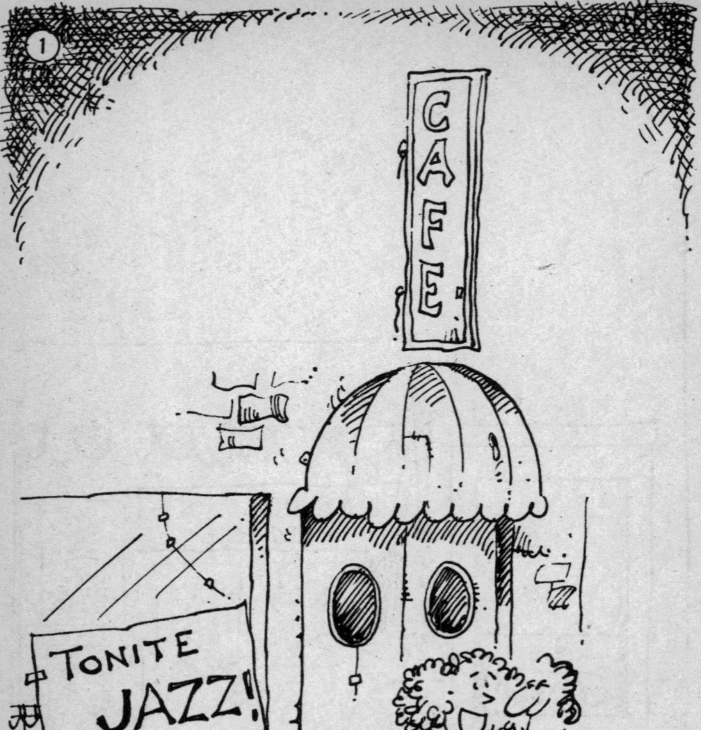
1
CAFE
TONITE
JAZZ!

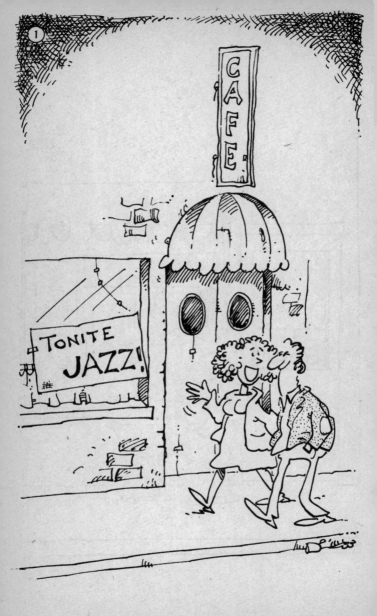

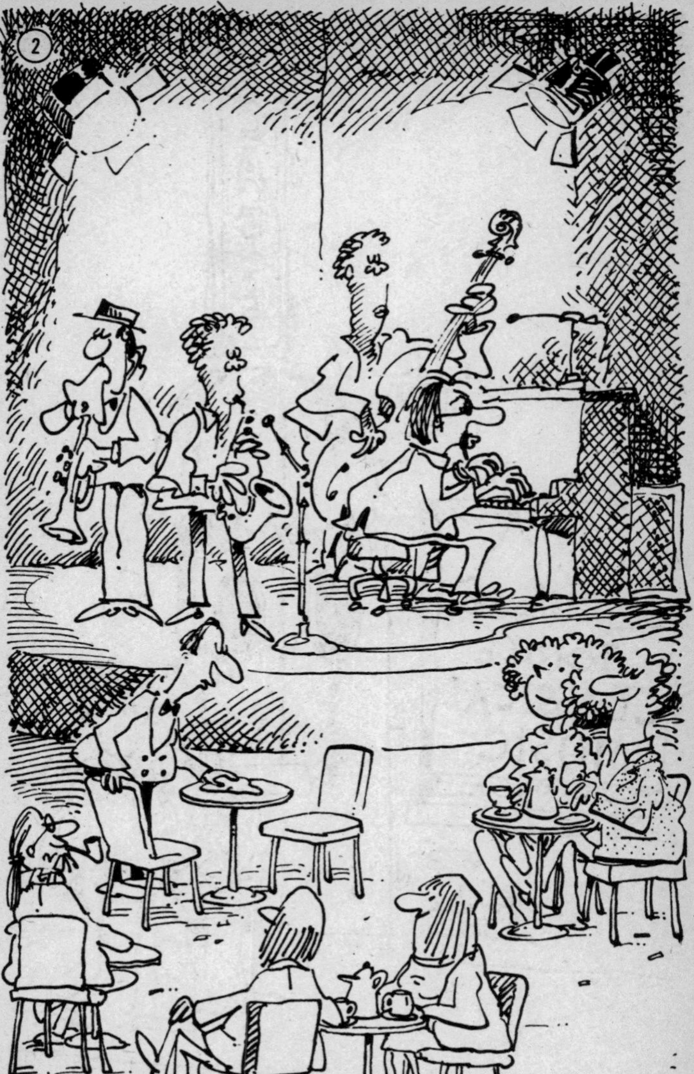
2

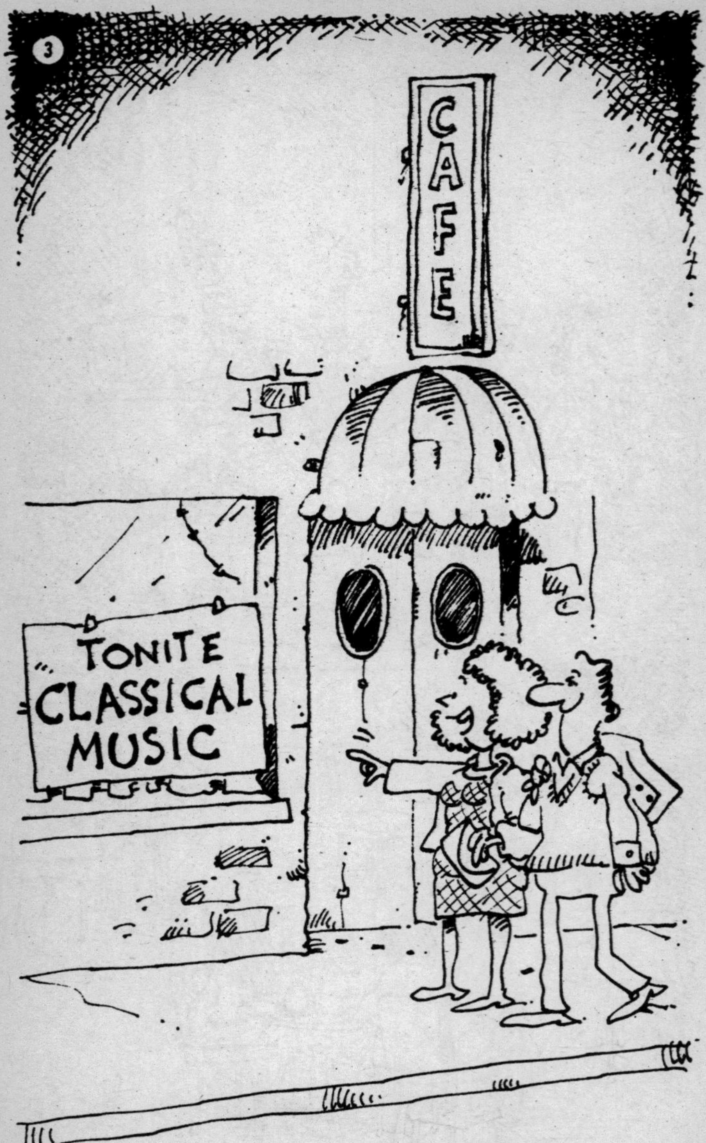
3
CAFE
TONITE
CLASSICAL
MUSIC

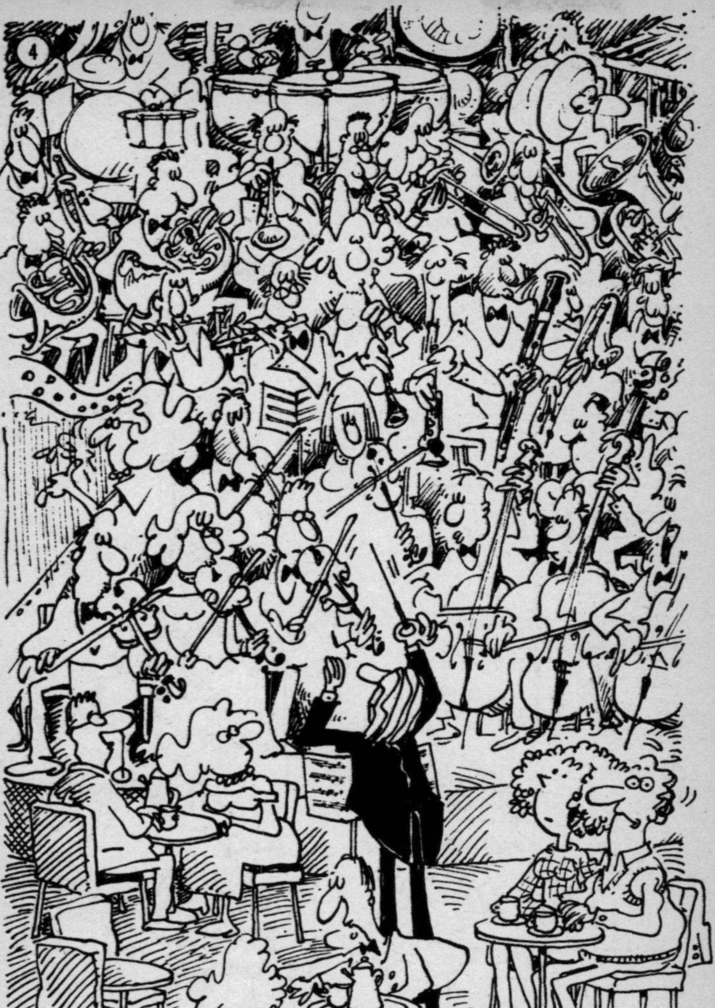
4

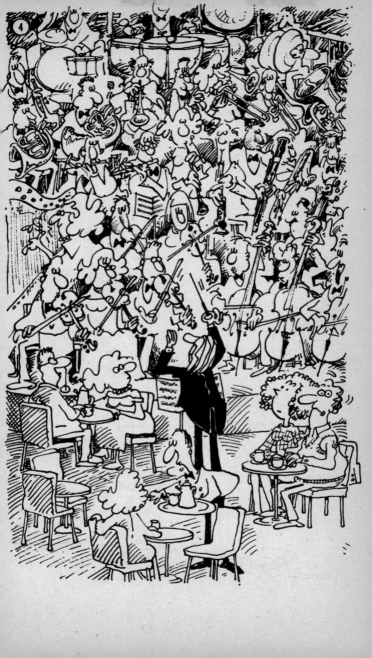

1

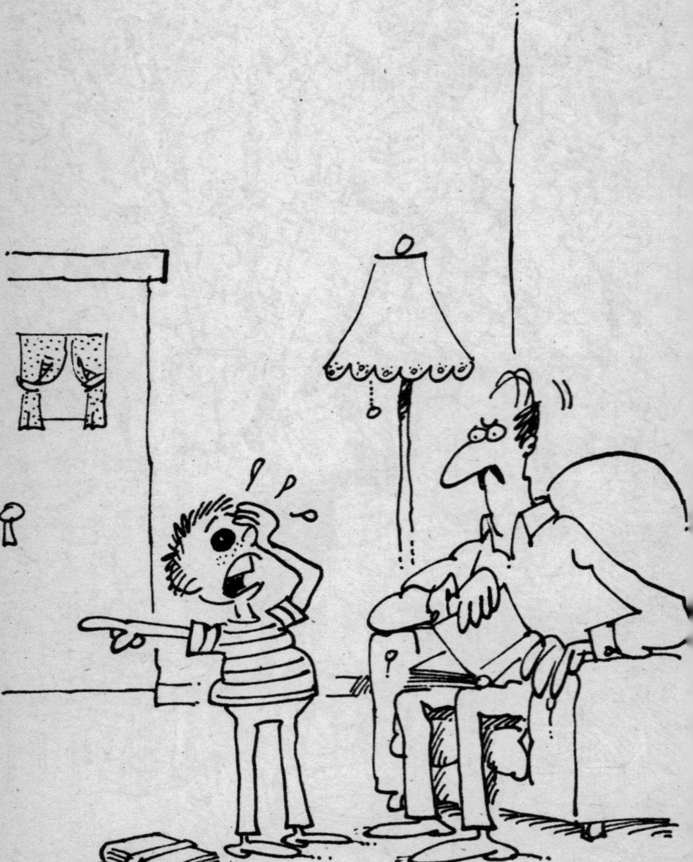

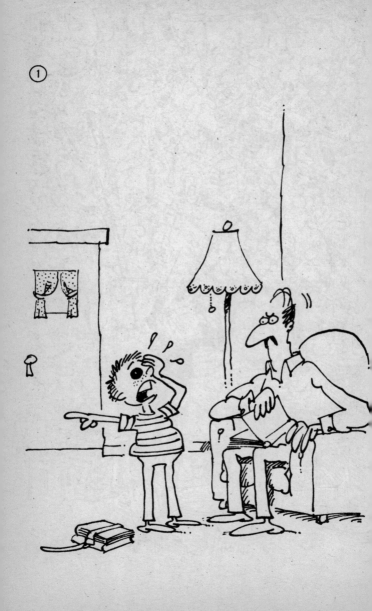

2

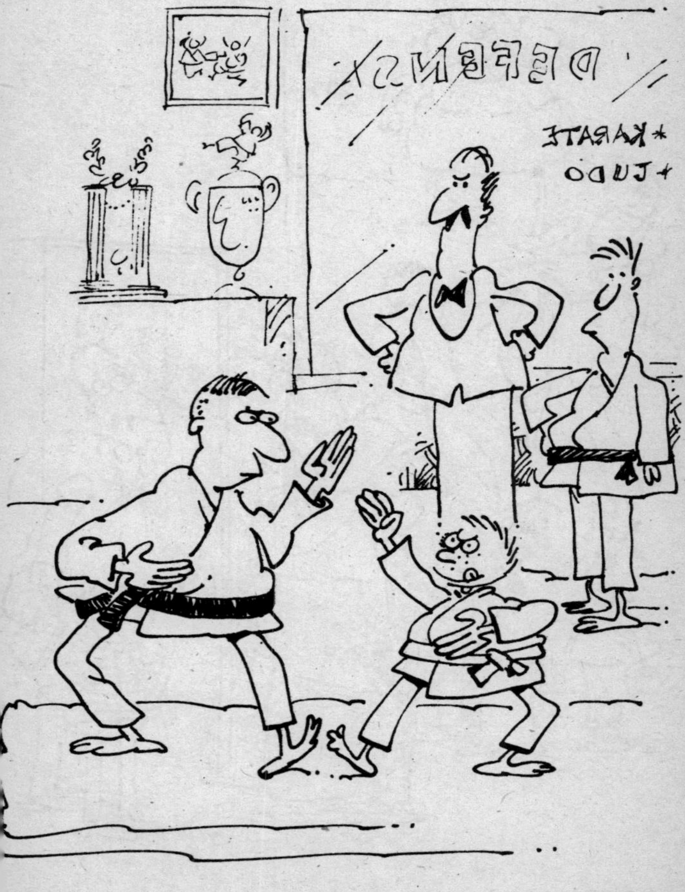

3

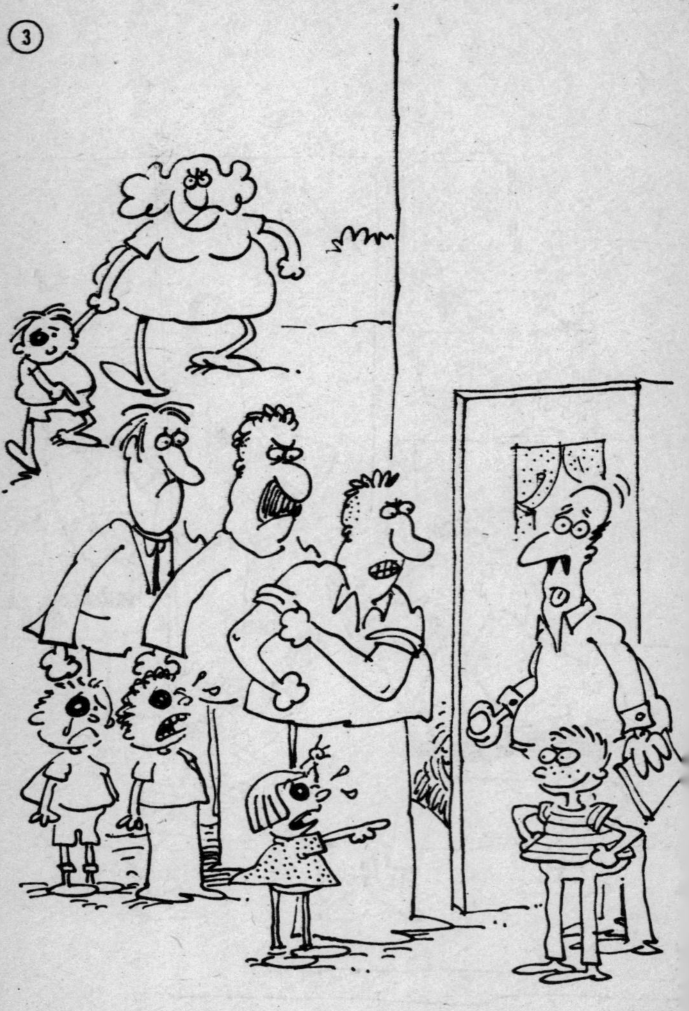

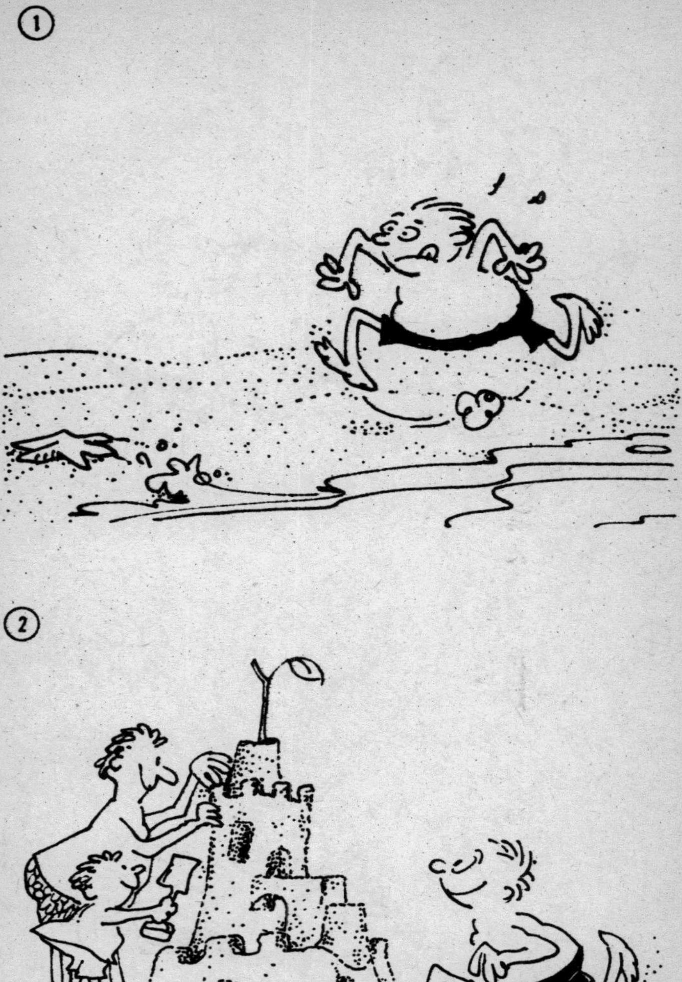
1
2

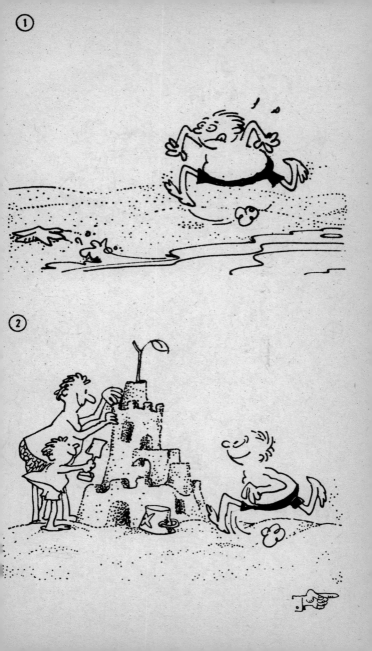

3

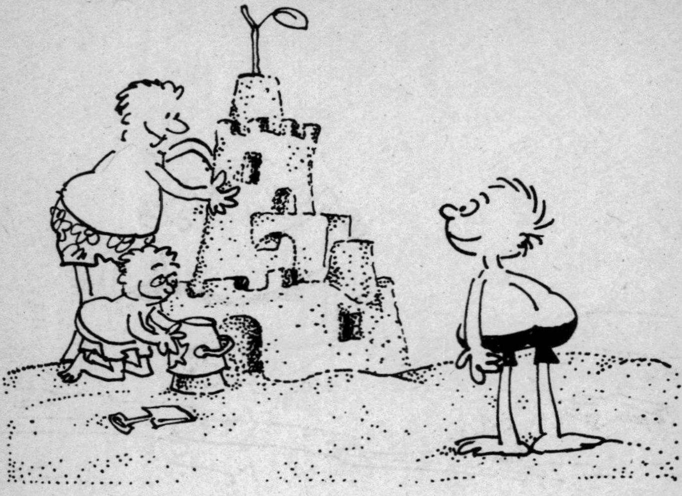

4

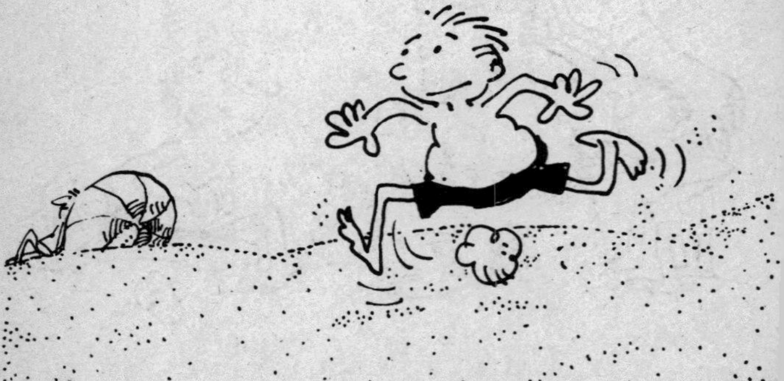

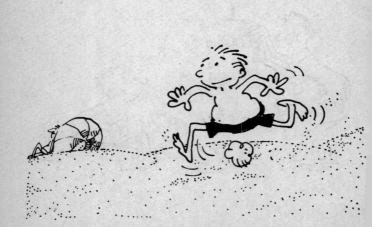

5

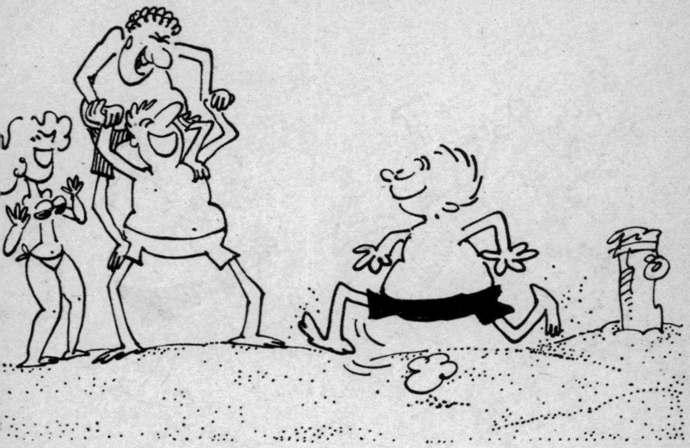

6

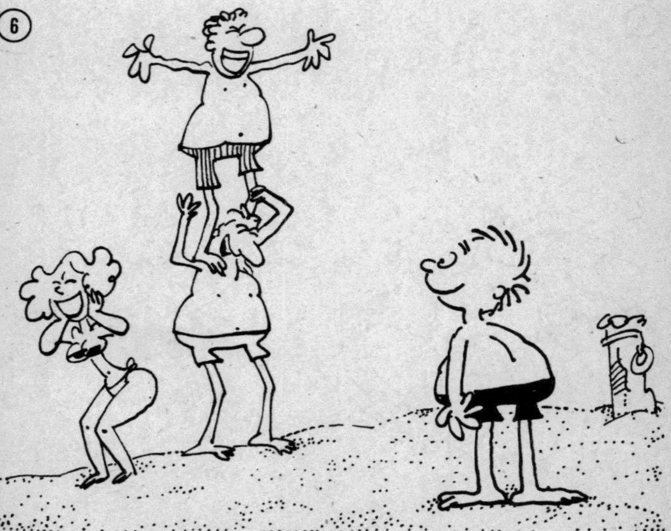

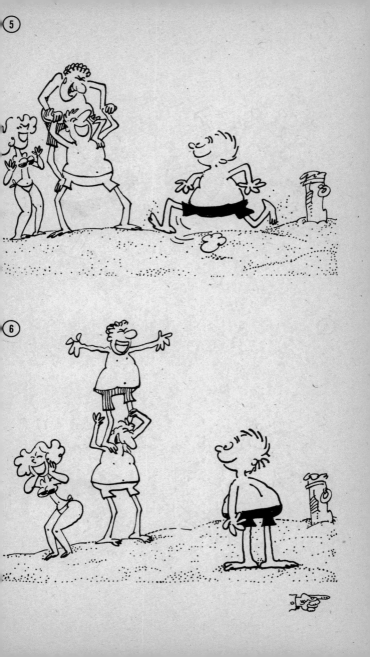

7

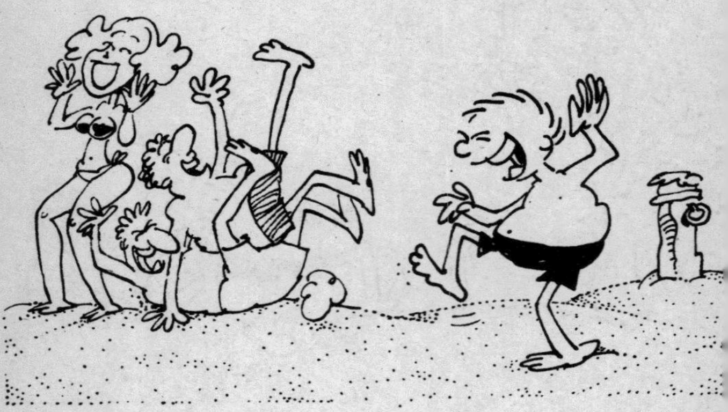

8

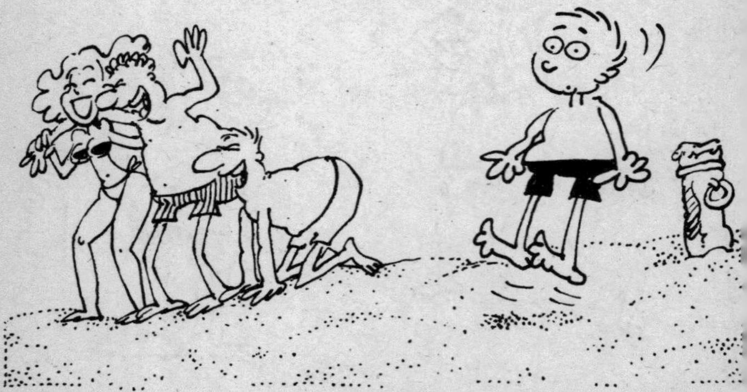

9

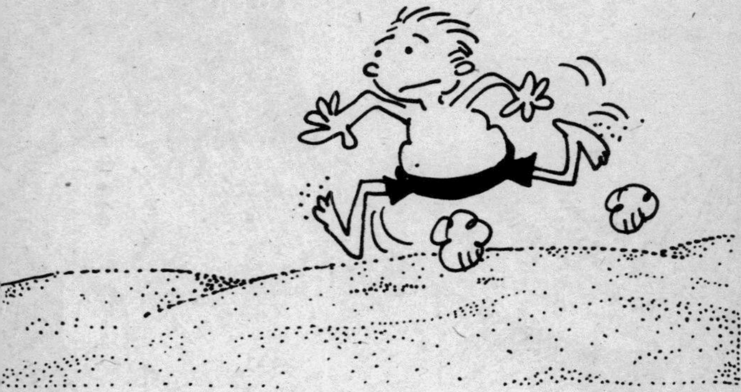

10

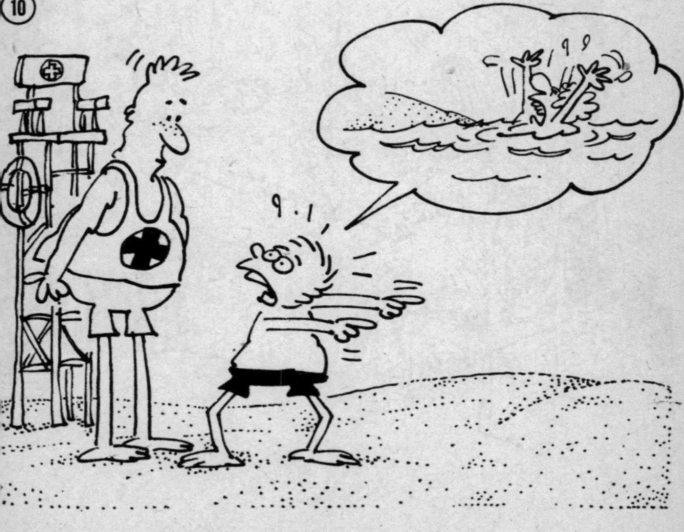

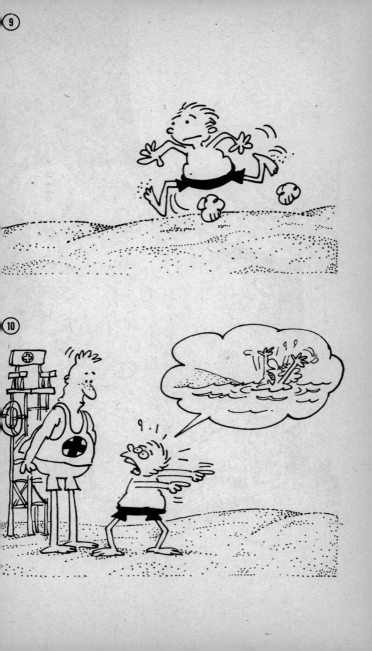

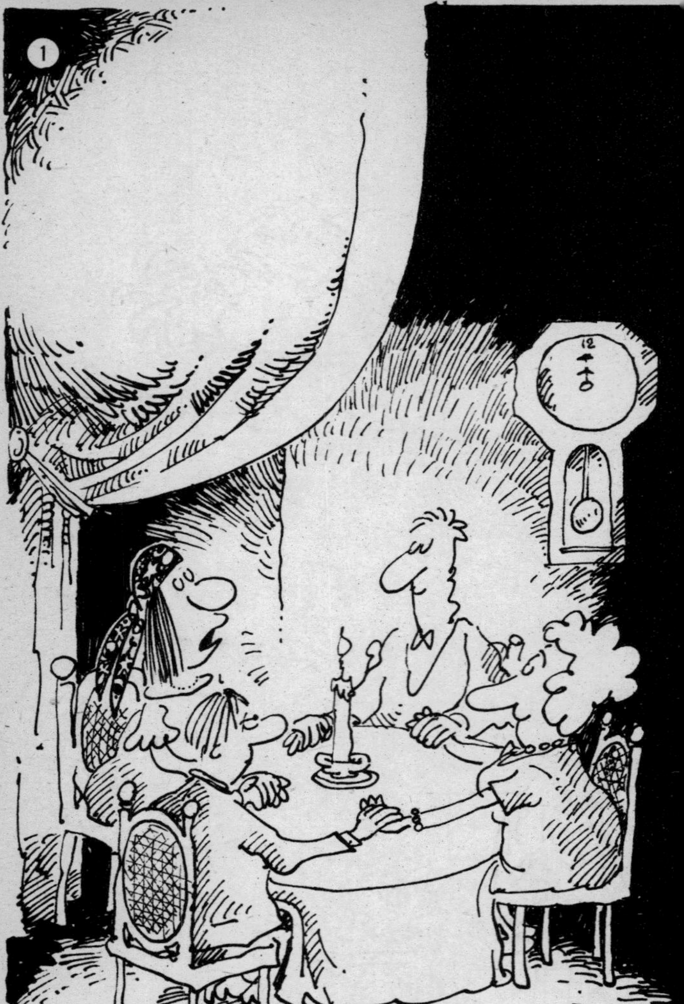

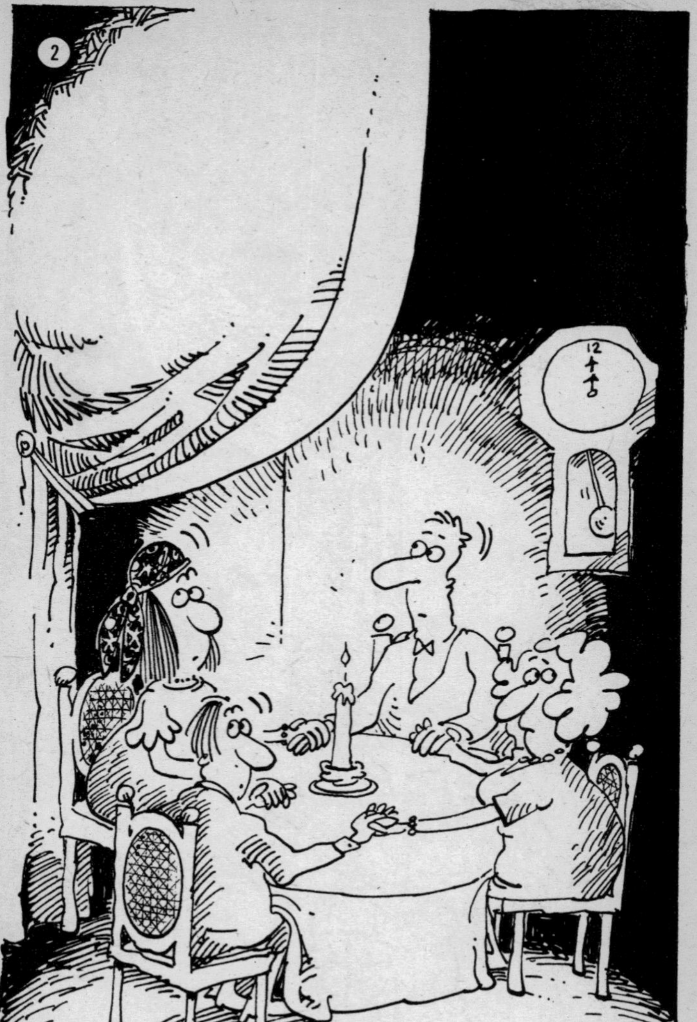
2

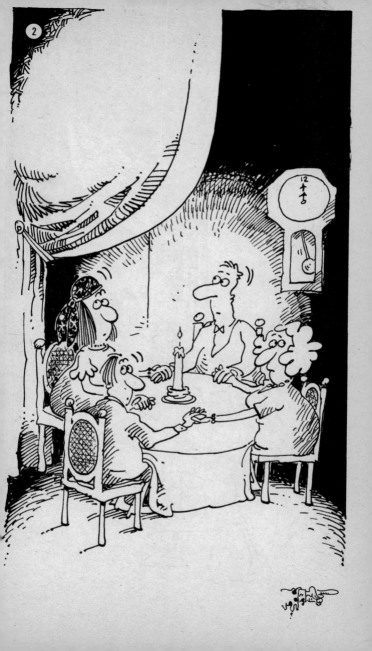

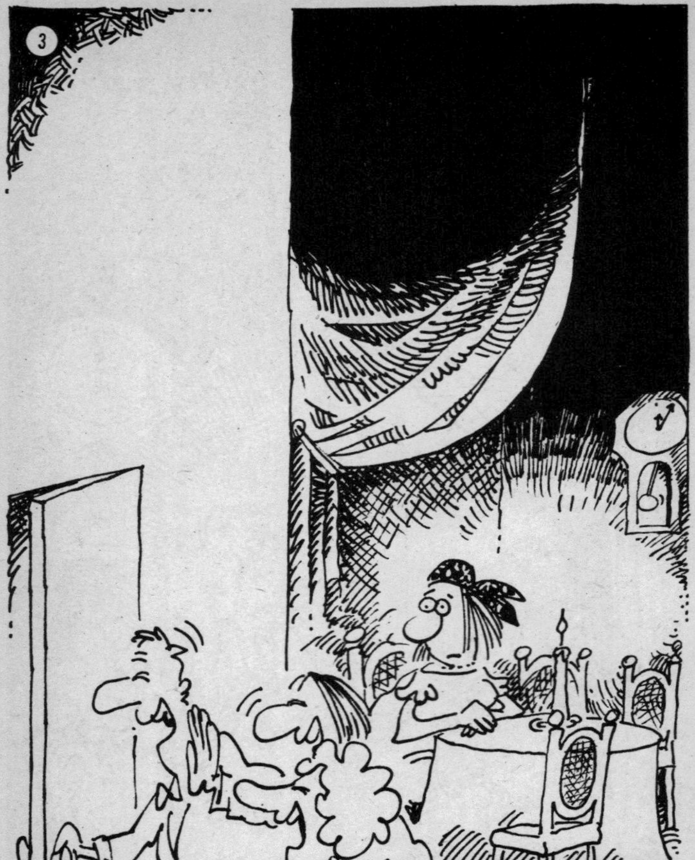
3

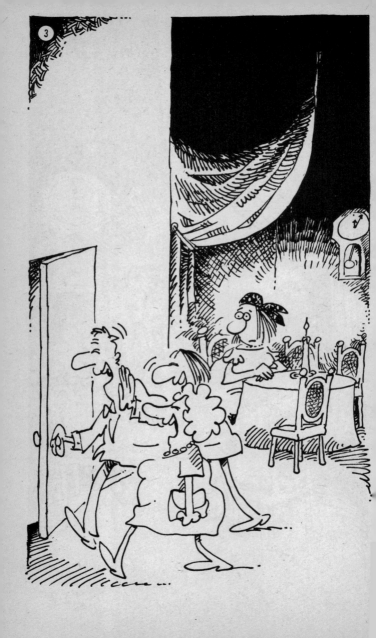

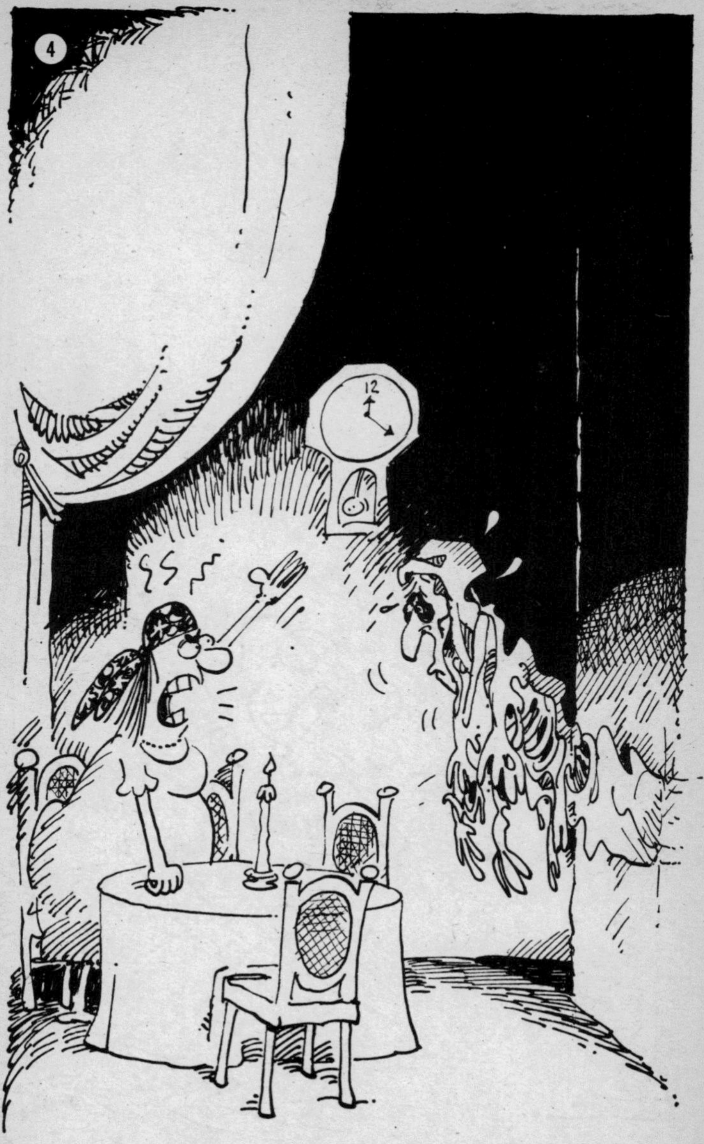
4
12

3

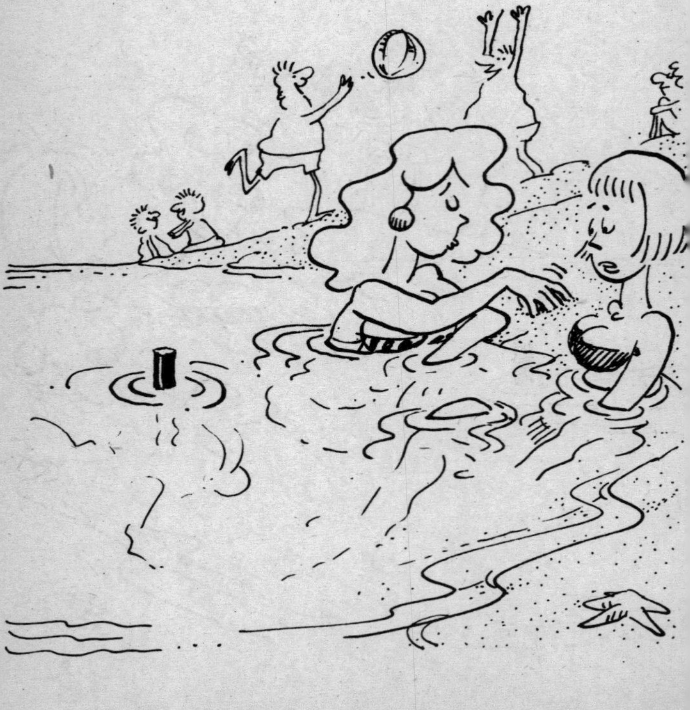

1

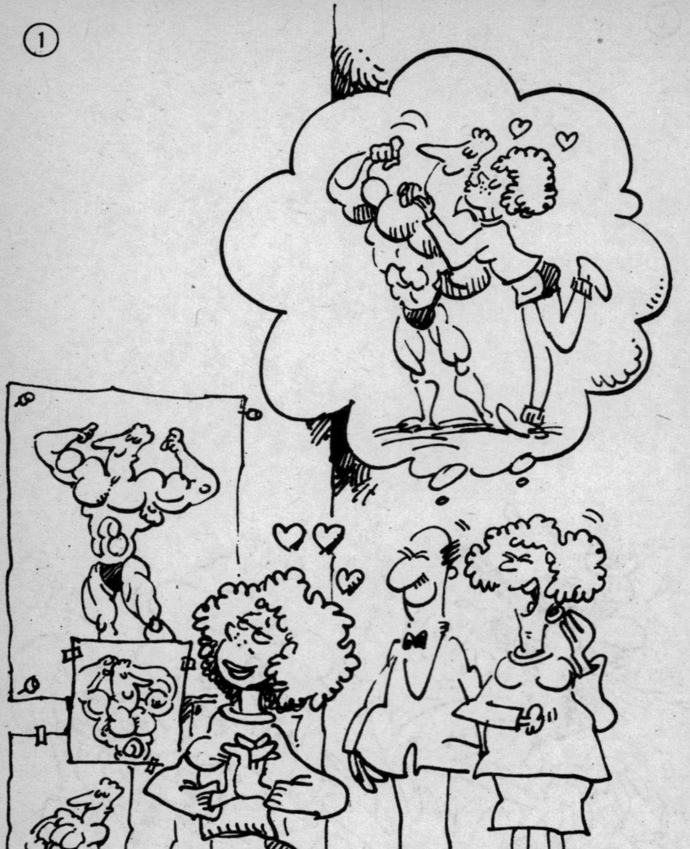

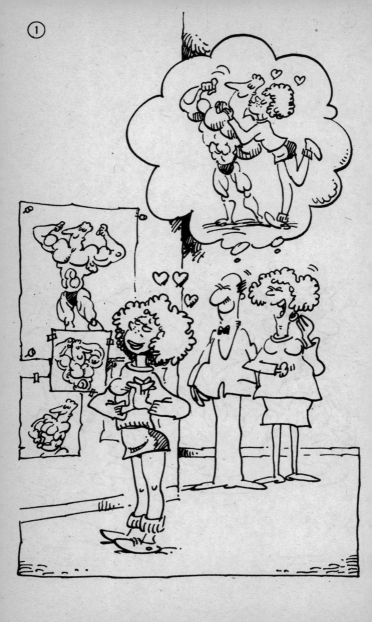

(2)

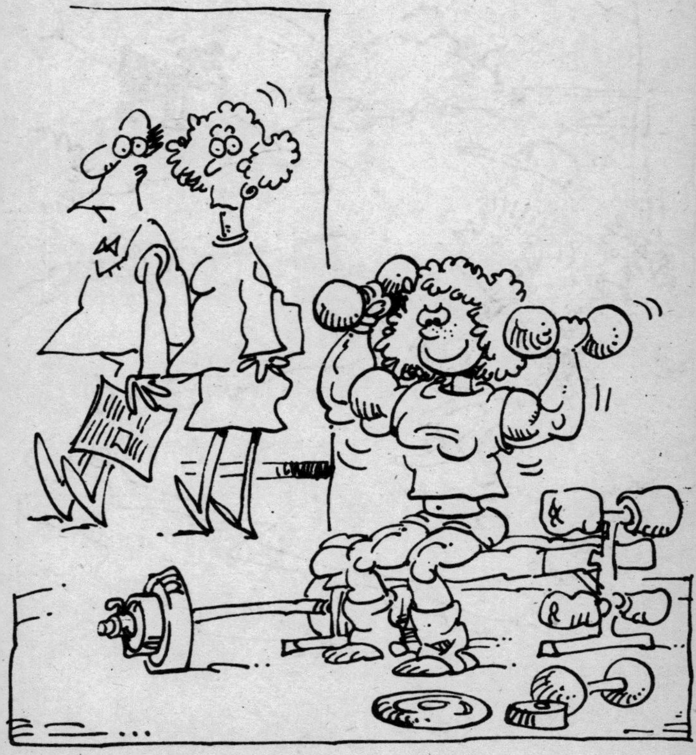

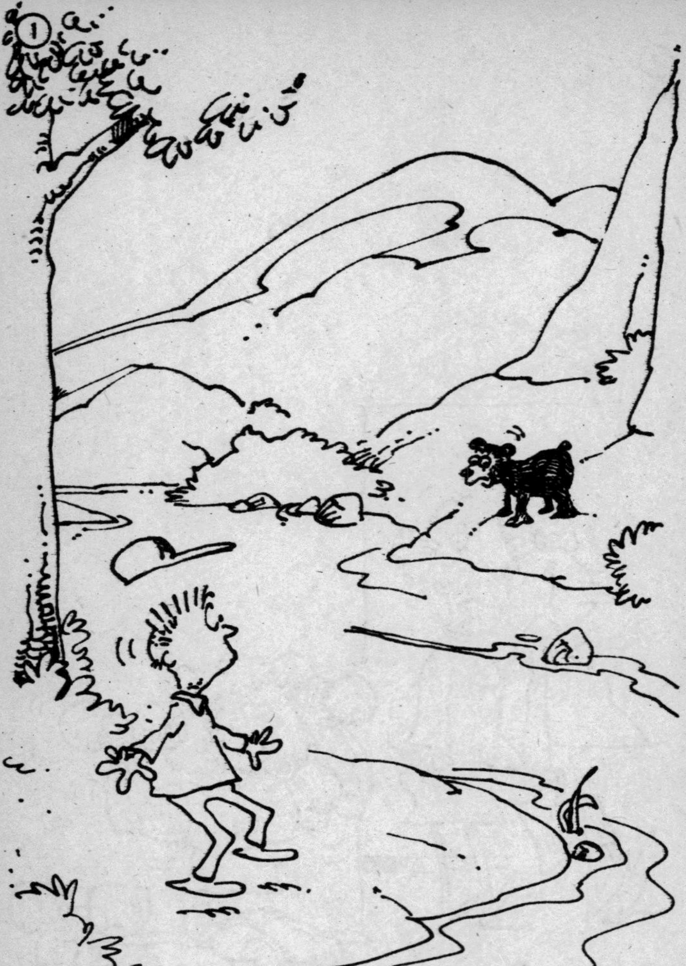
1

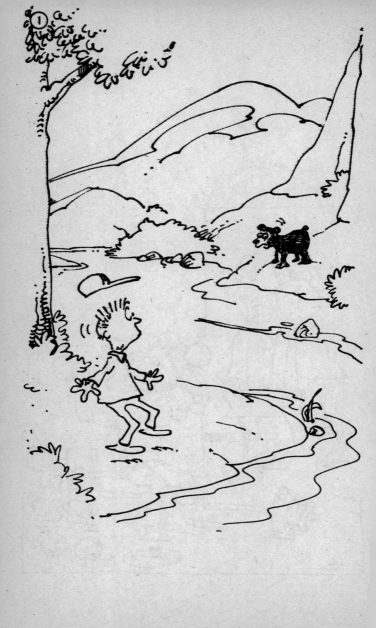

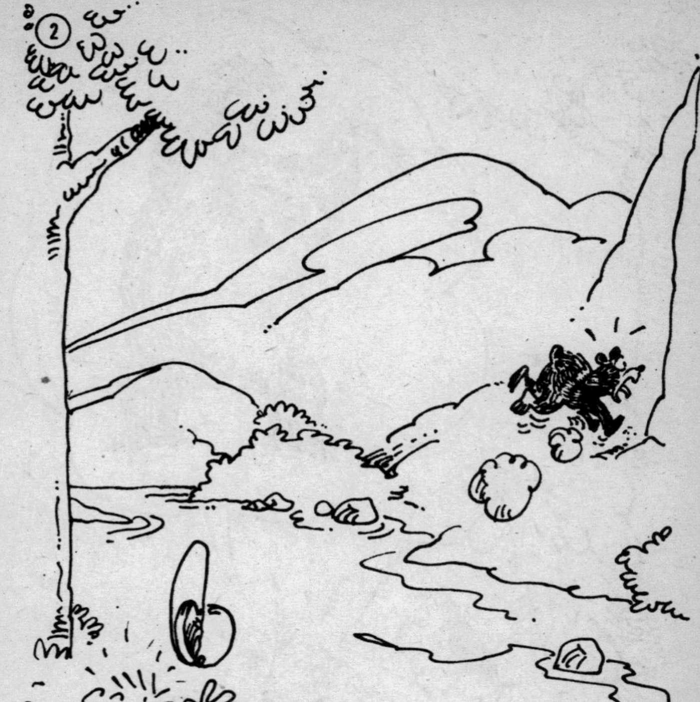

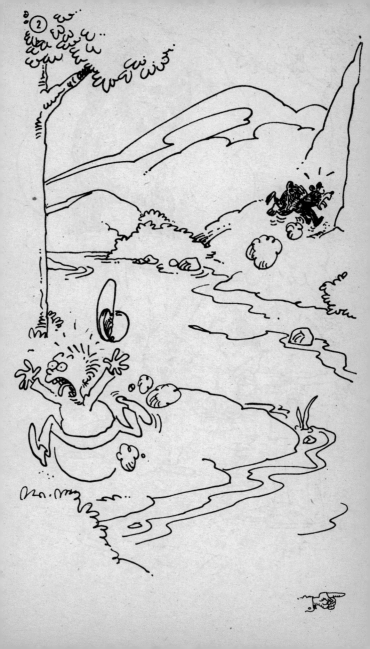

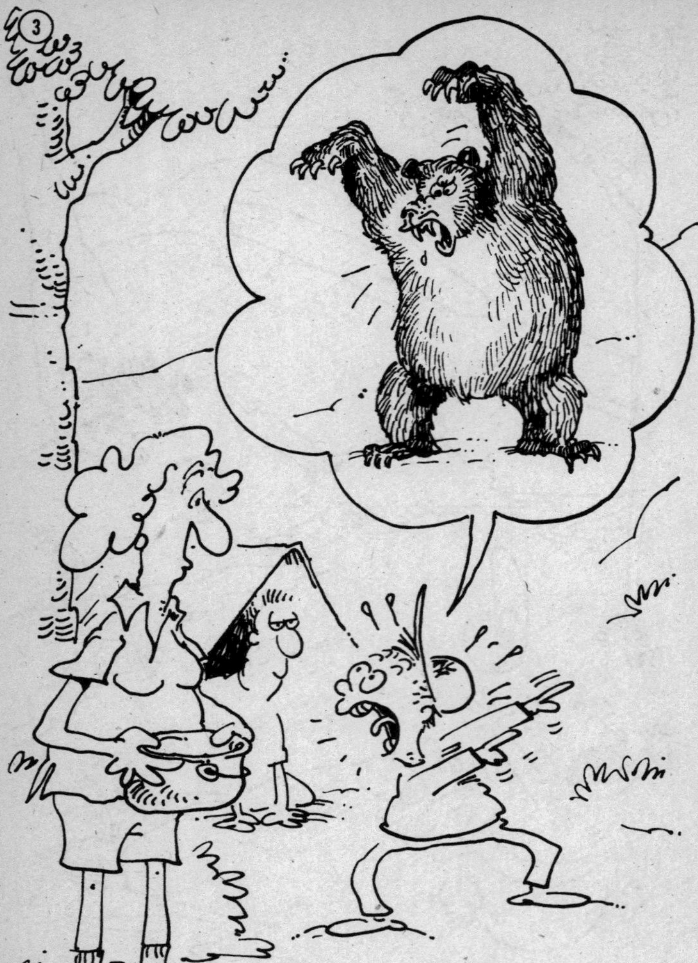

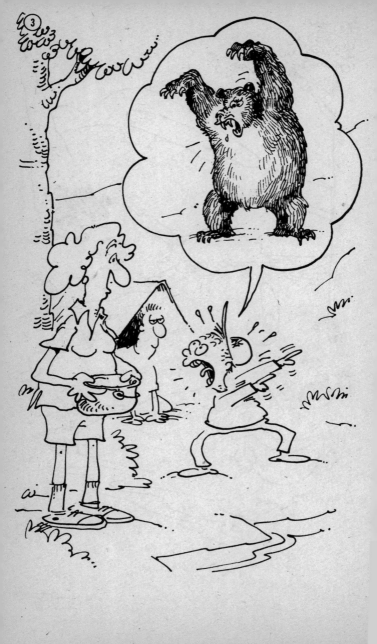

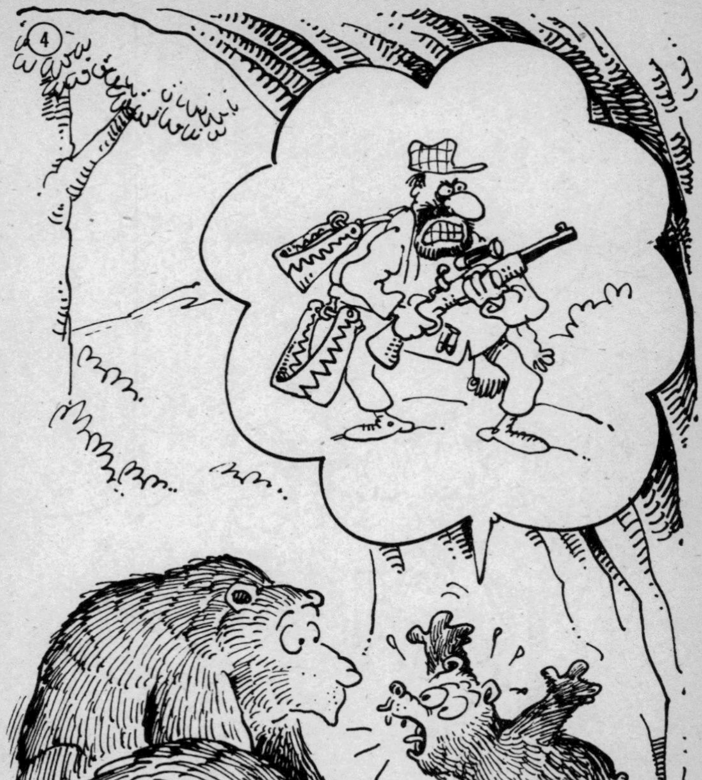
4

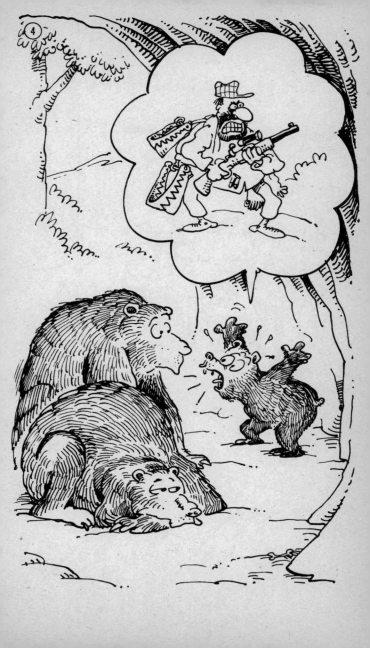

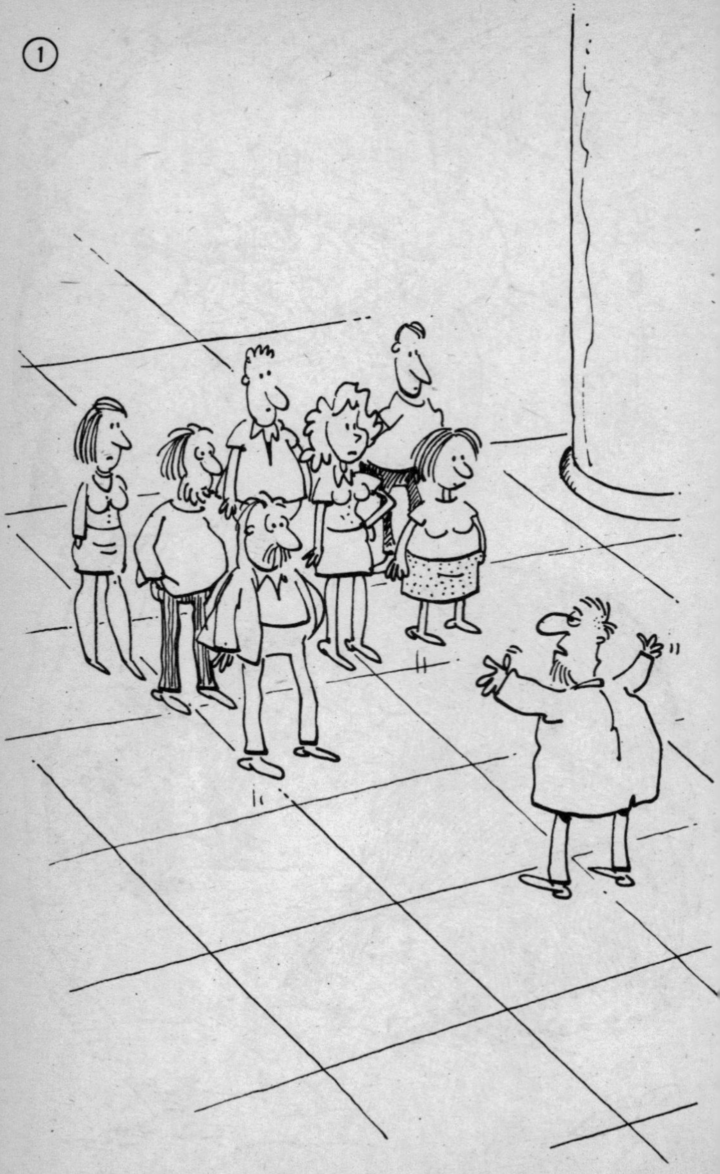
1

2

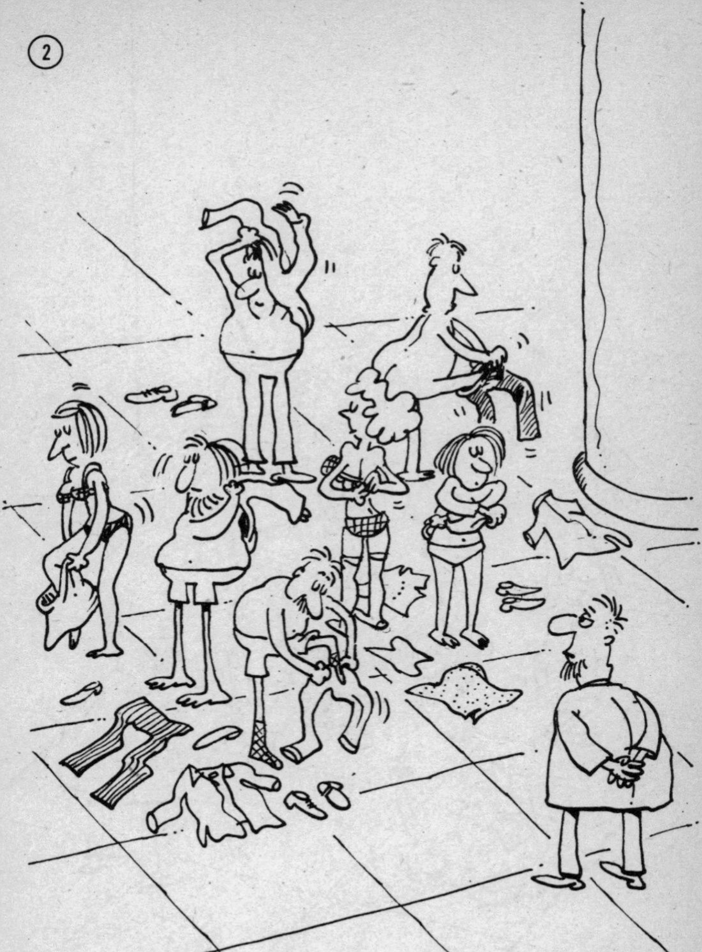

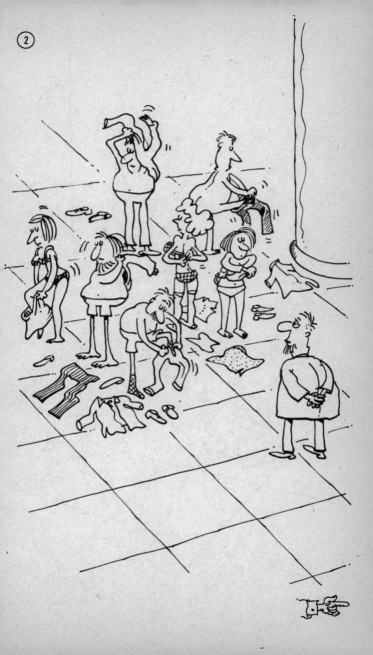

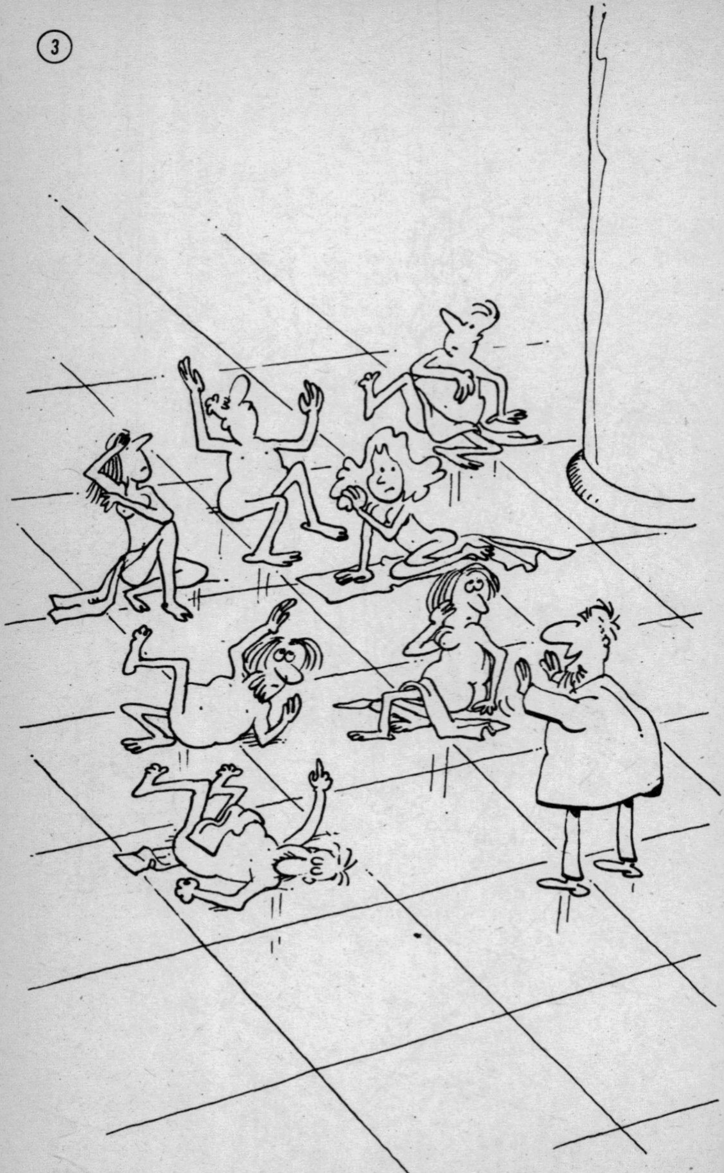
3

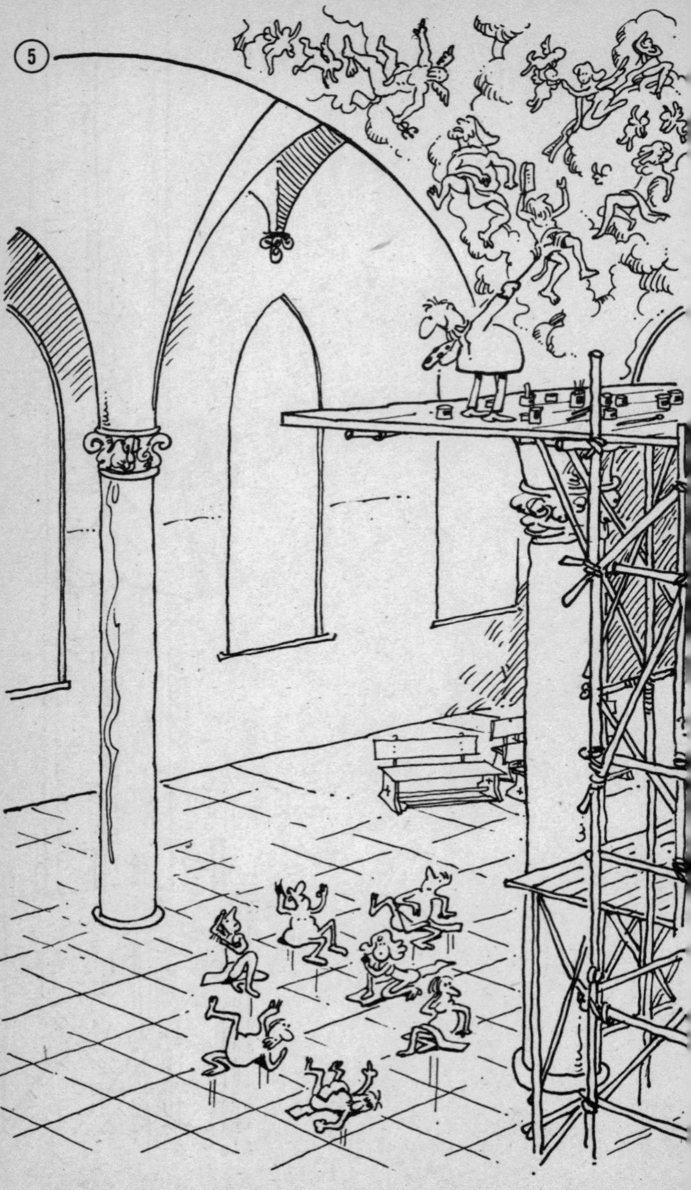

(1)

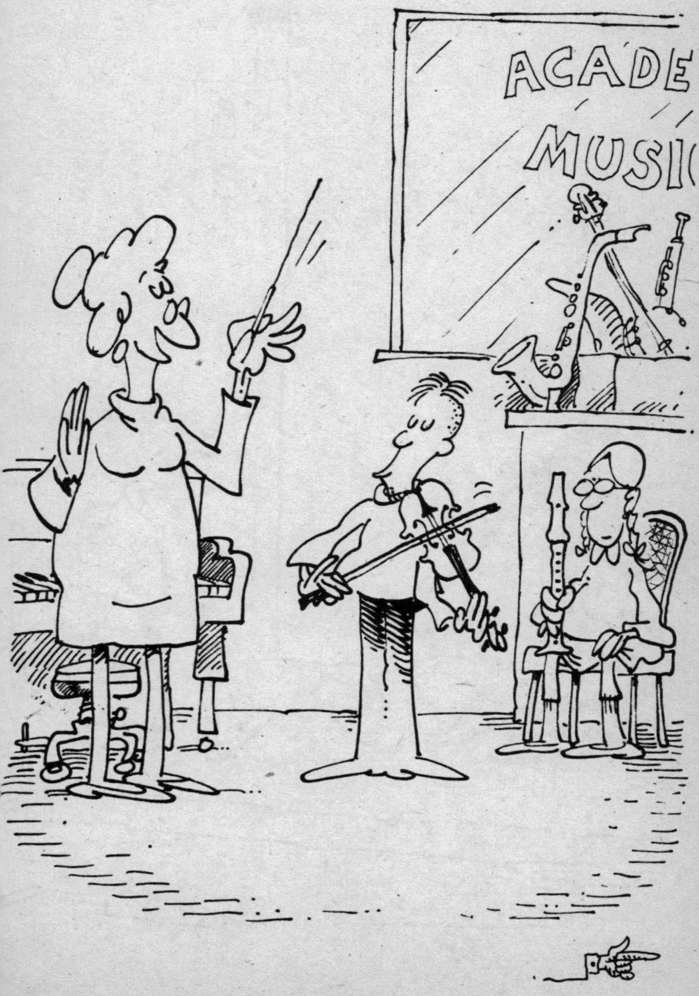
ACADE
MUSI

②

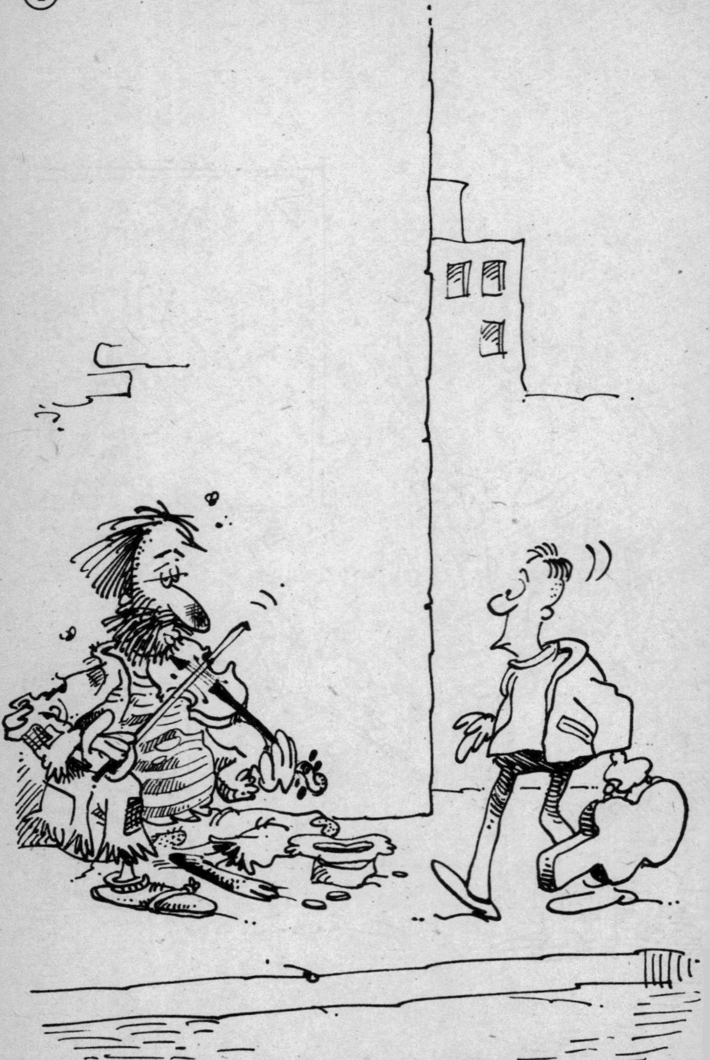

3

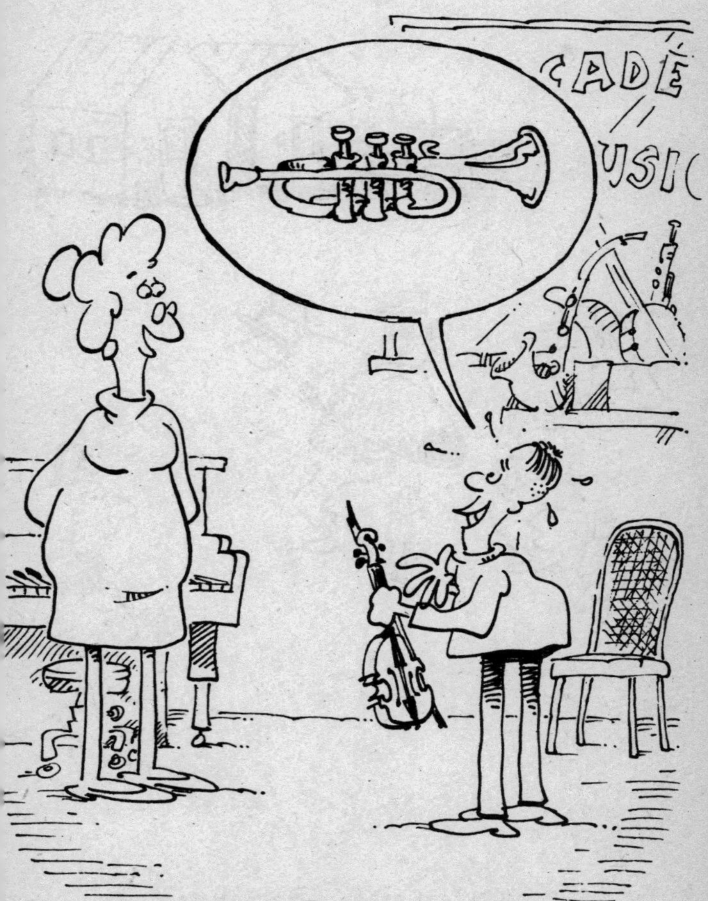
CADÉ
USI

1

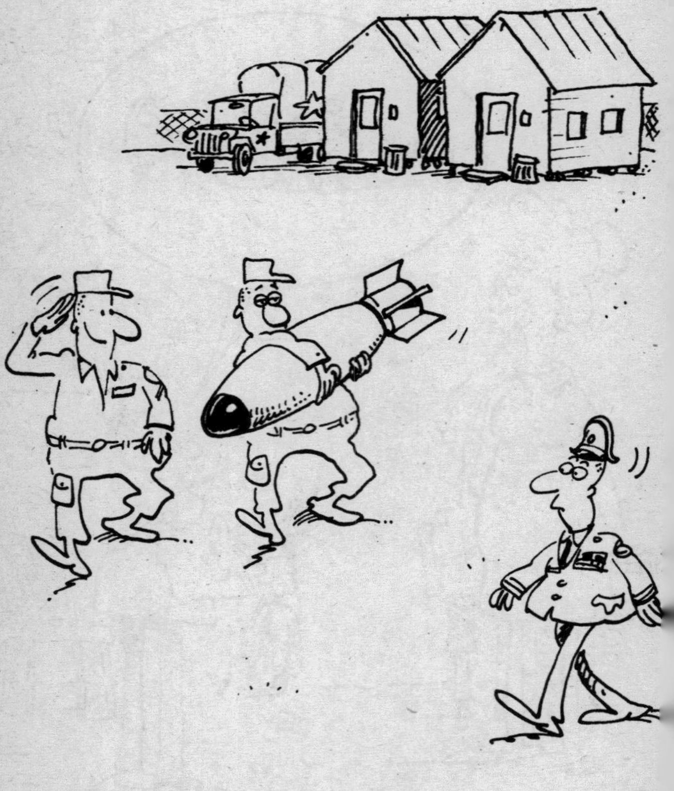

2

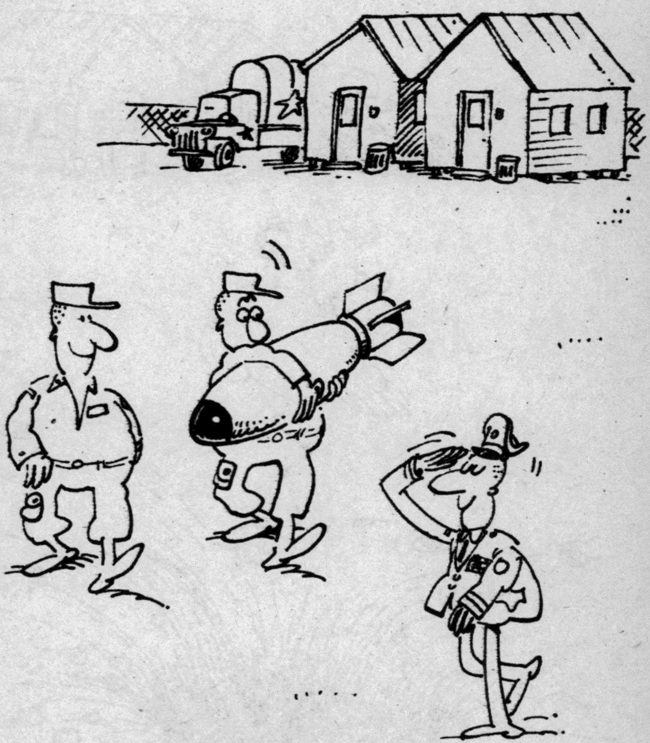

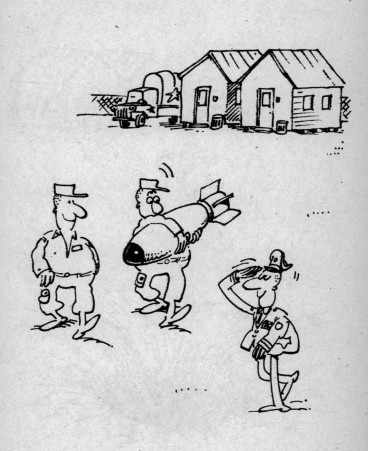

3

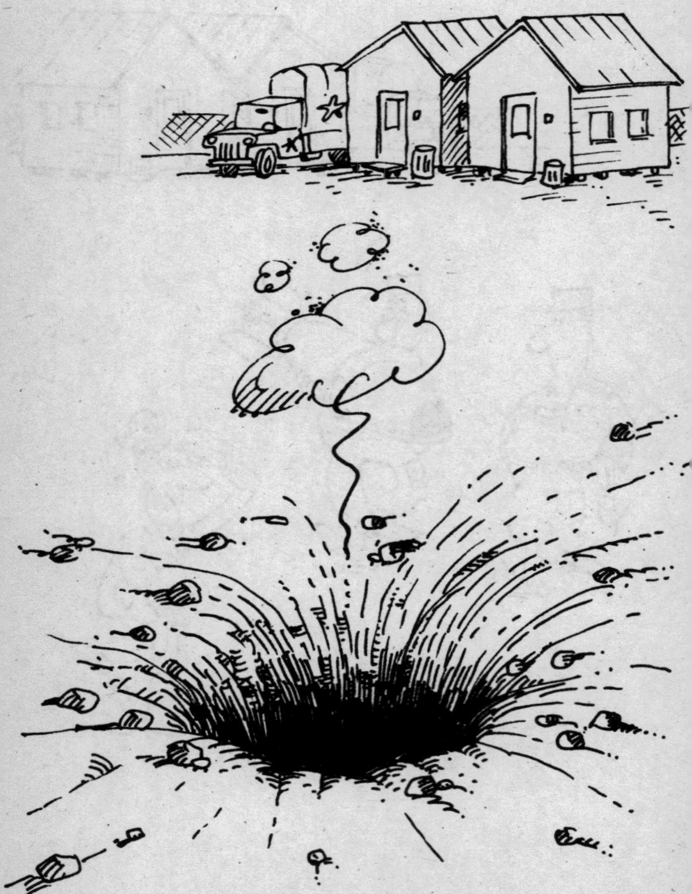

①

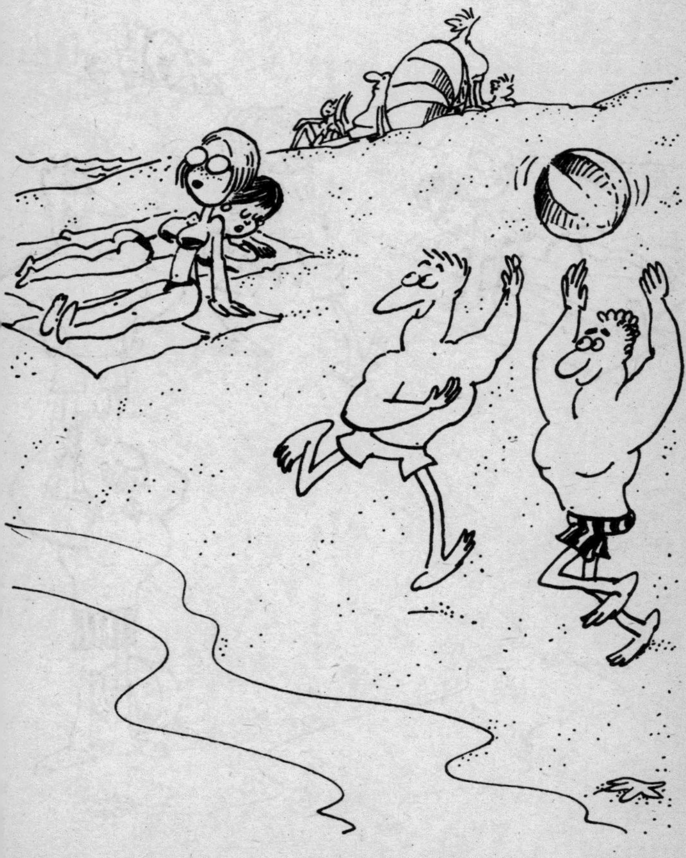

3

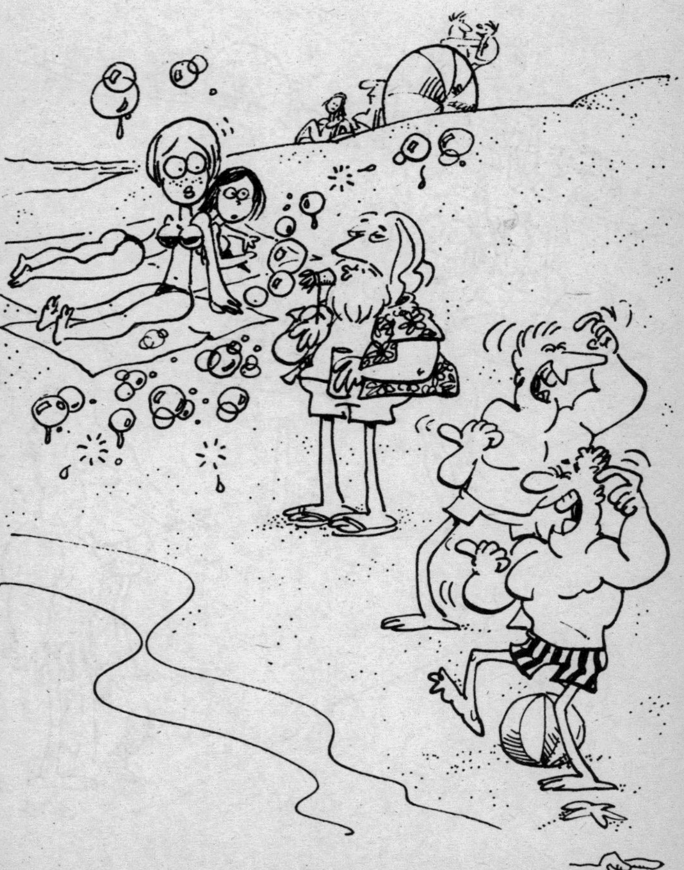

4

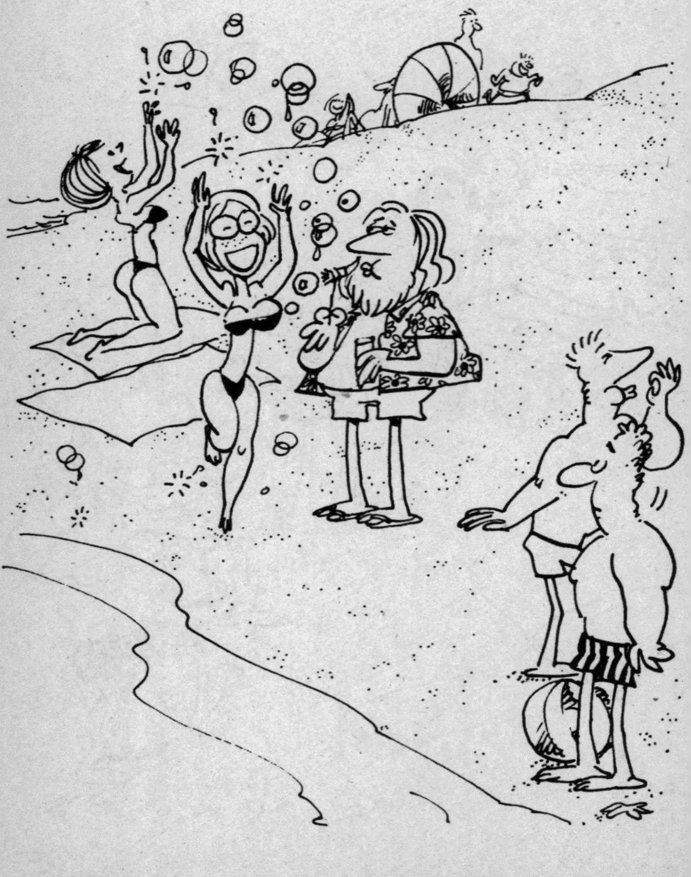

5

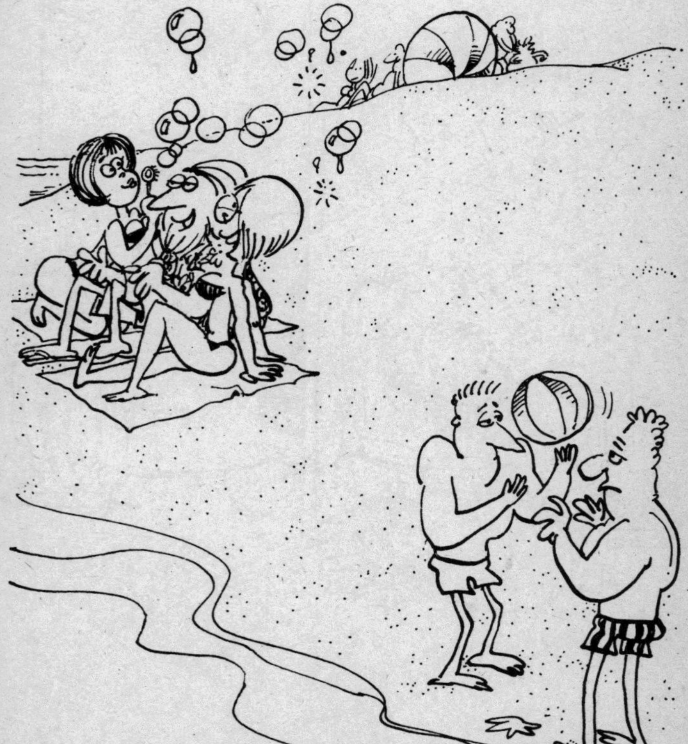

2

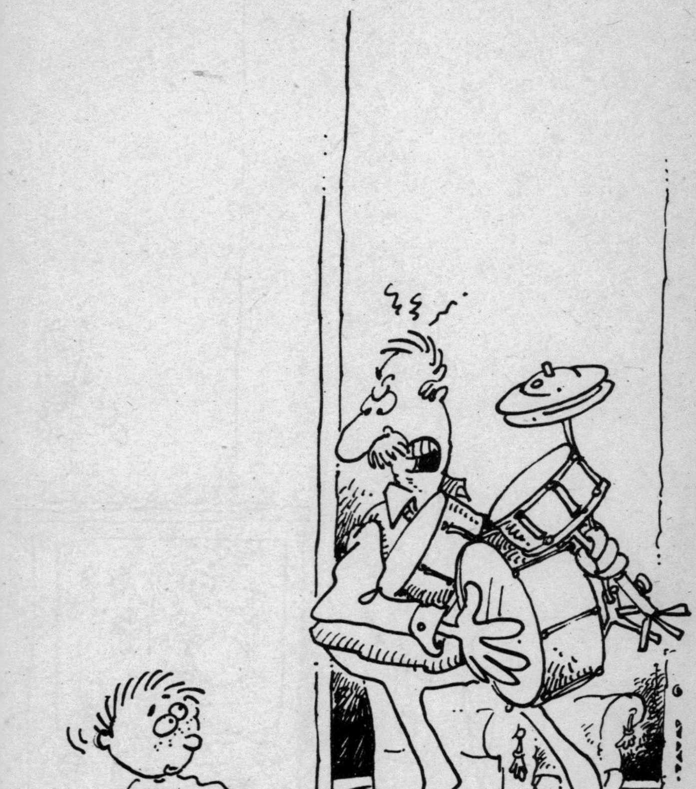

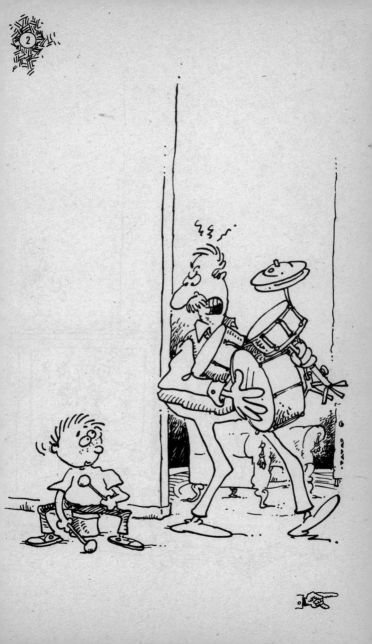

3

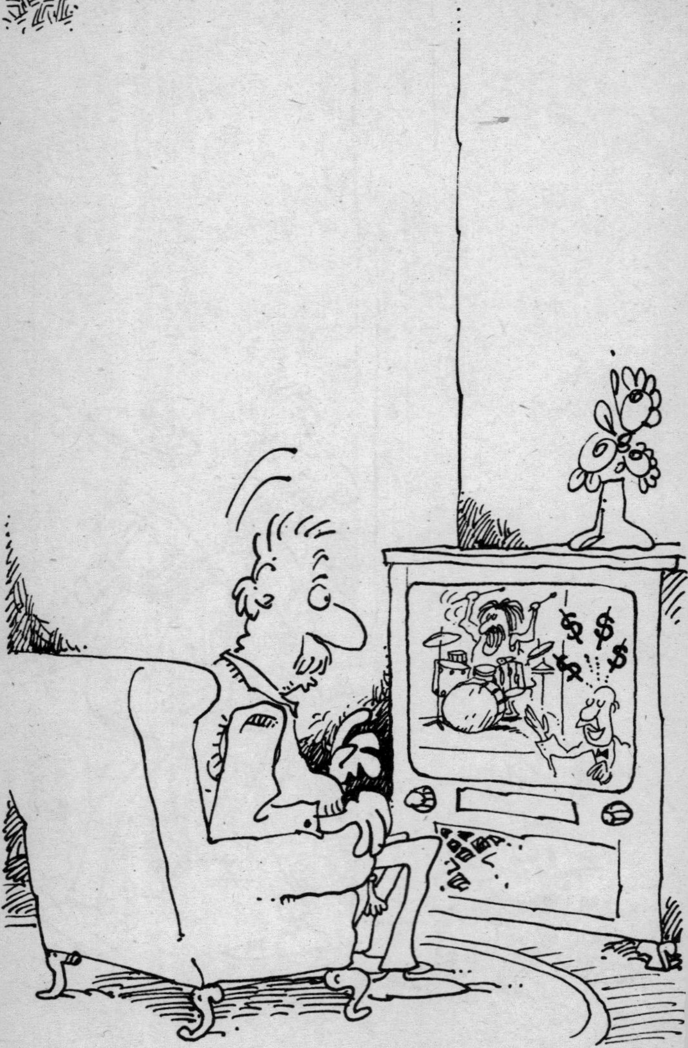

4

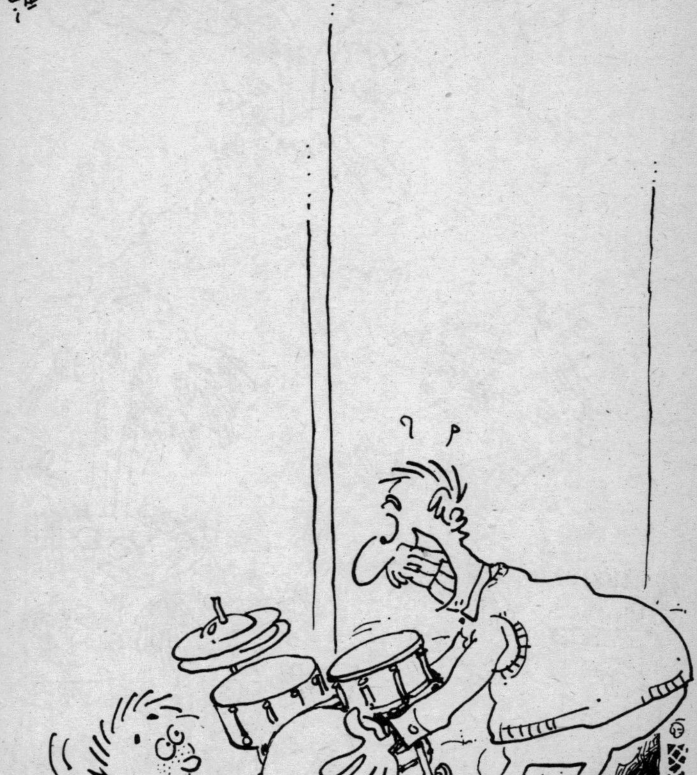

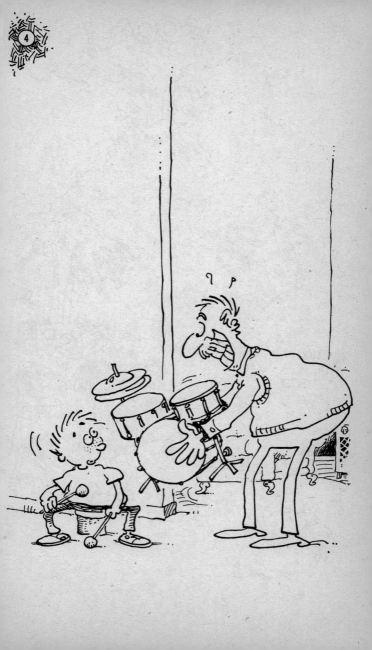

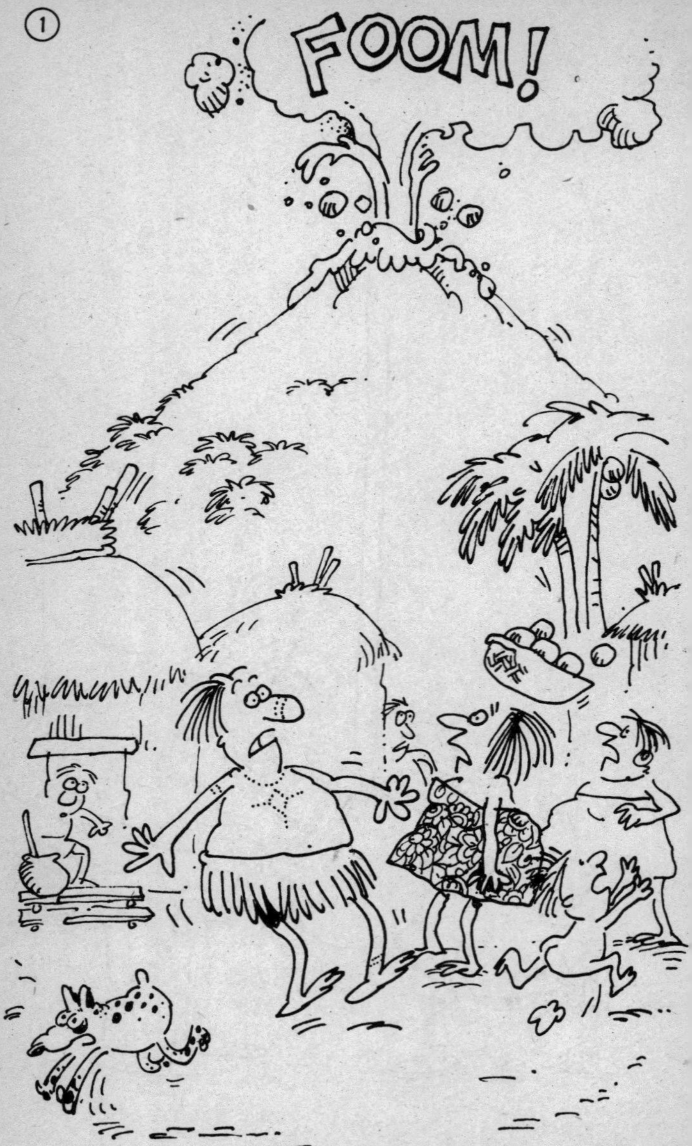
1
FOOM!

2

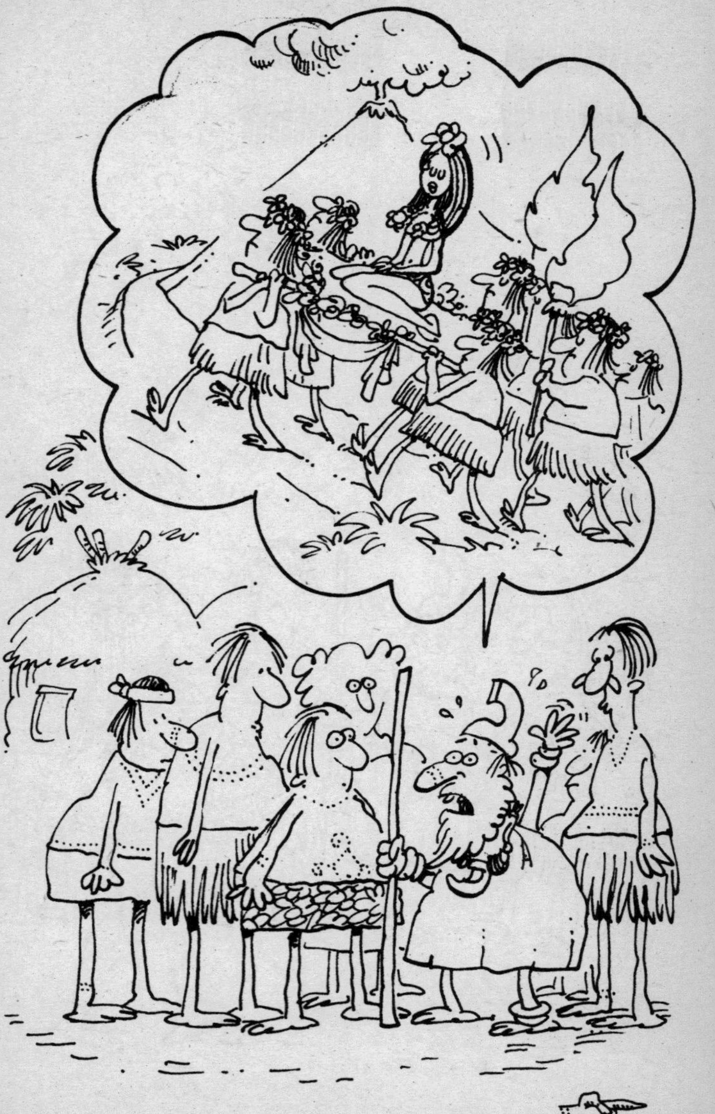

3

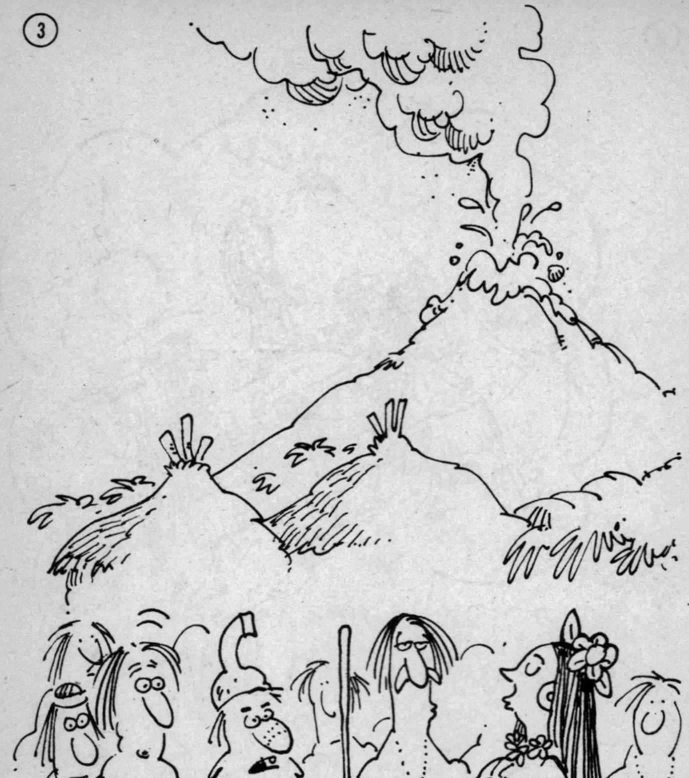

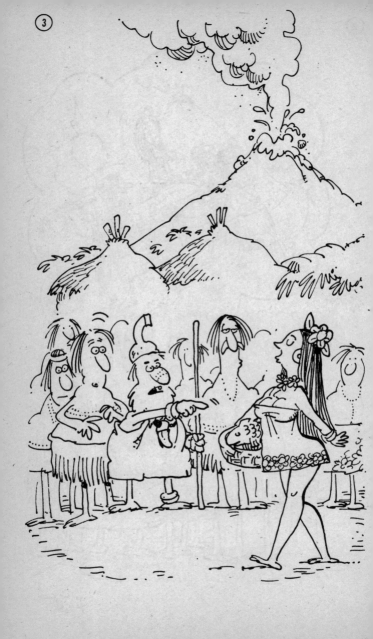

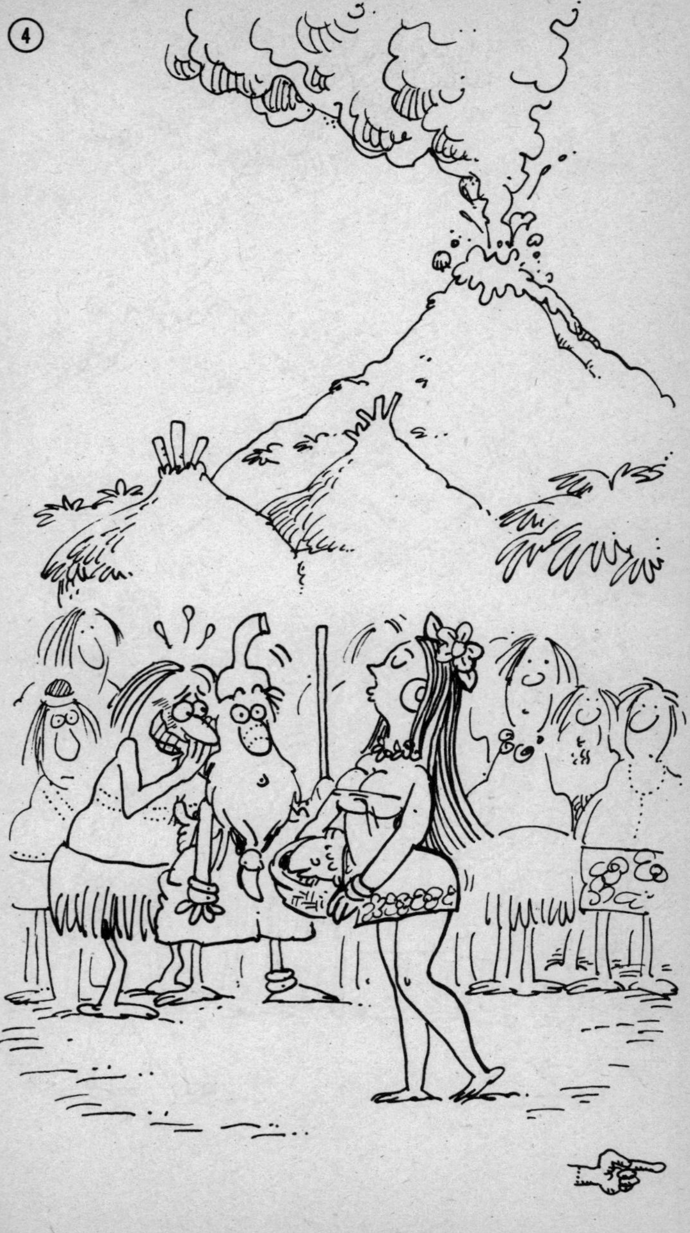
4

5

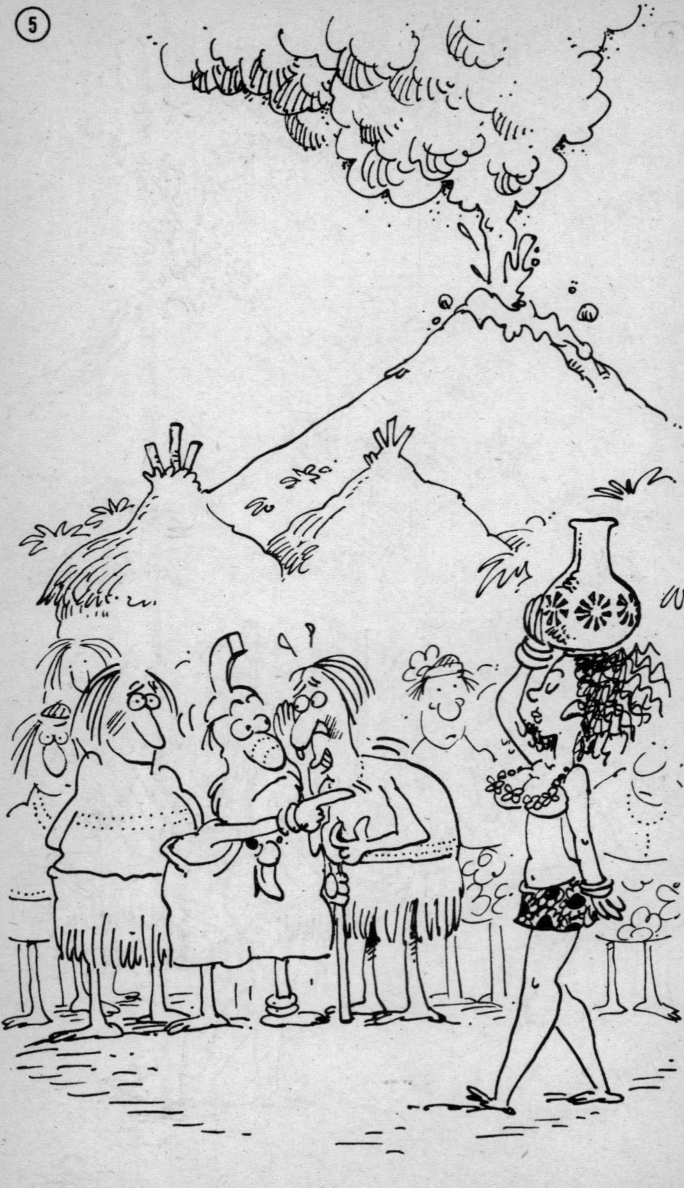

6

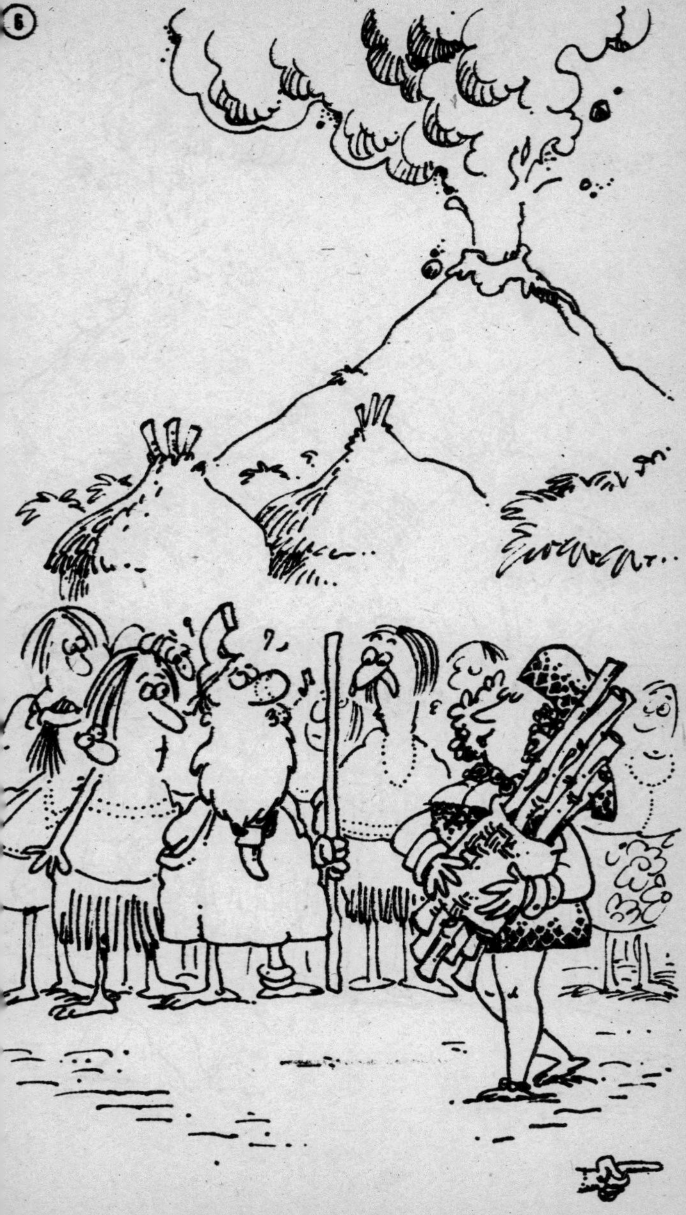

7

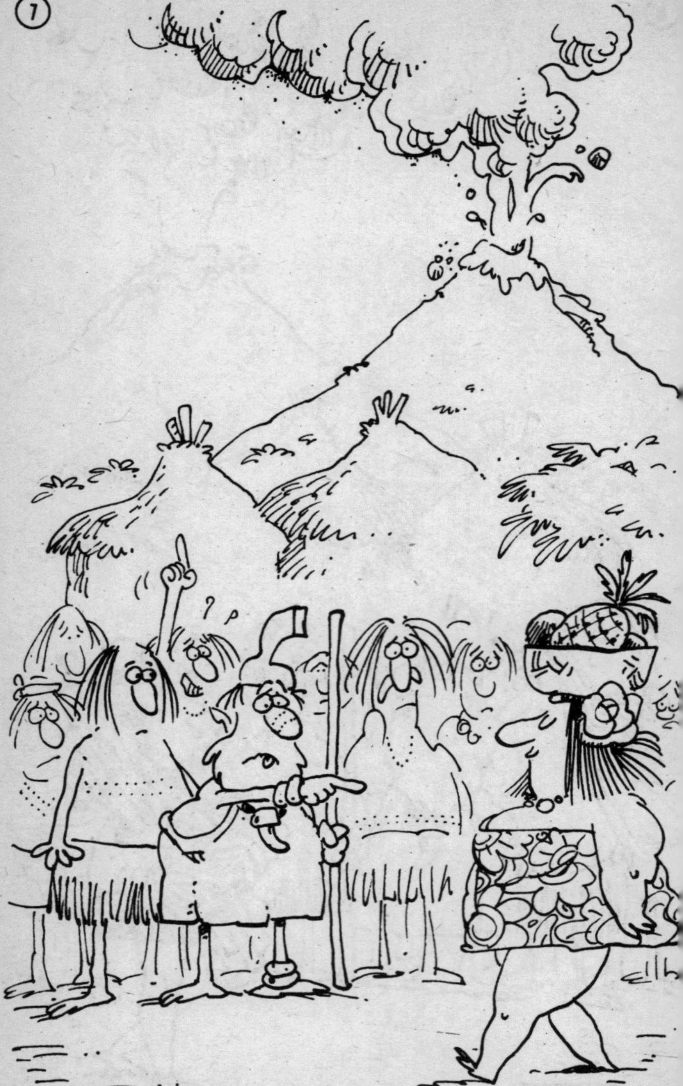

8

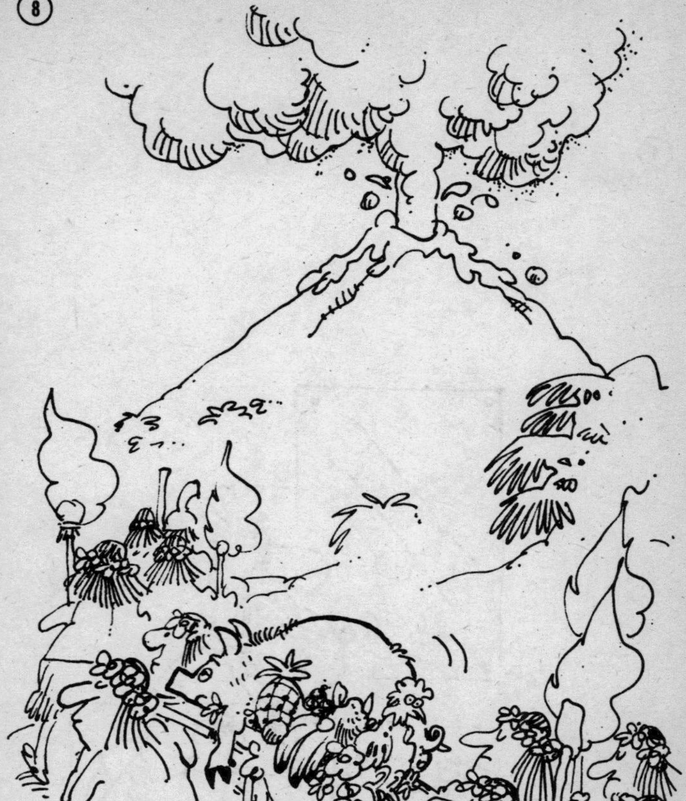

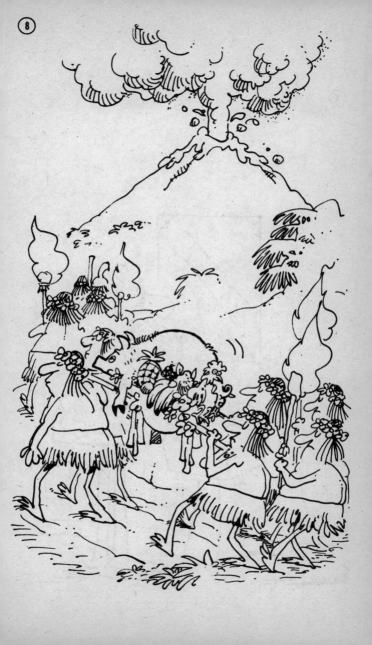

②

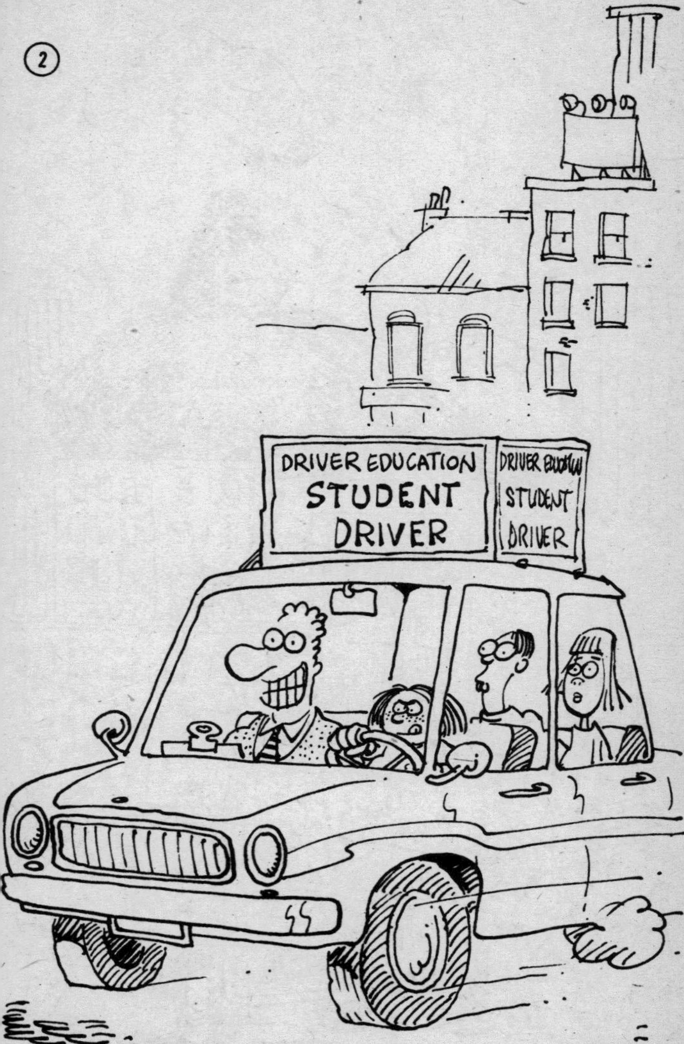
DRIVER EDUCATION
STUDENT
DRIVER
STUDENT
DRIVER

1

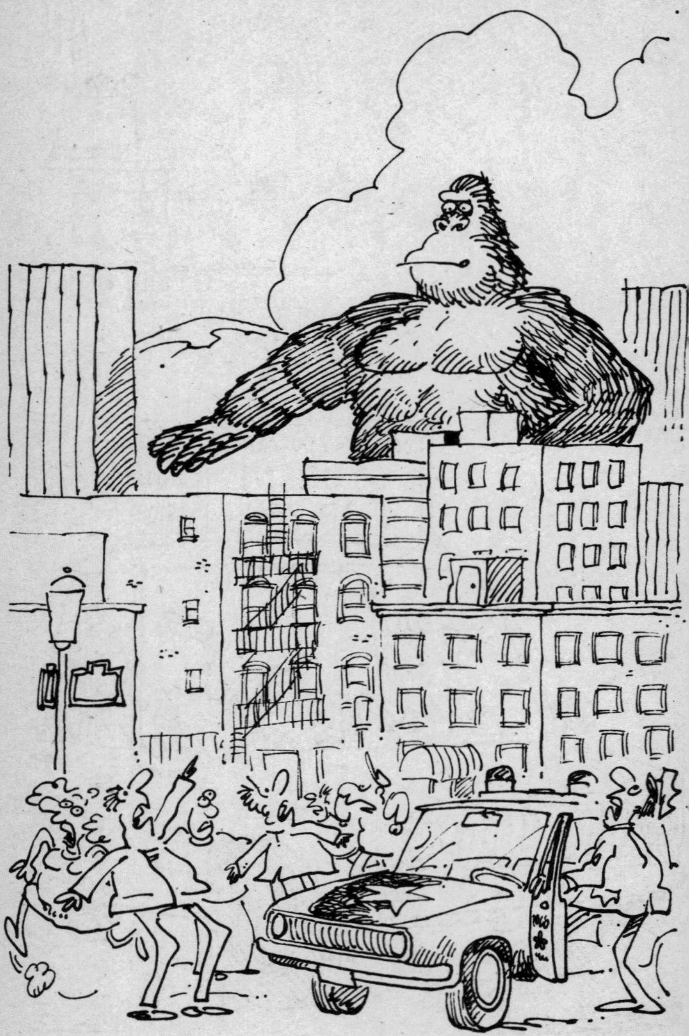

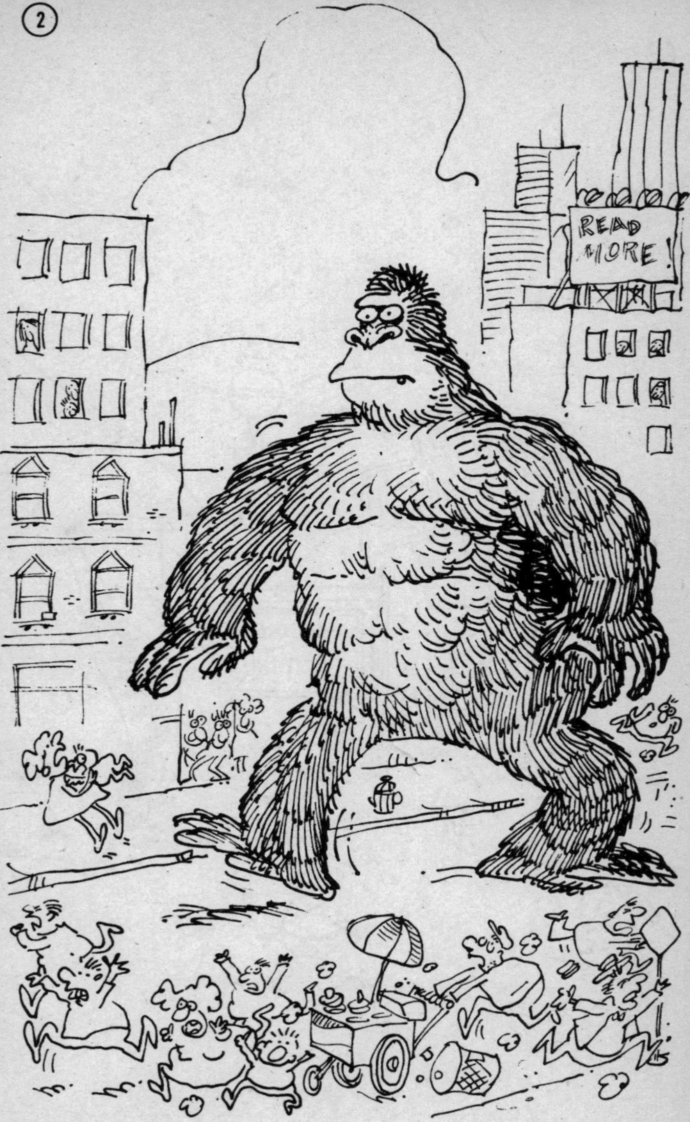
2
READ MORE!

③

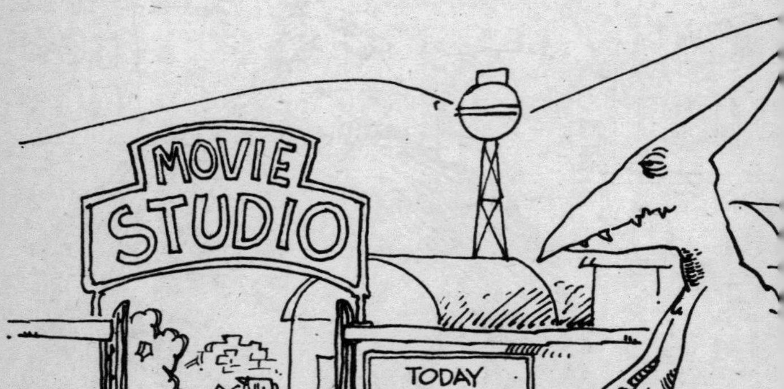
MOVIE
STUDIO
TODAY
CASTING

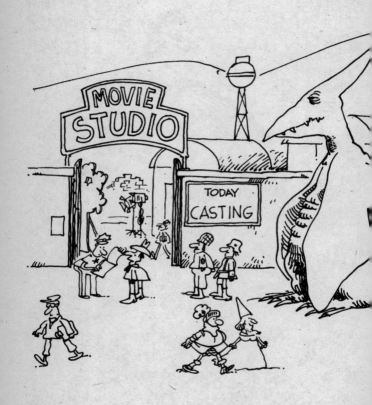

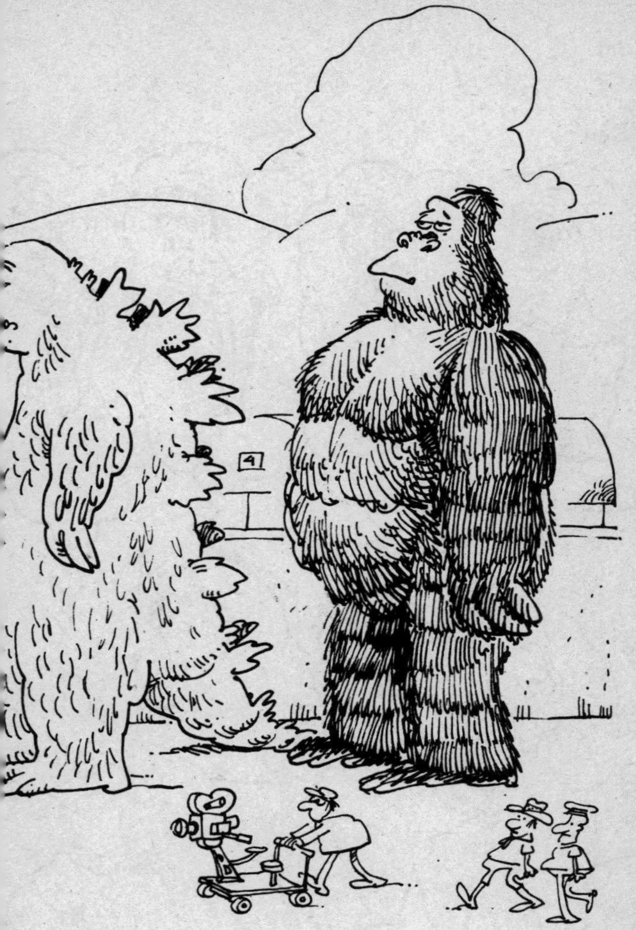
4

1

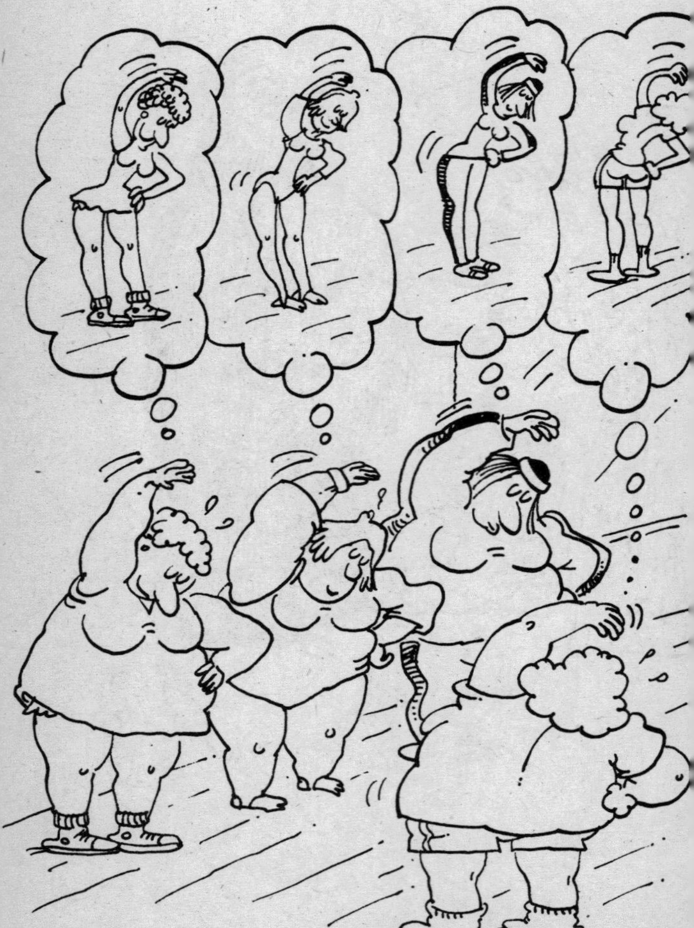

2

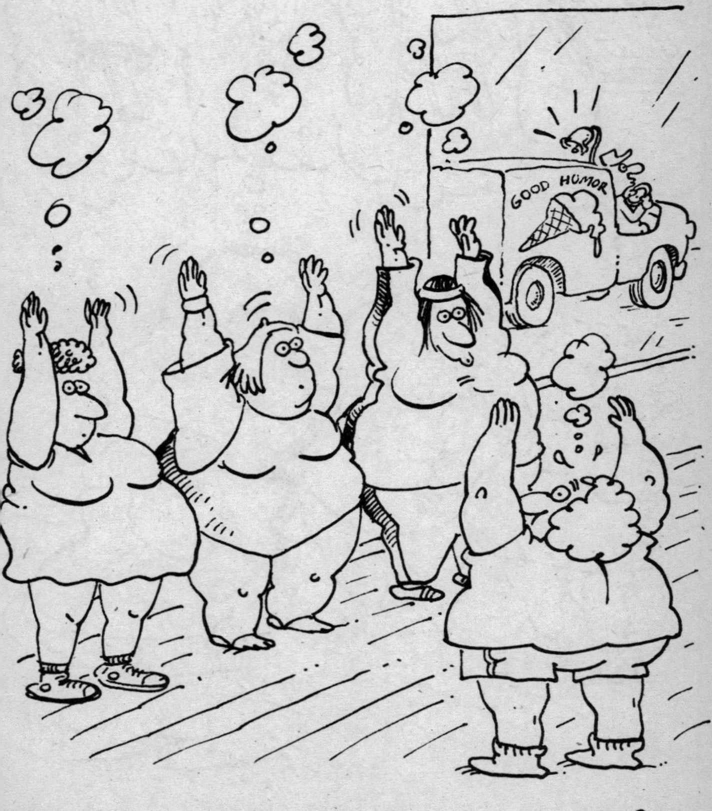
GOOD HUMOR

③

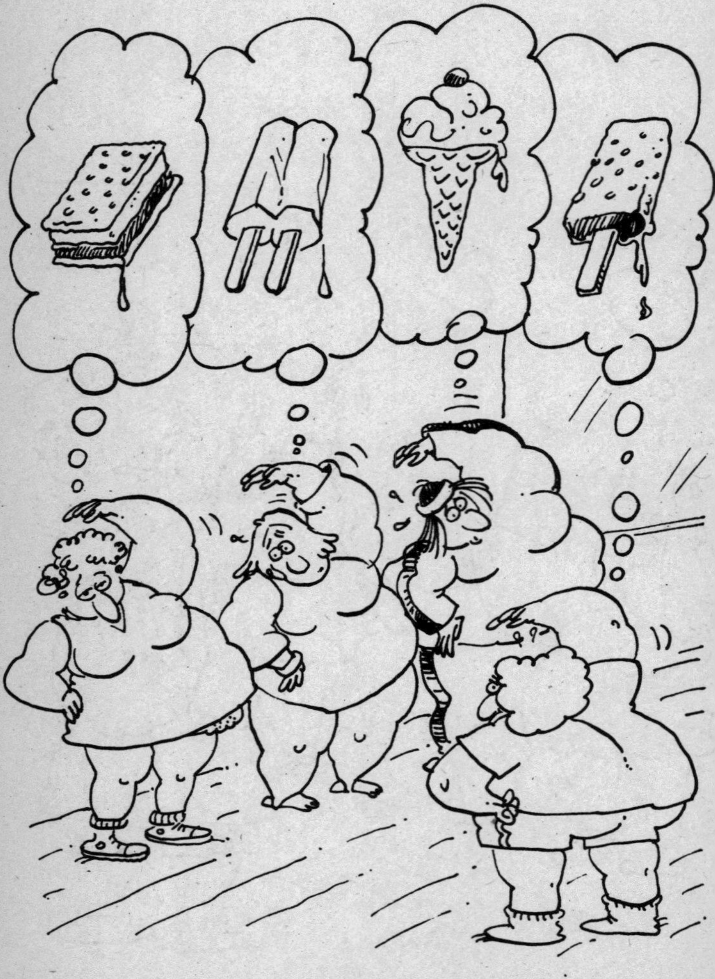

1

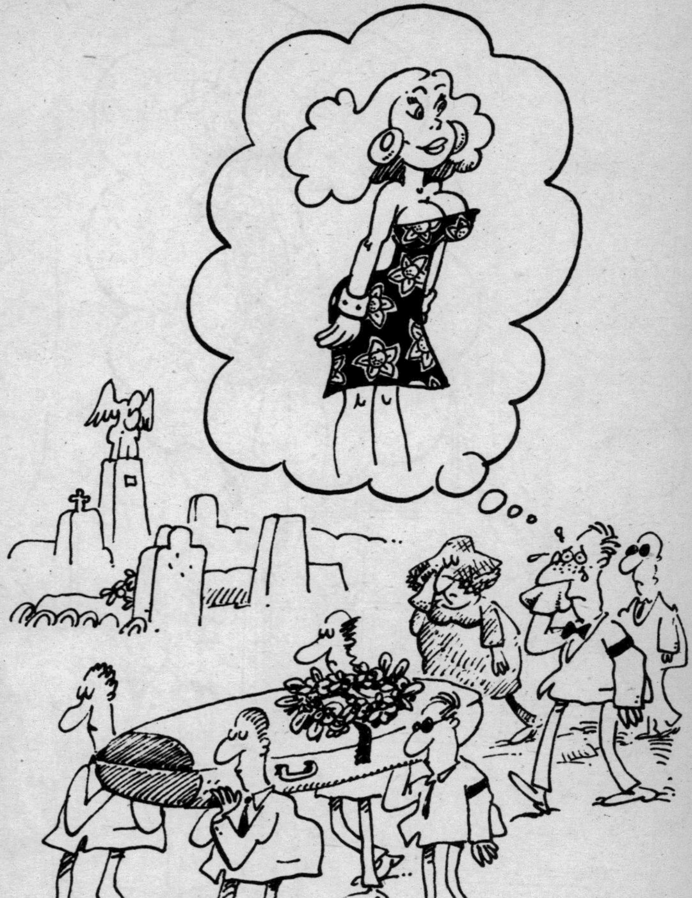

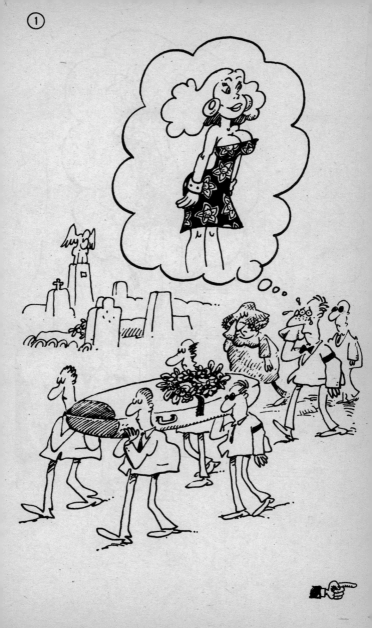

②

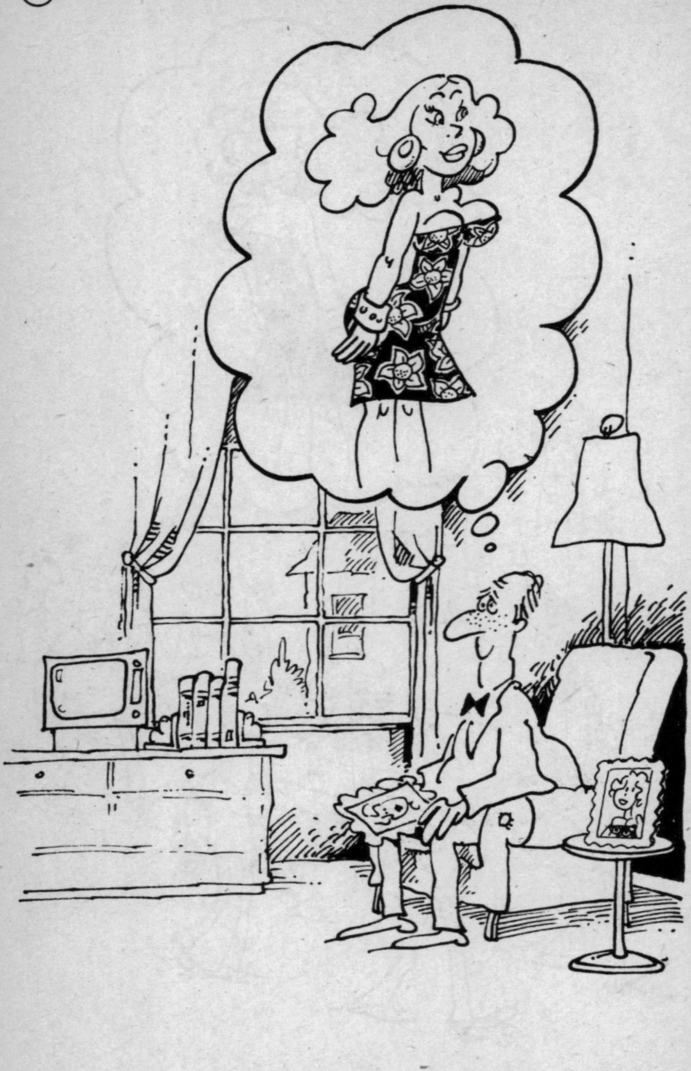

3

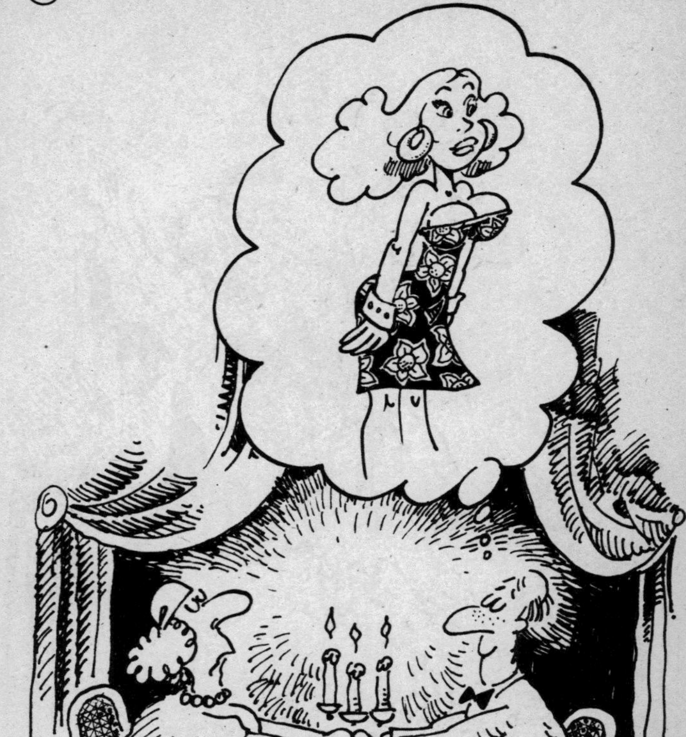

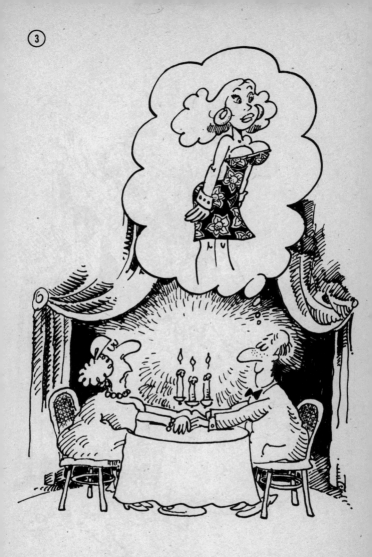

4

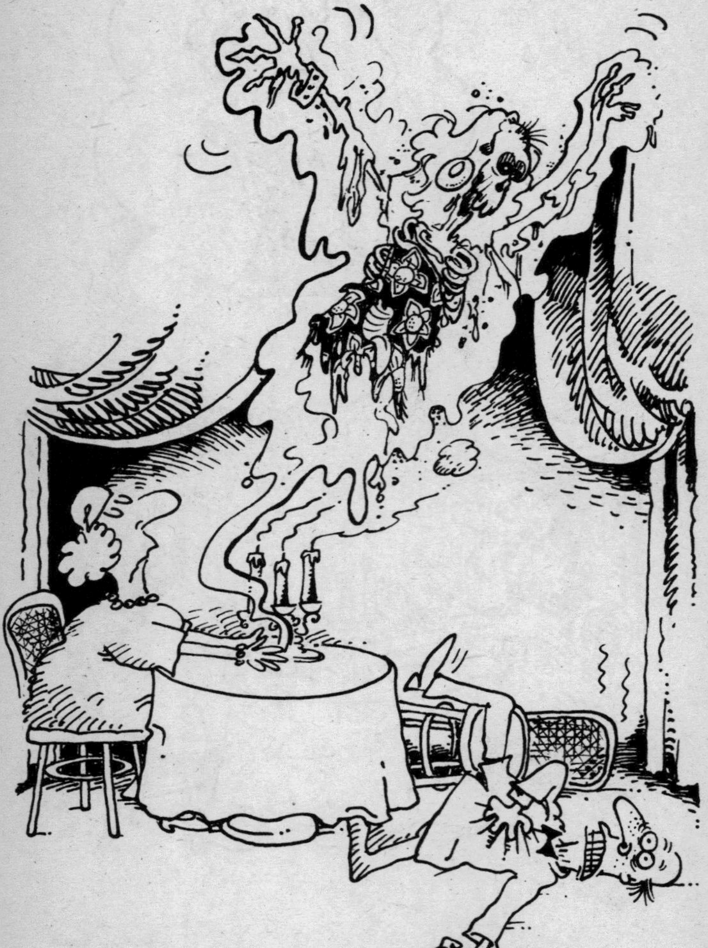

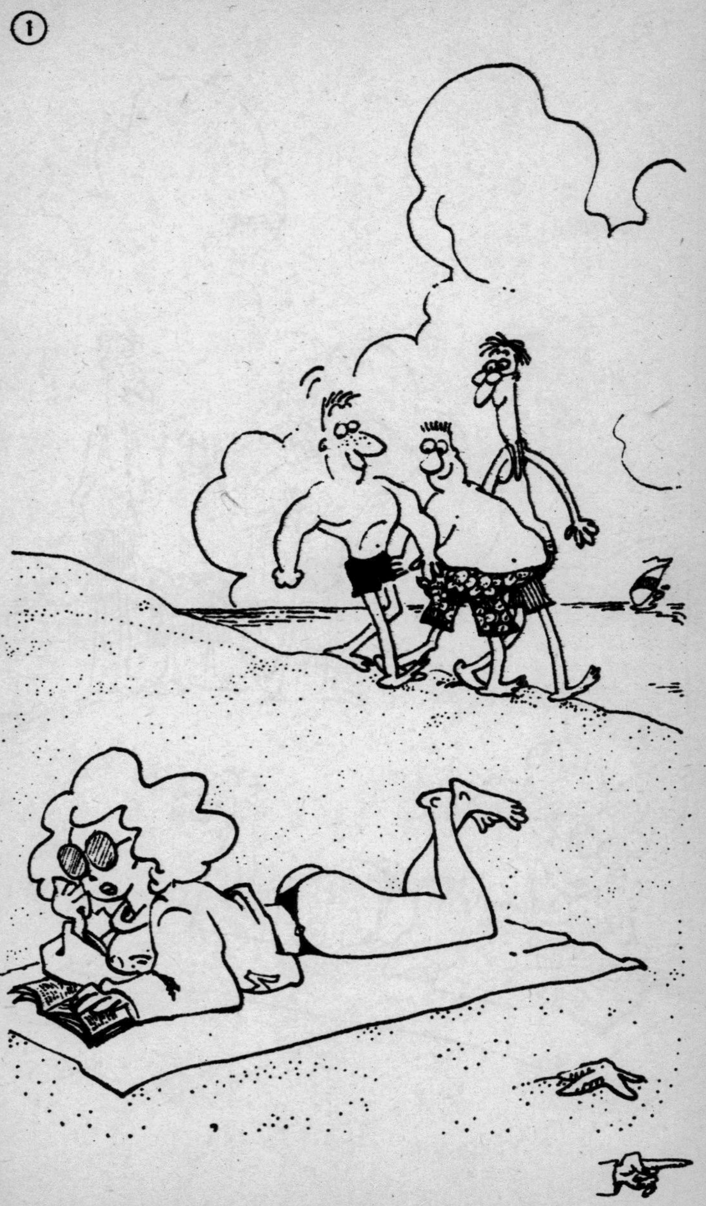
1

2

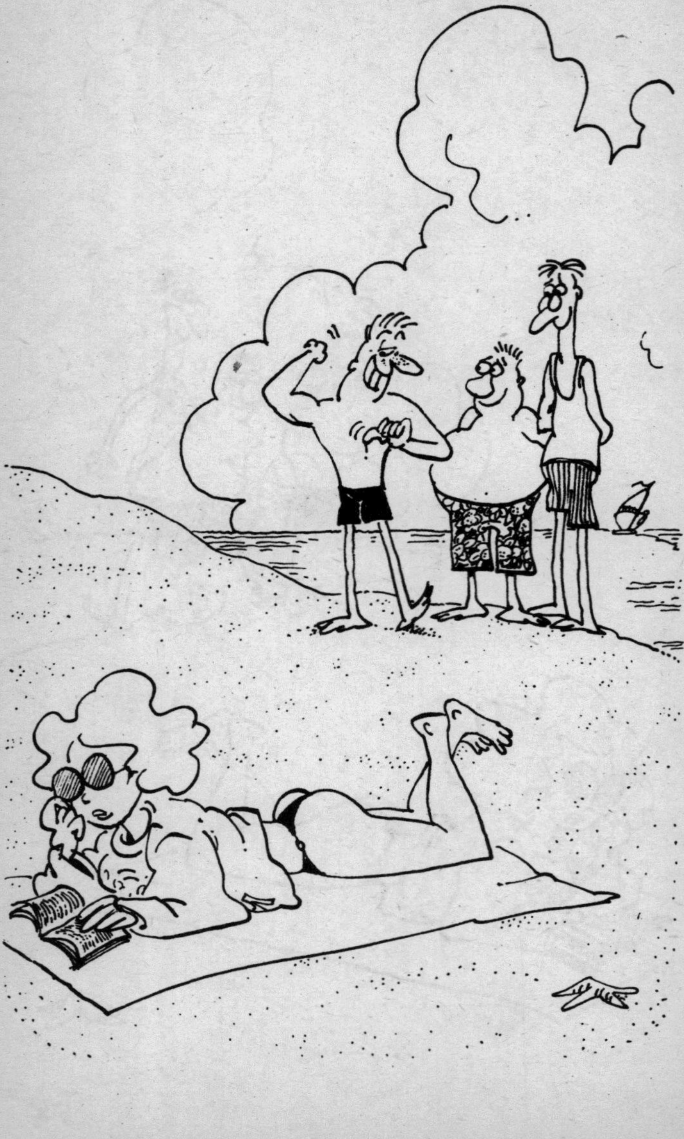

3

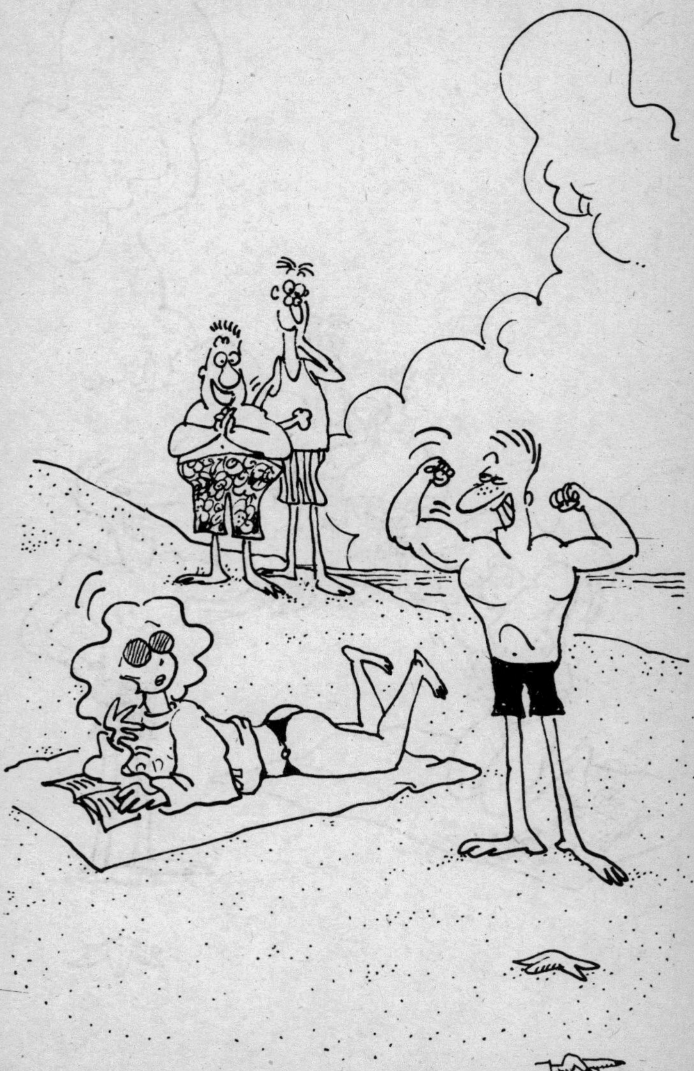

4

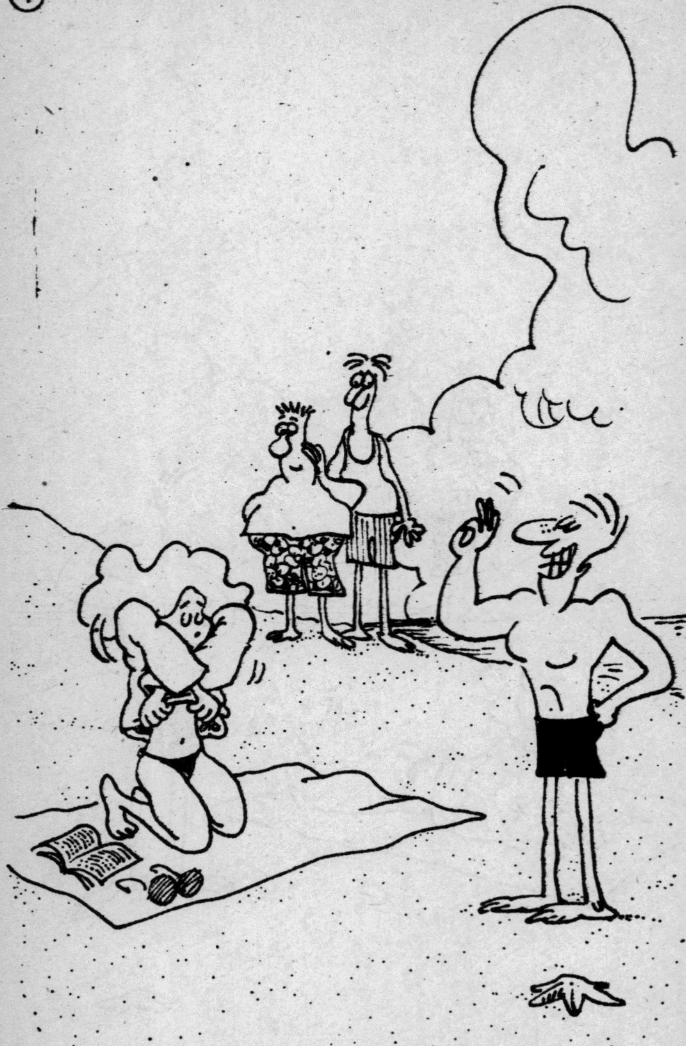

5

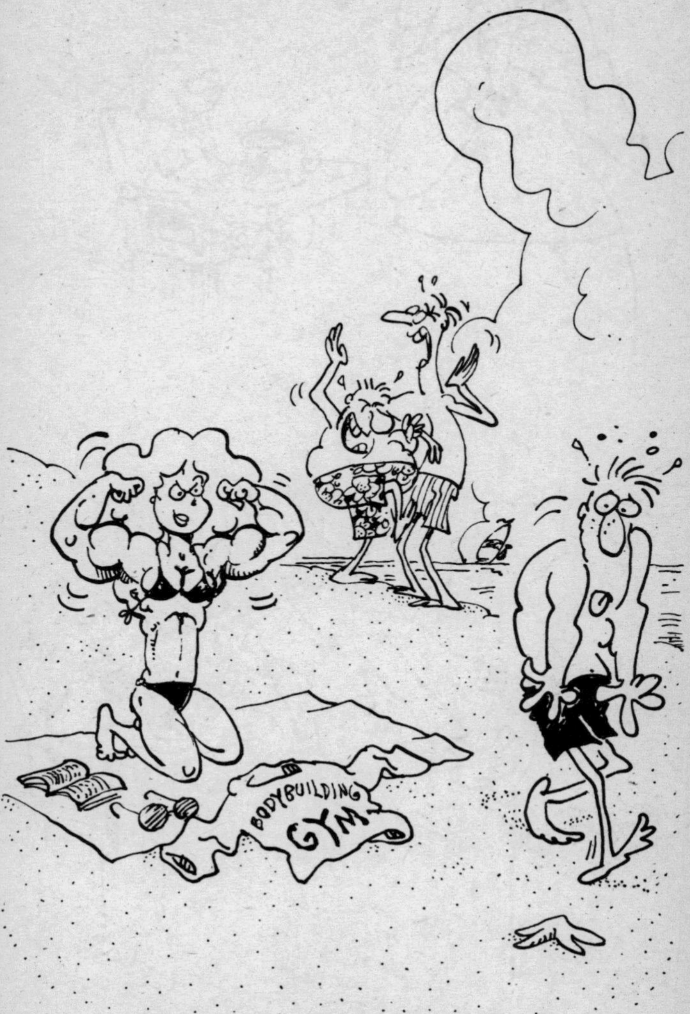
BODYBUILDING
GYM

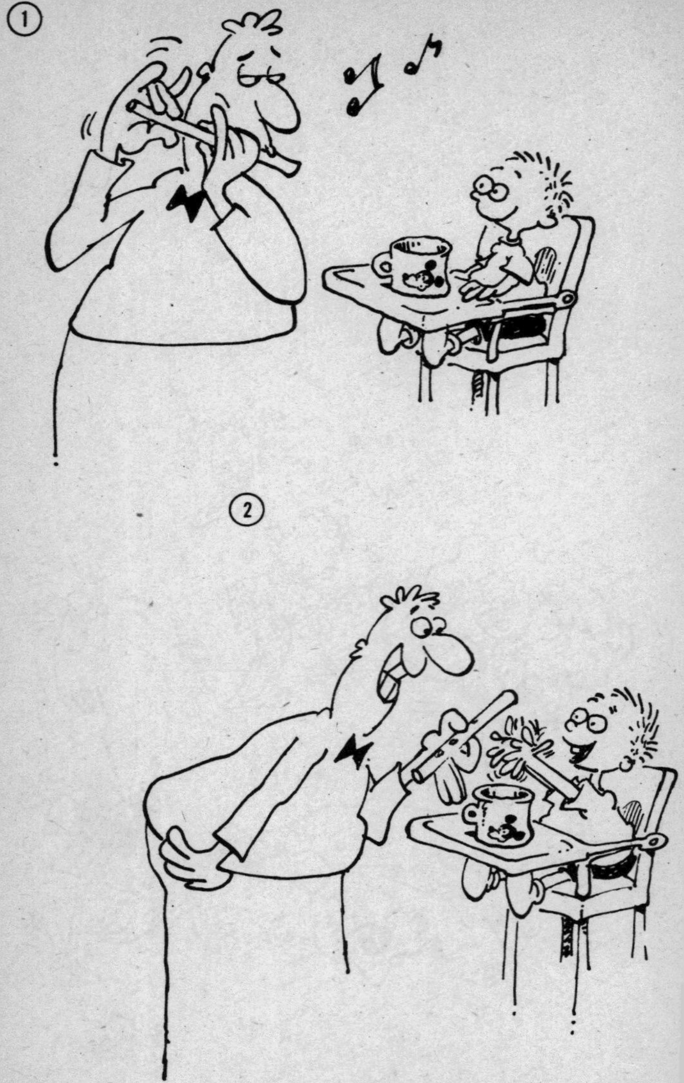
1
2

1

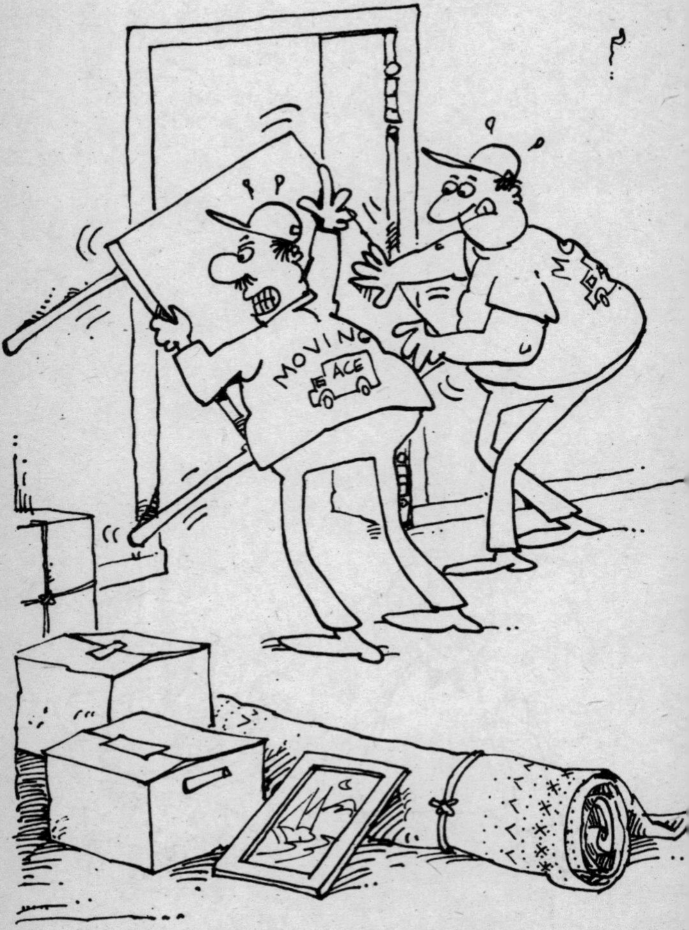
MOVIN
ACE

2

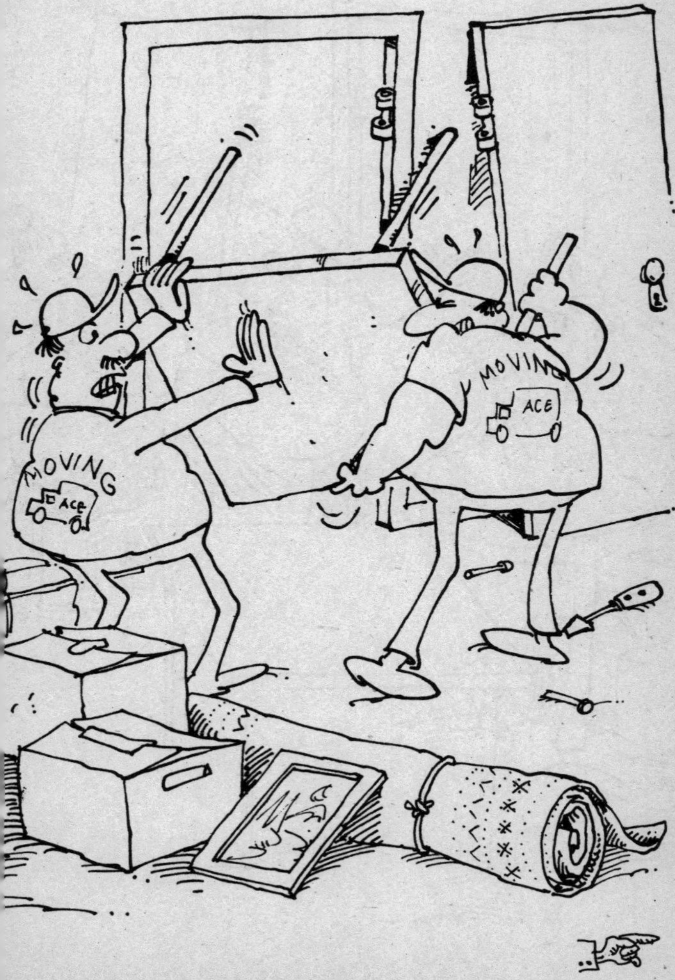
MOVING
ACE
MOVING
ACE

3

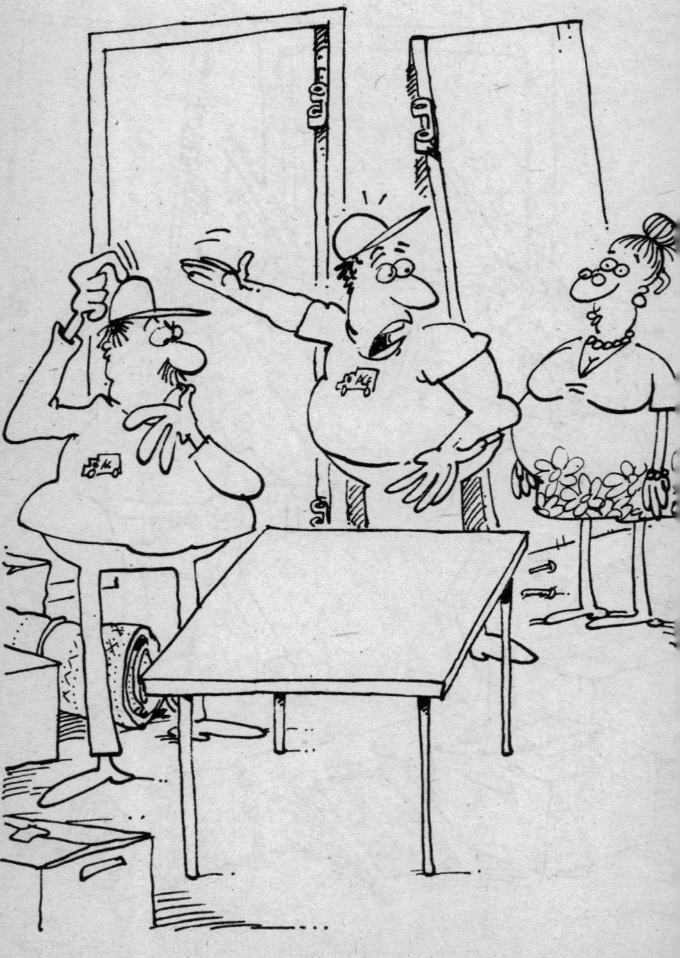
ACE

4

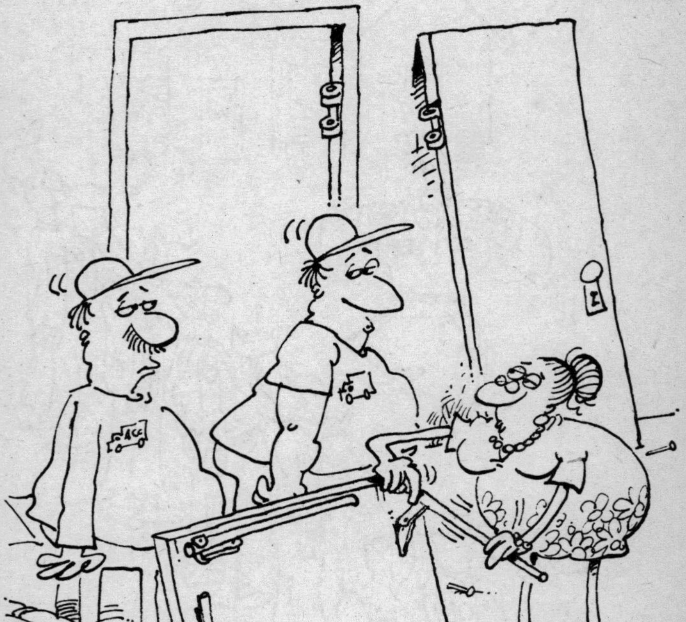
ACC

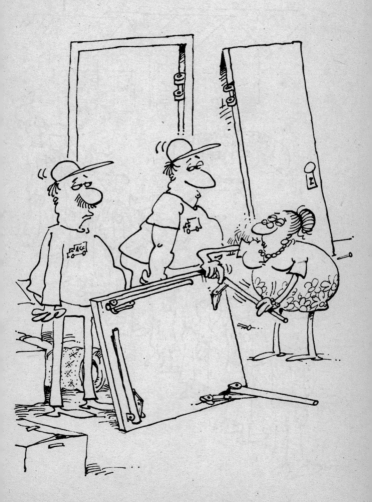

1

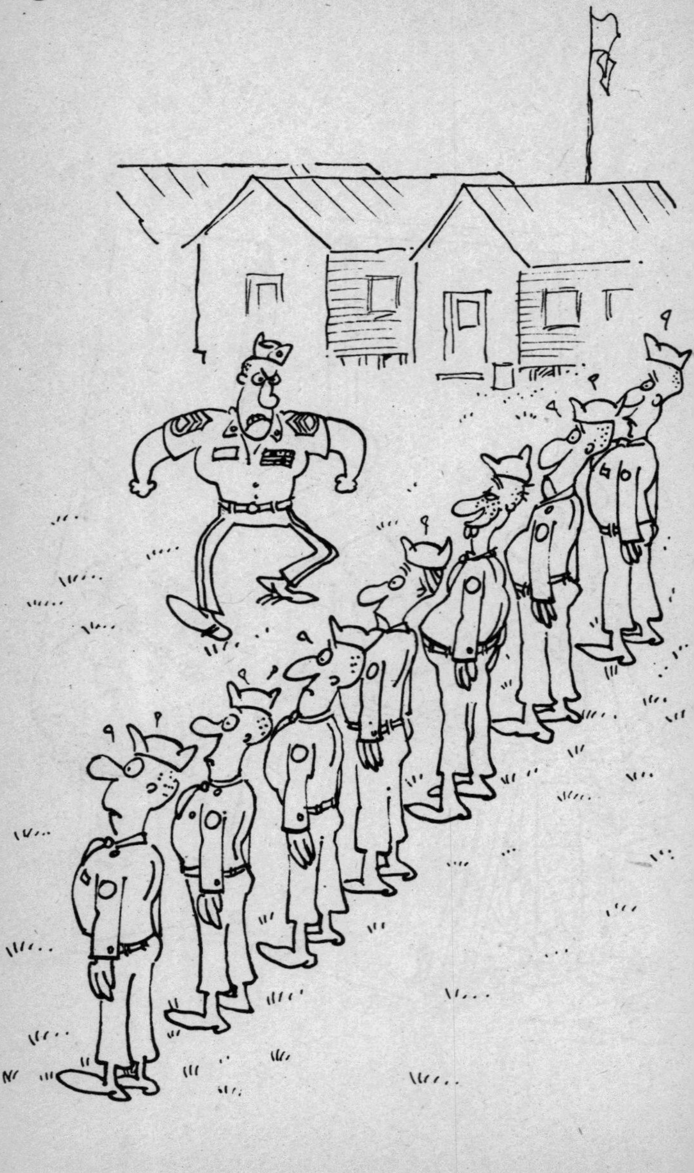

(2)

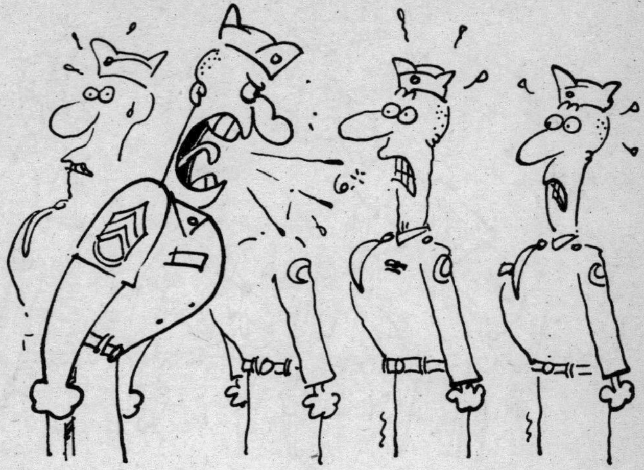

(3)

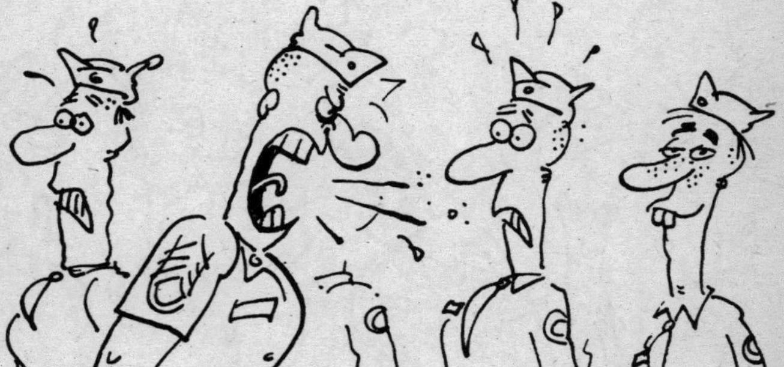

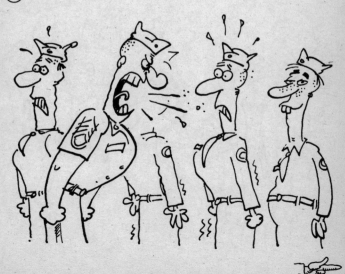

4

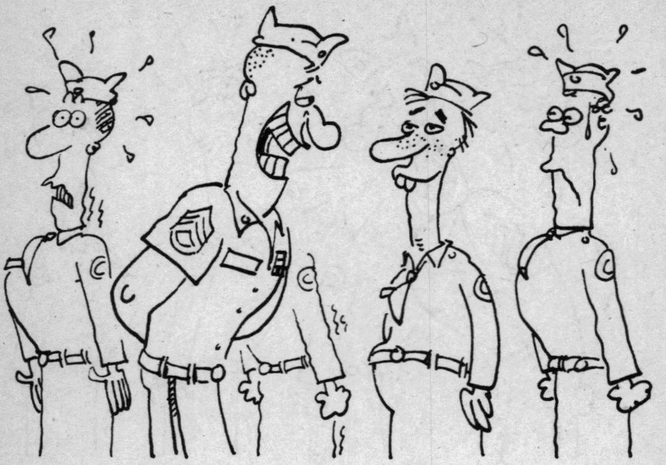

5

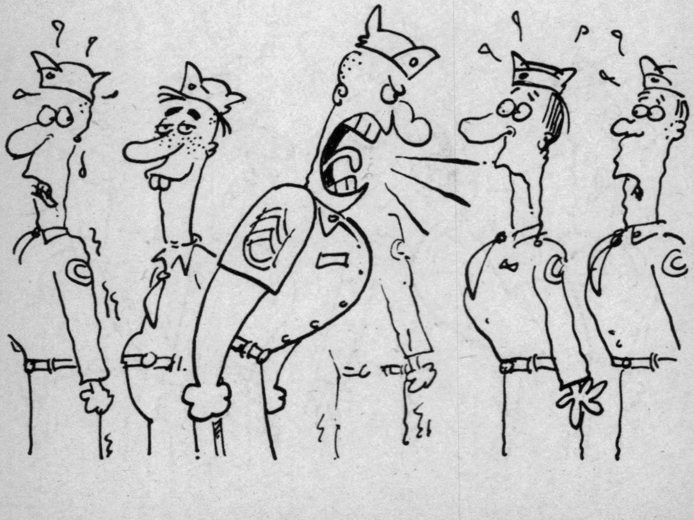

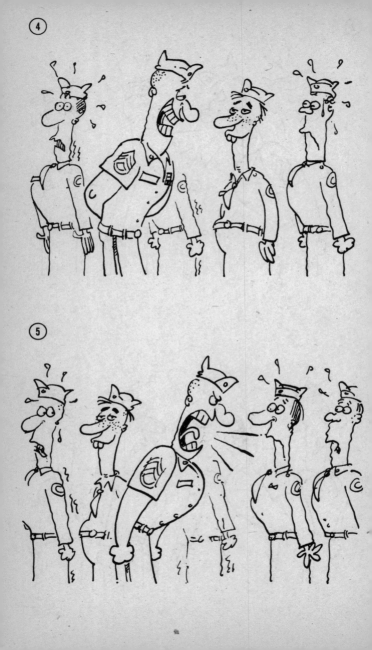

6

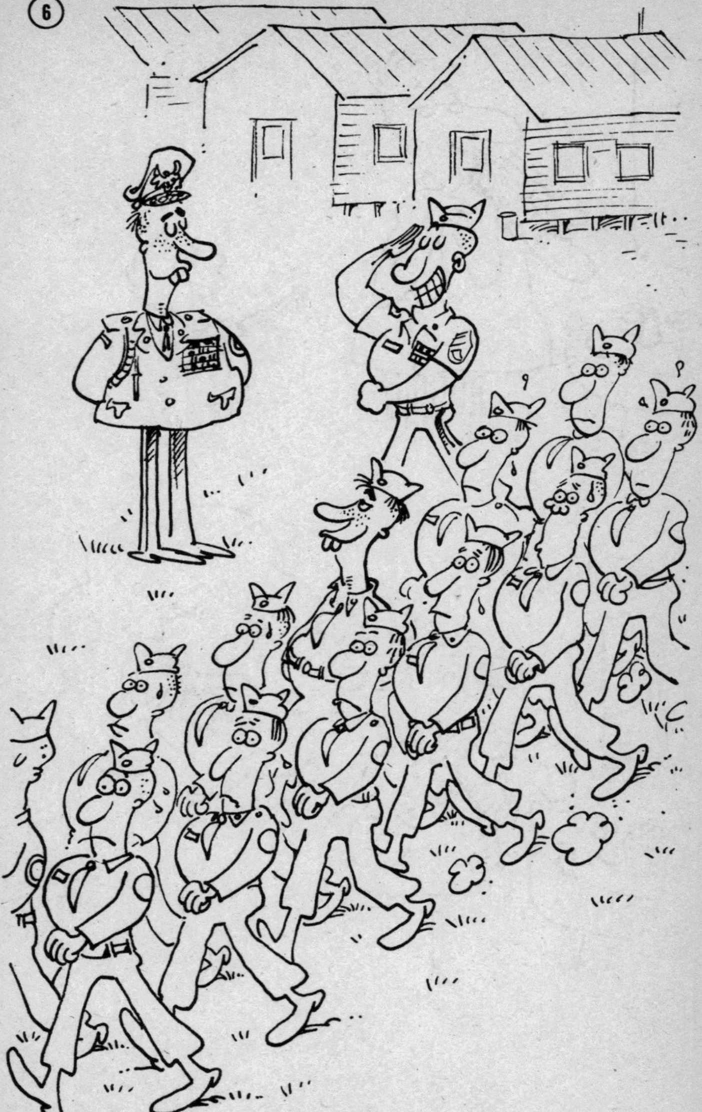

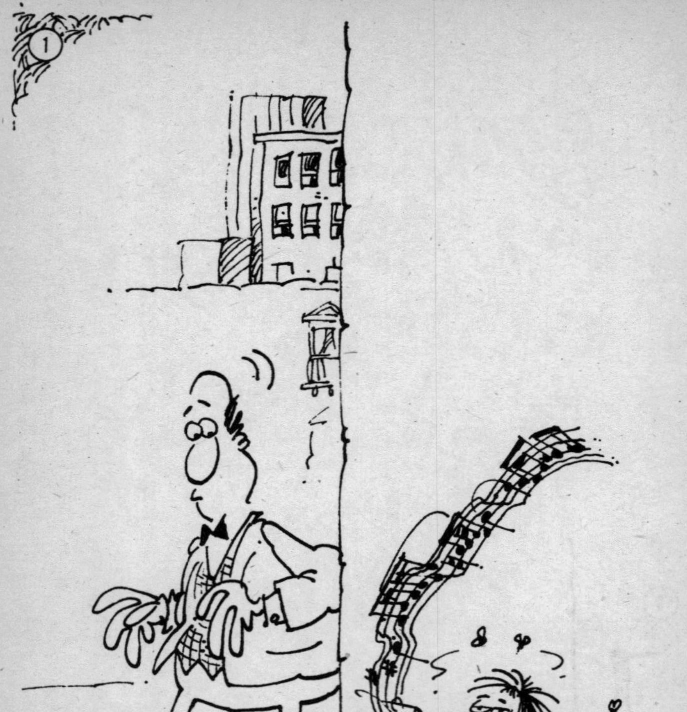
1

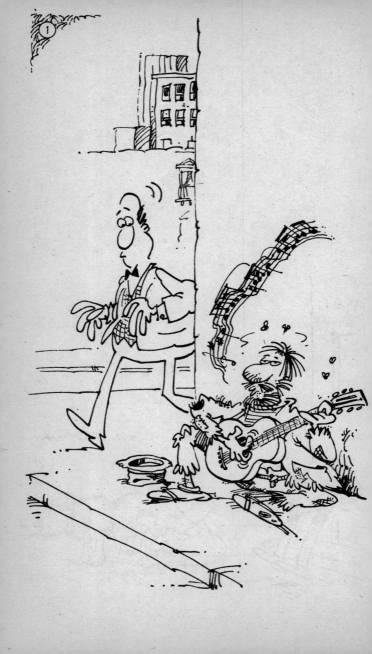

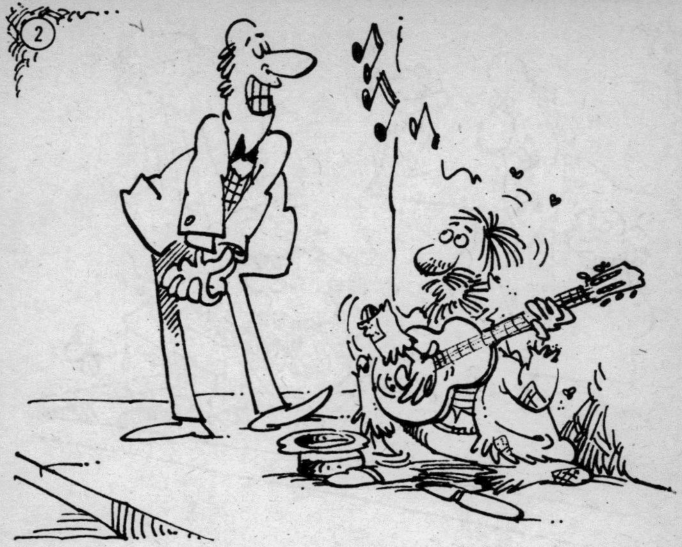
2

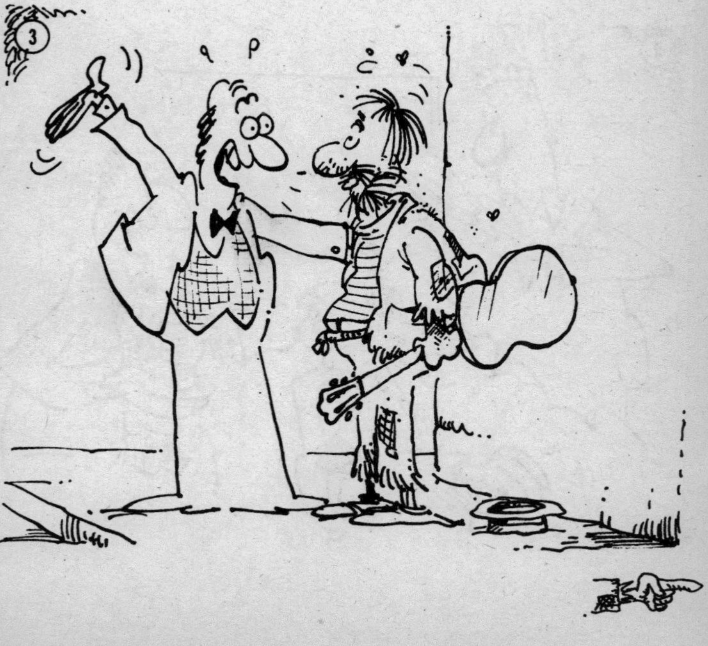
3

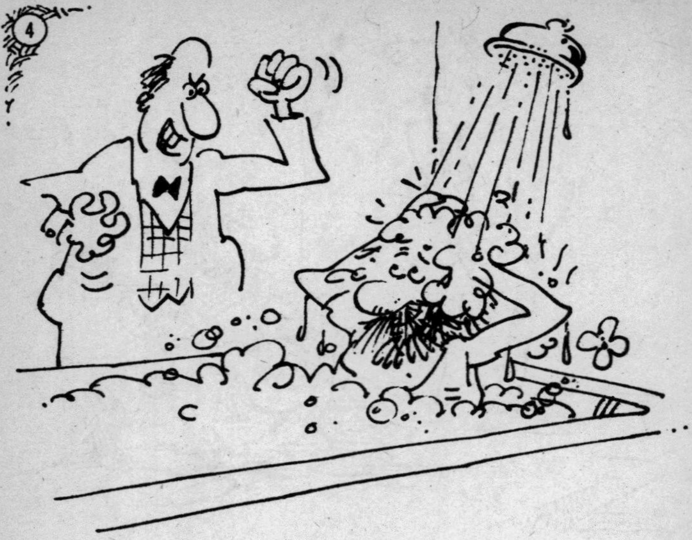
4

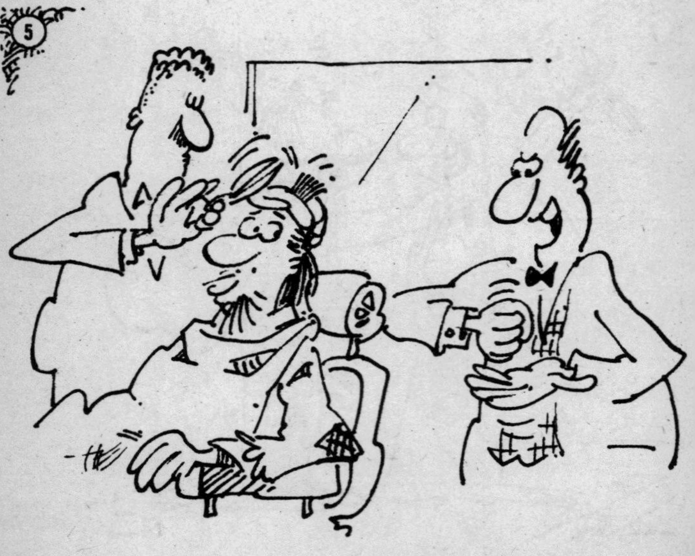
5

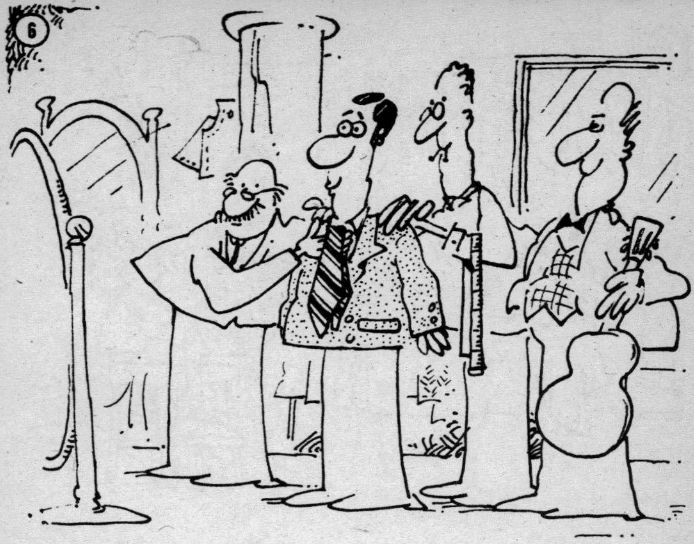
6

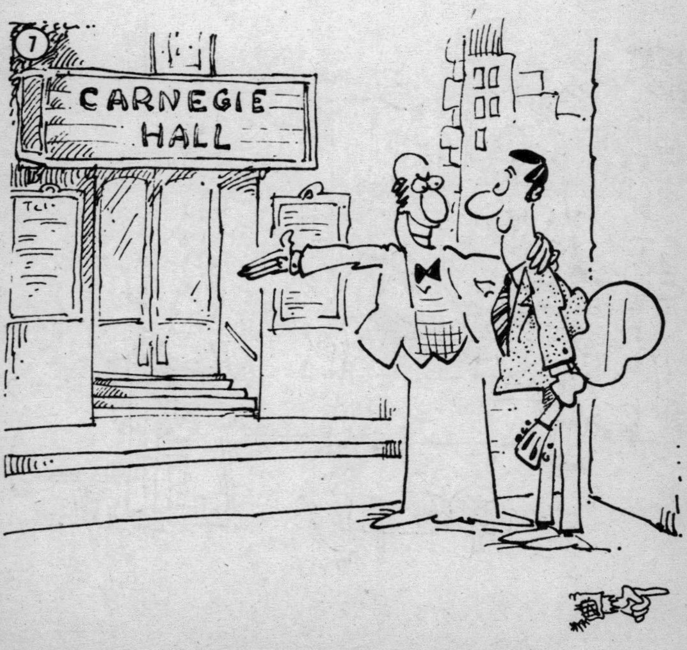
7
CARNEGIE
HALL

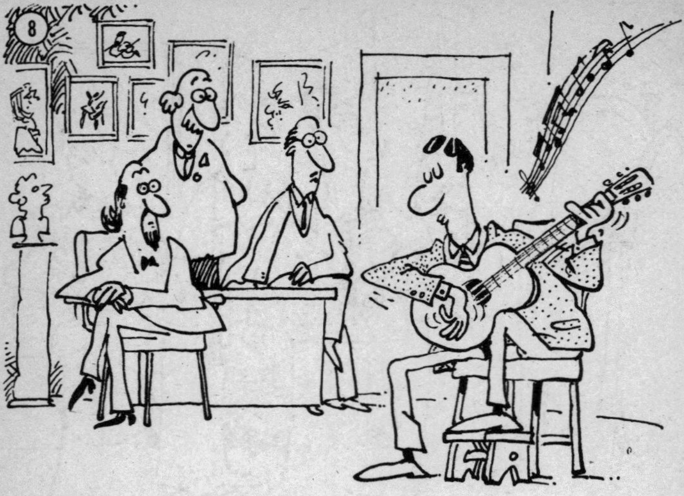
8

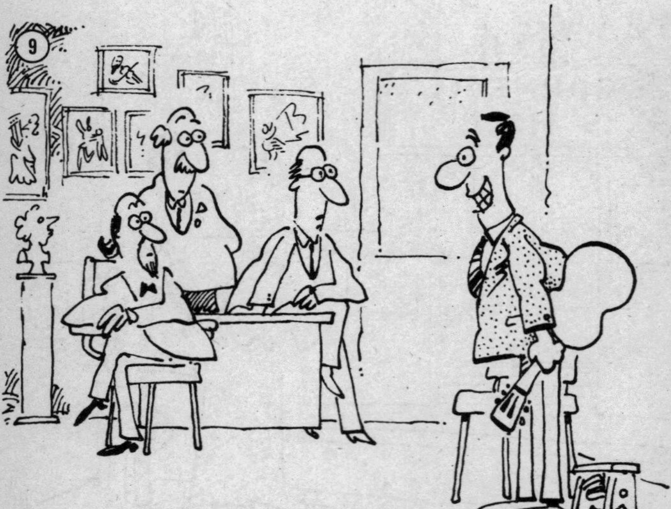
9

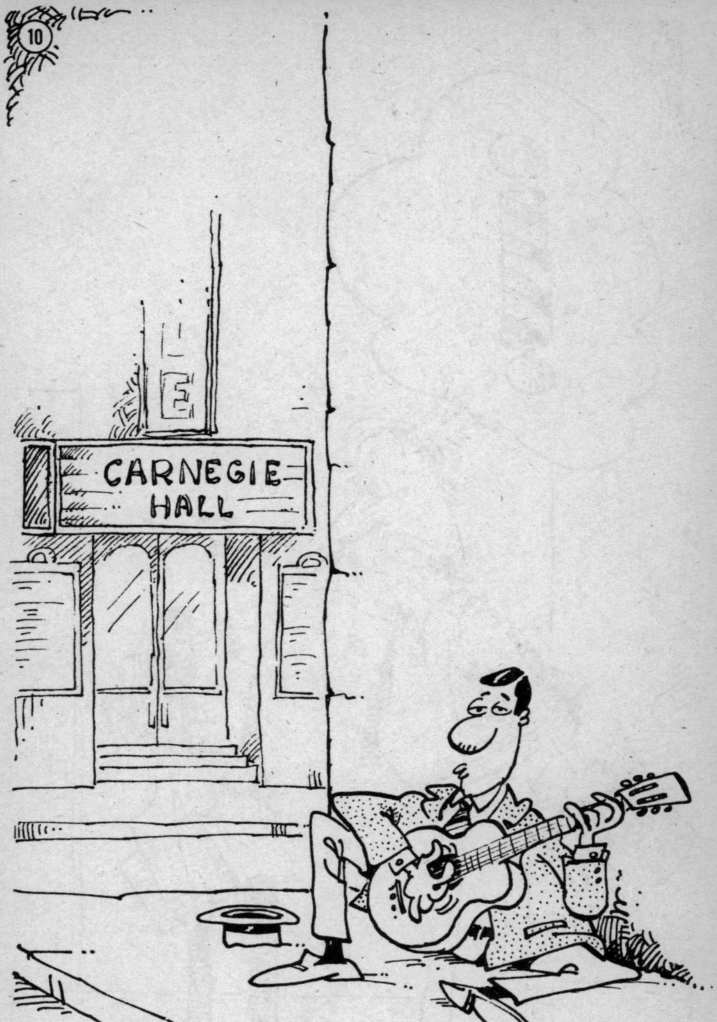
10
CARNEGIE
HALL

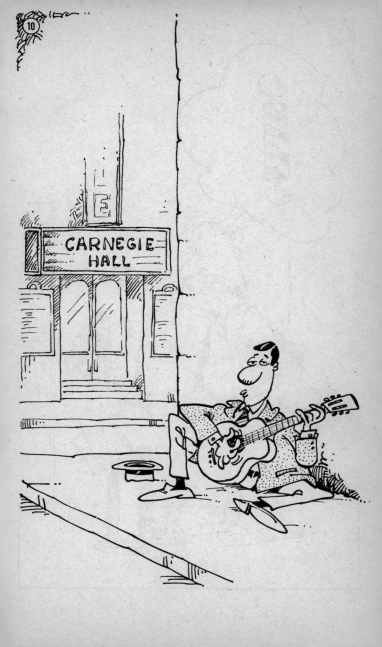

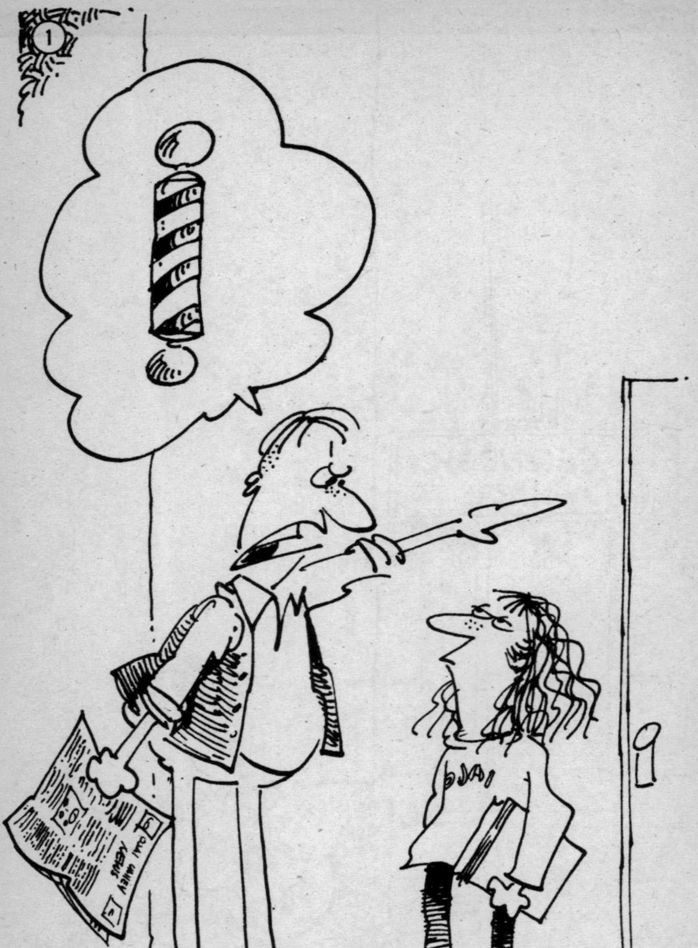
1
OJAI VALLEY NEWS
OJAI

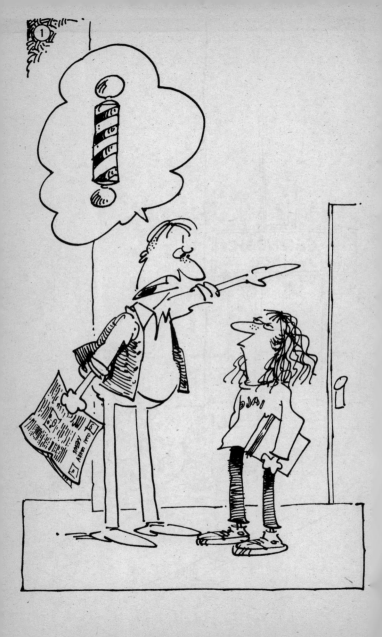

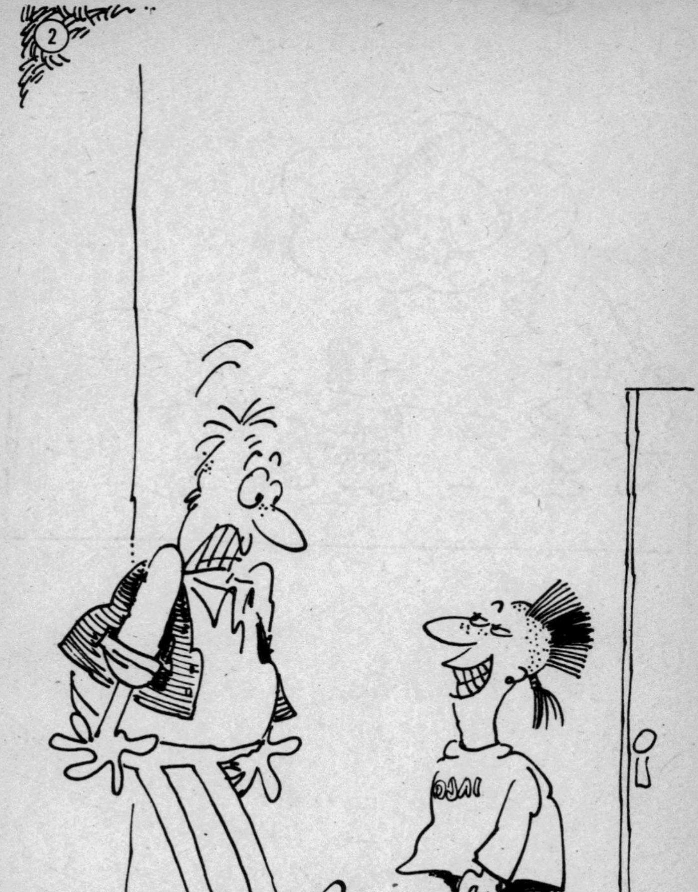
2

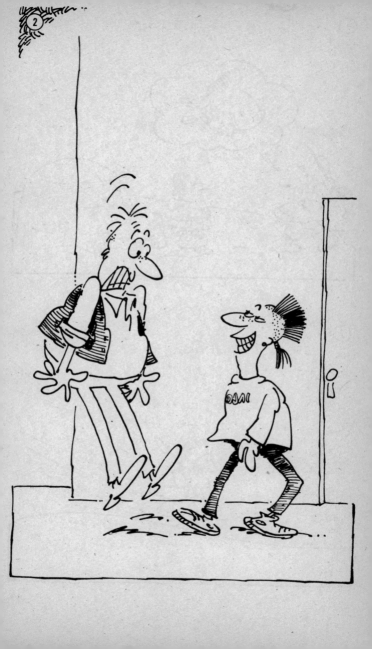

①

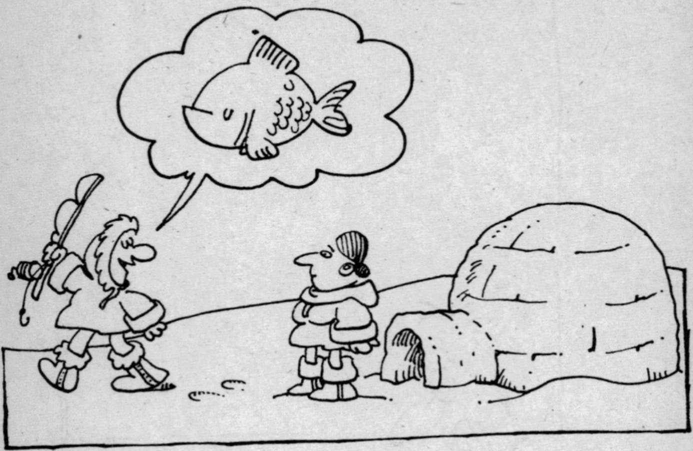

②

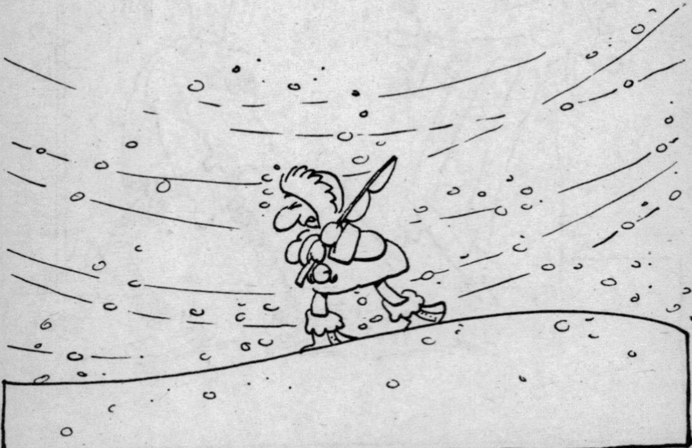

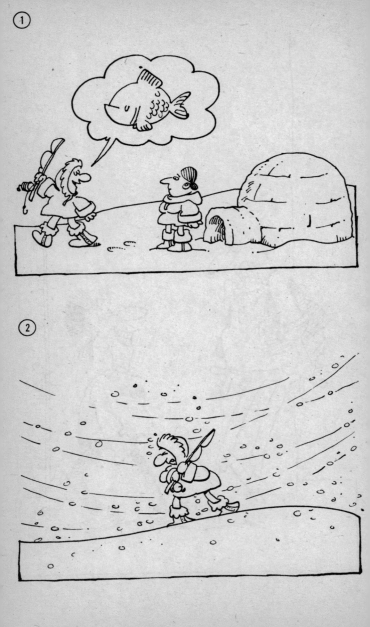

3

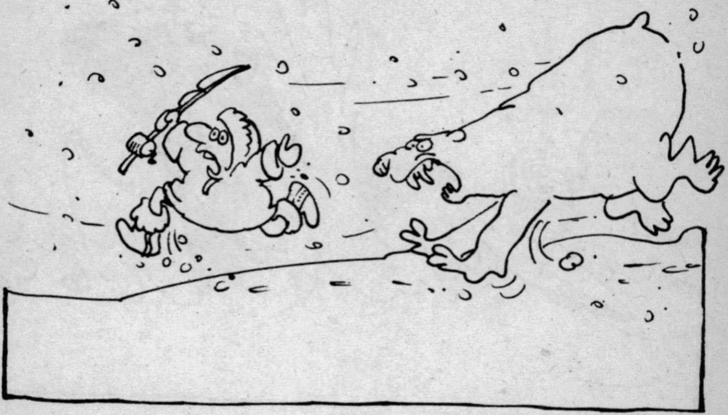

4

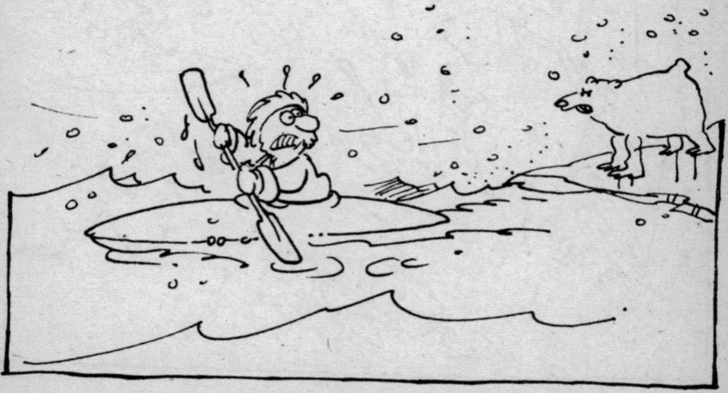

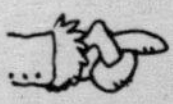

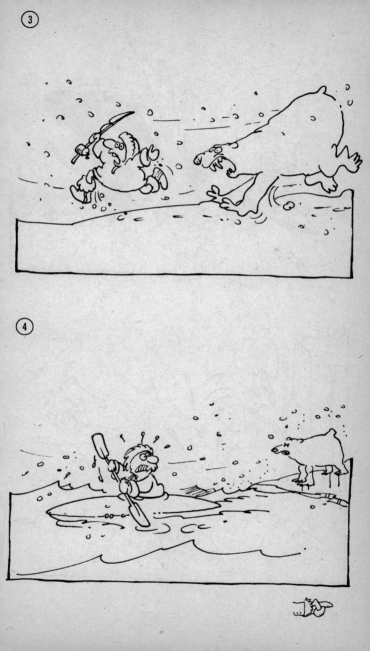

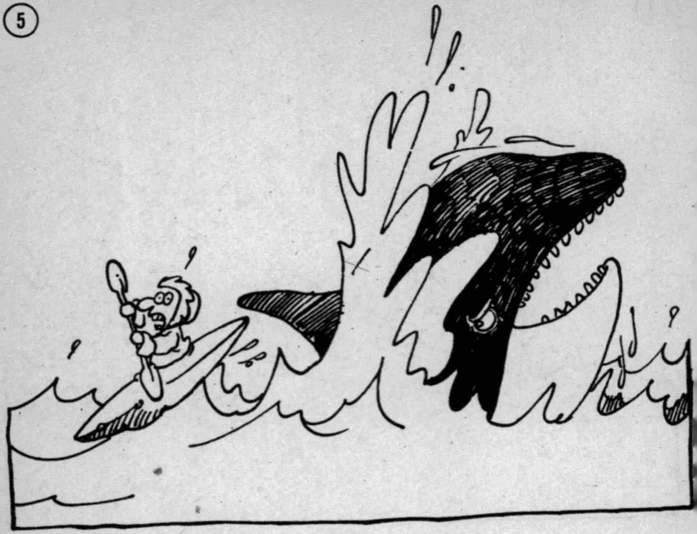
5

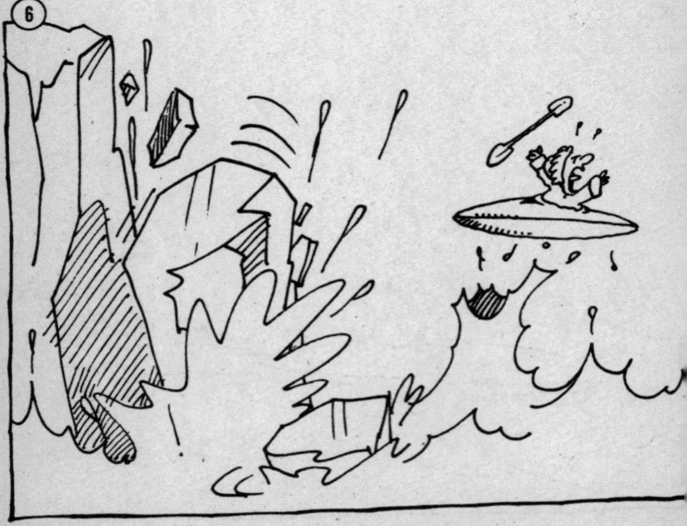
6

7

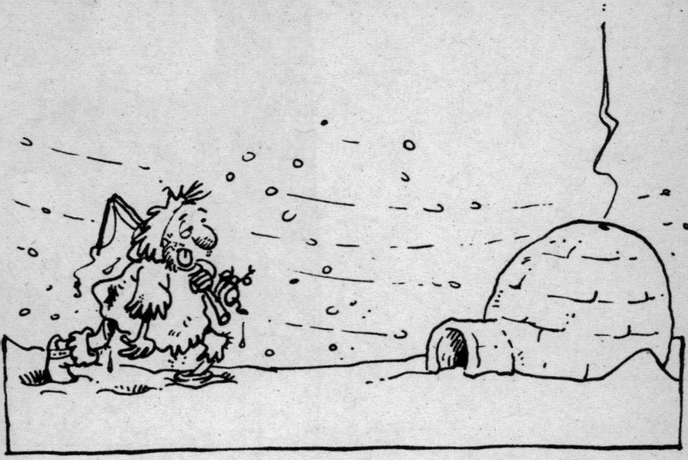

8

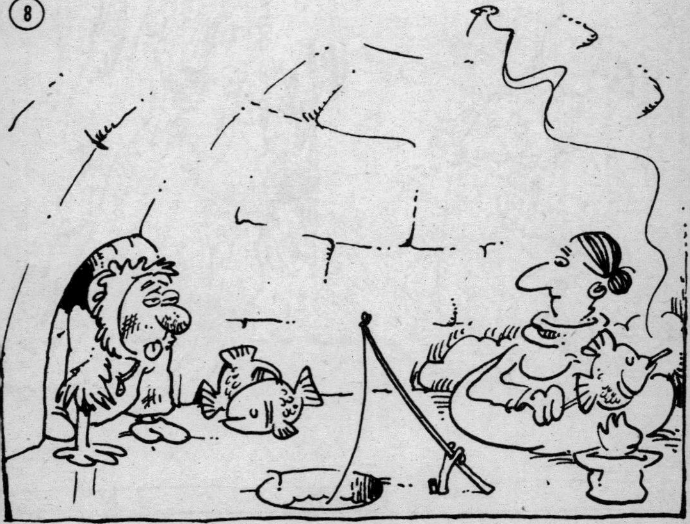

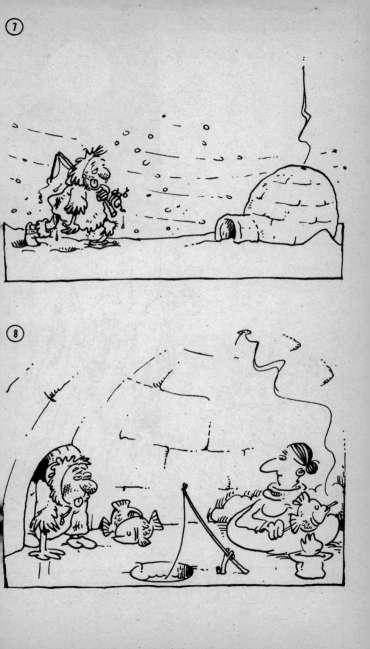

1

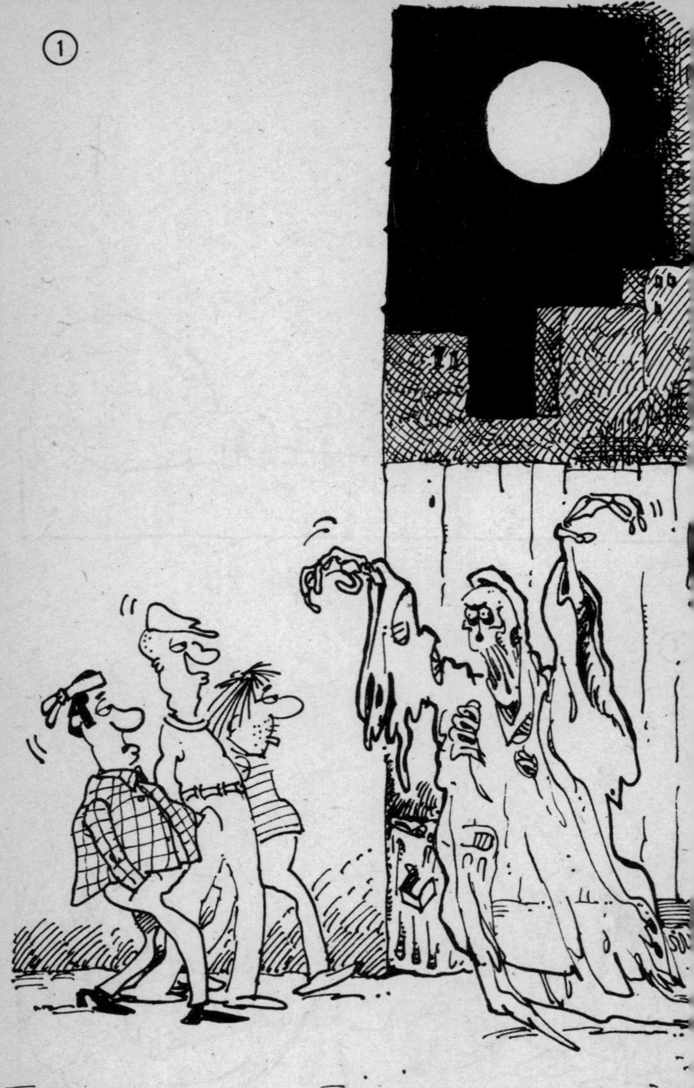

2

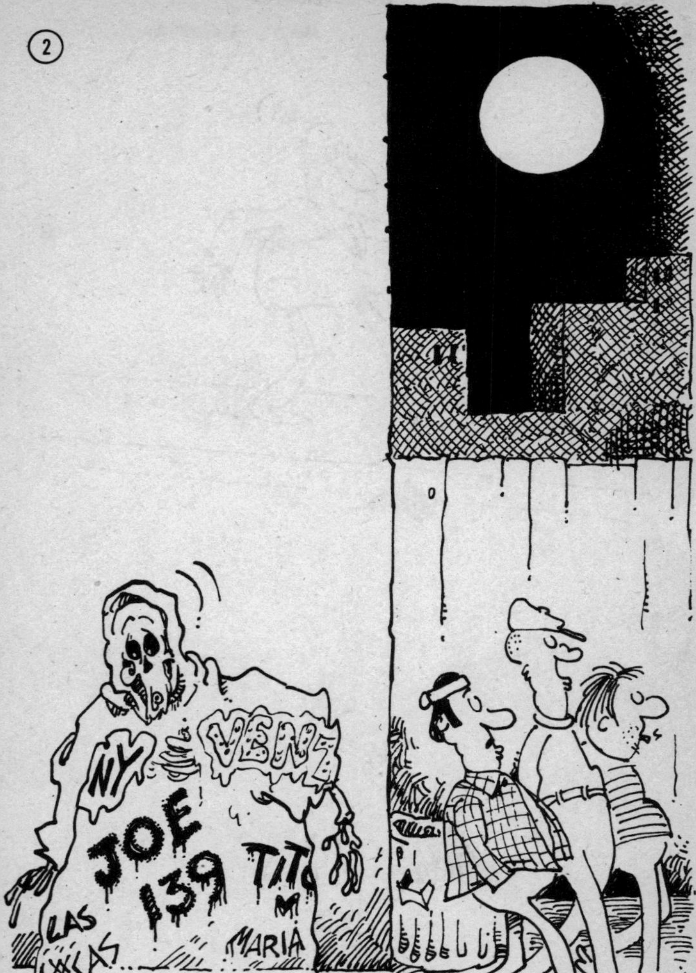
NY
VENZ
JOE
139
LAS
MARIA
VIVA
XAIME

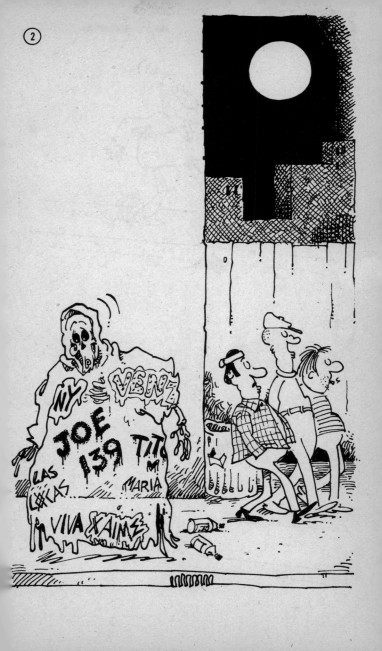

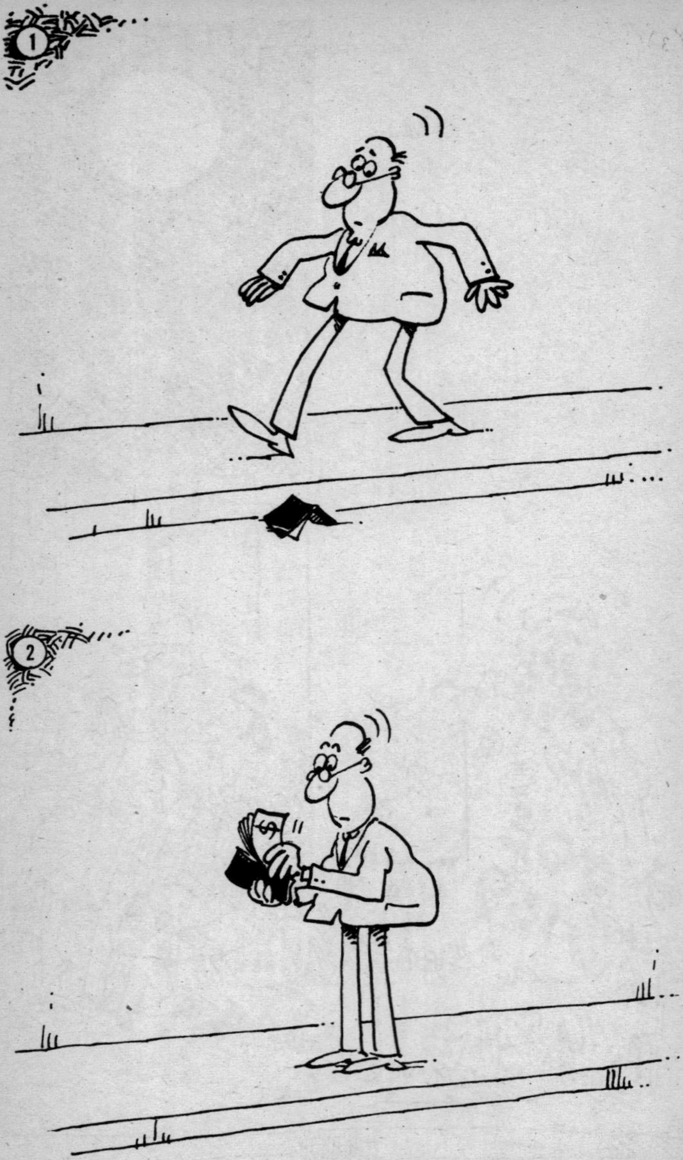
1
2

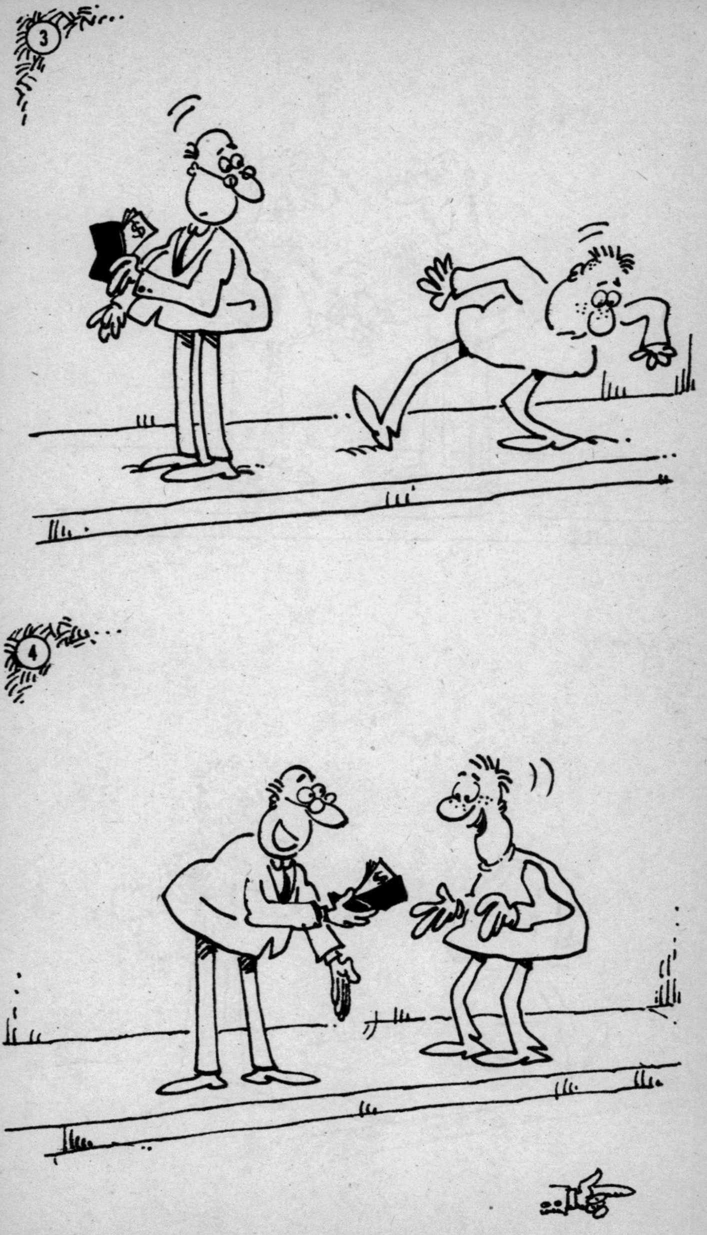
3
4

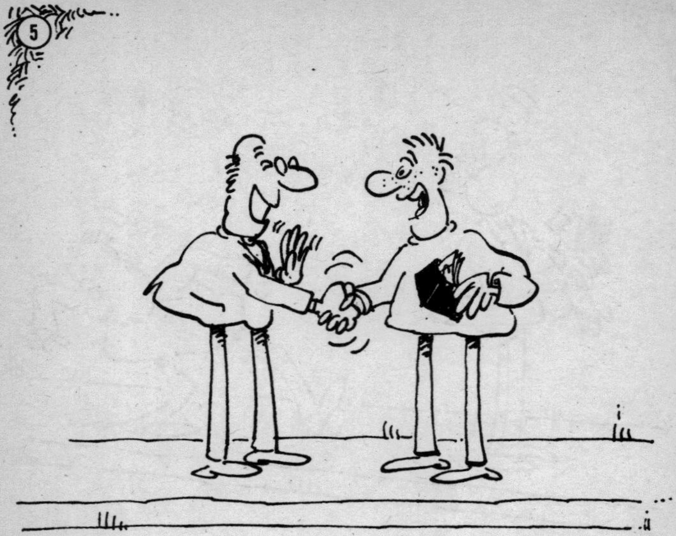

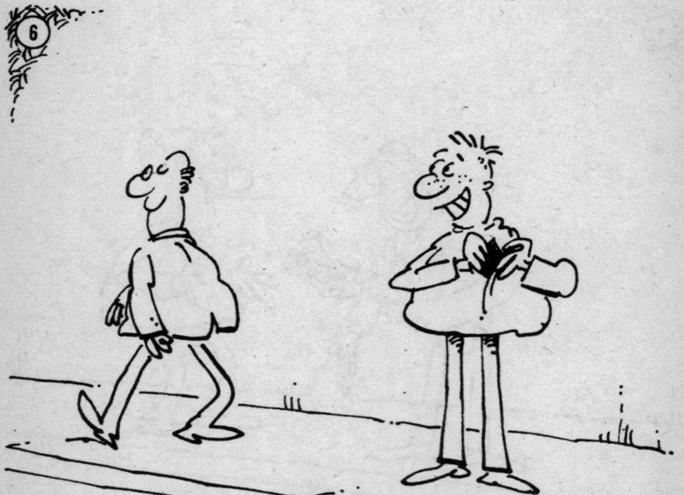

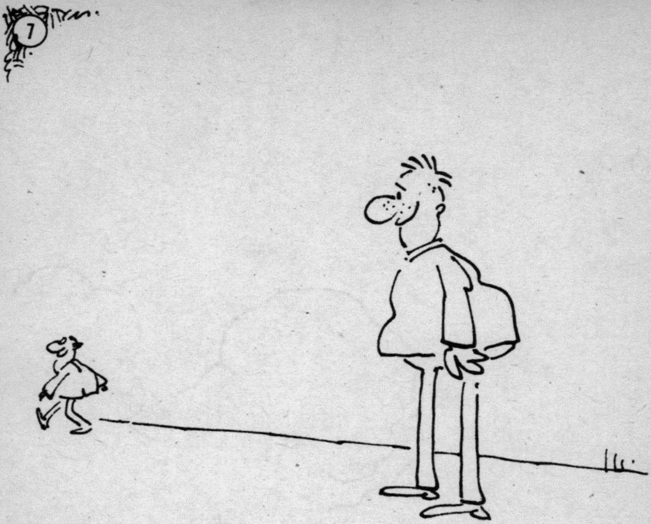
7

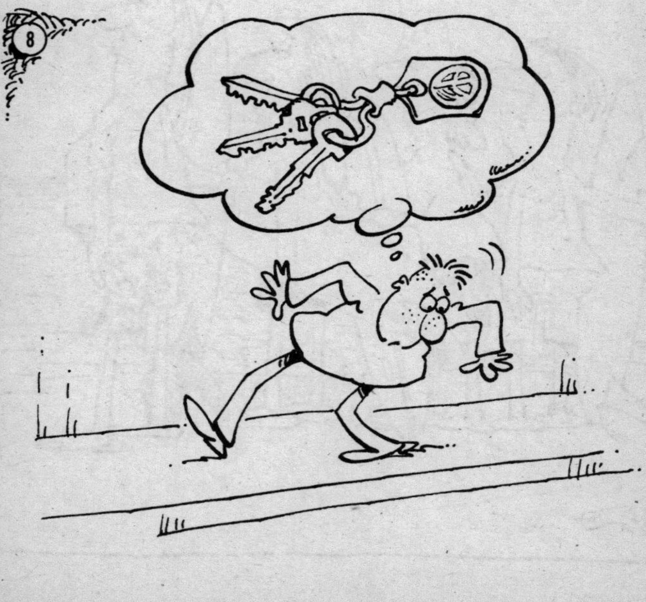
8

①

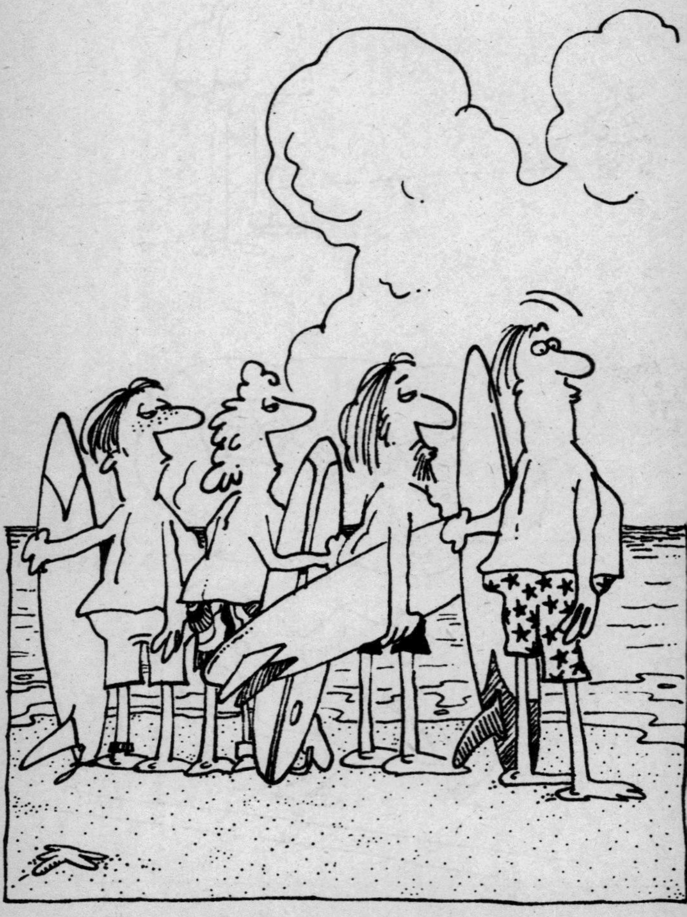

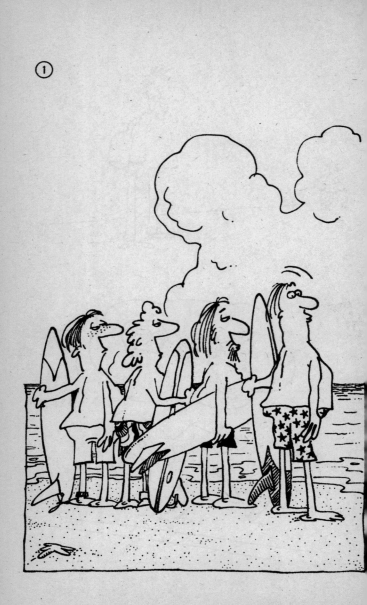

2

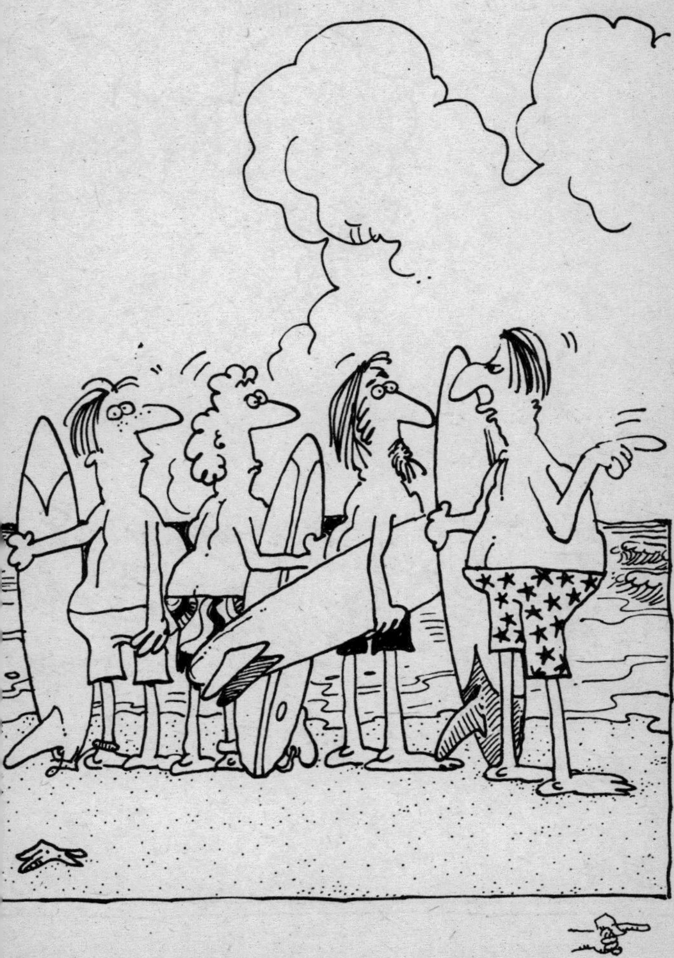

(3)

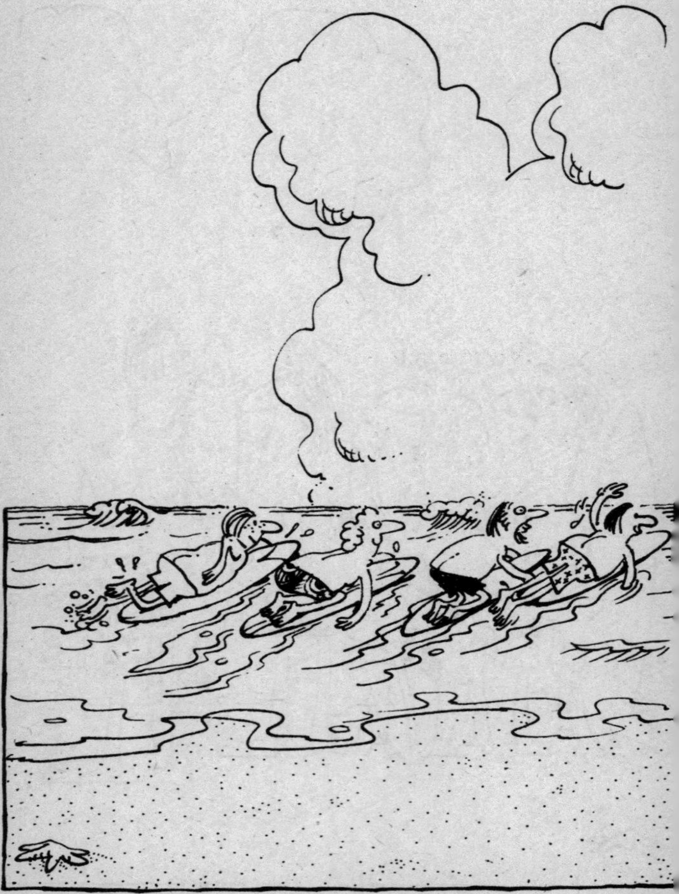

4

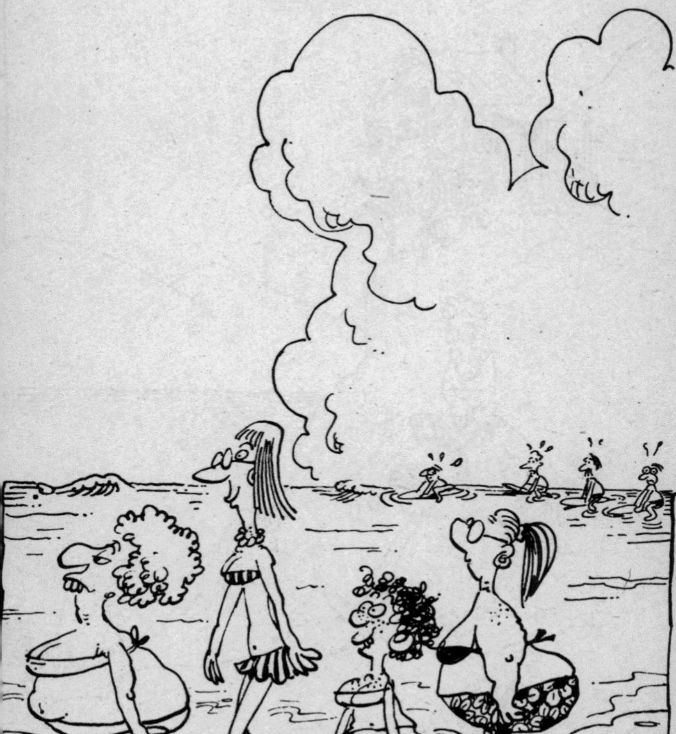

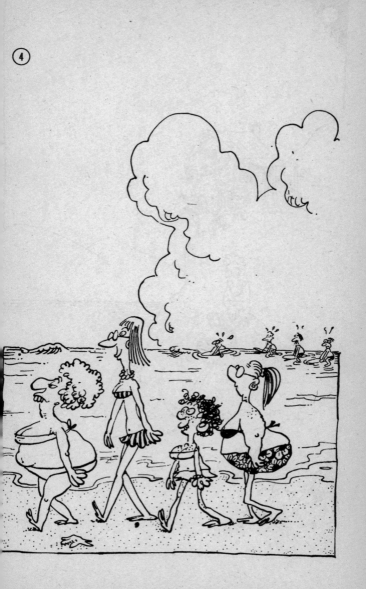

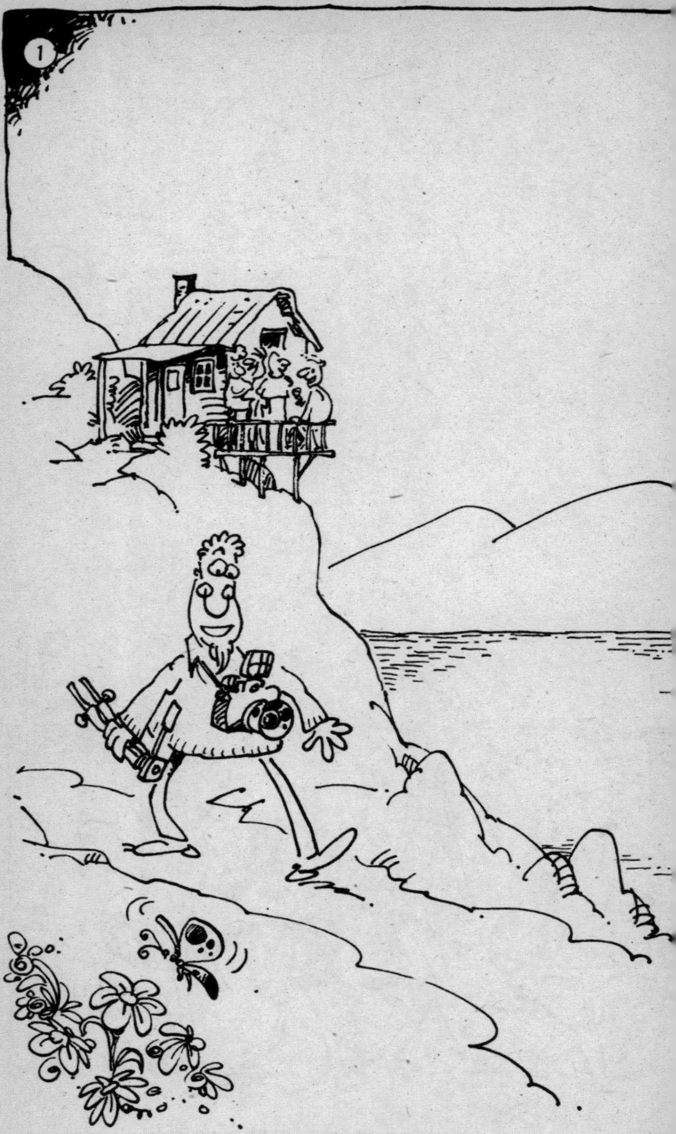
1

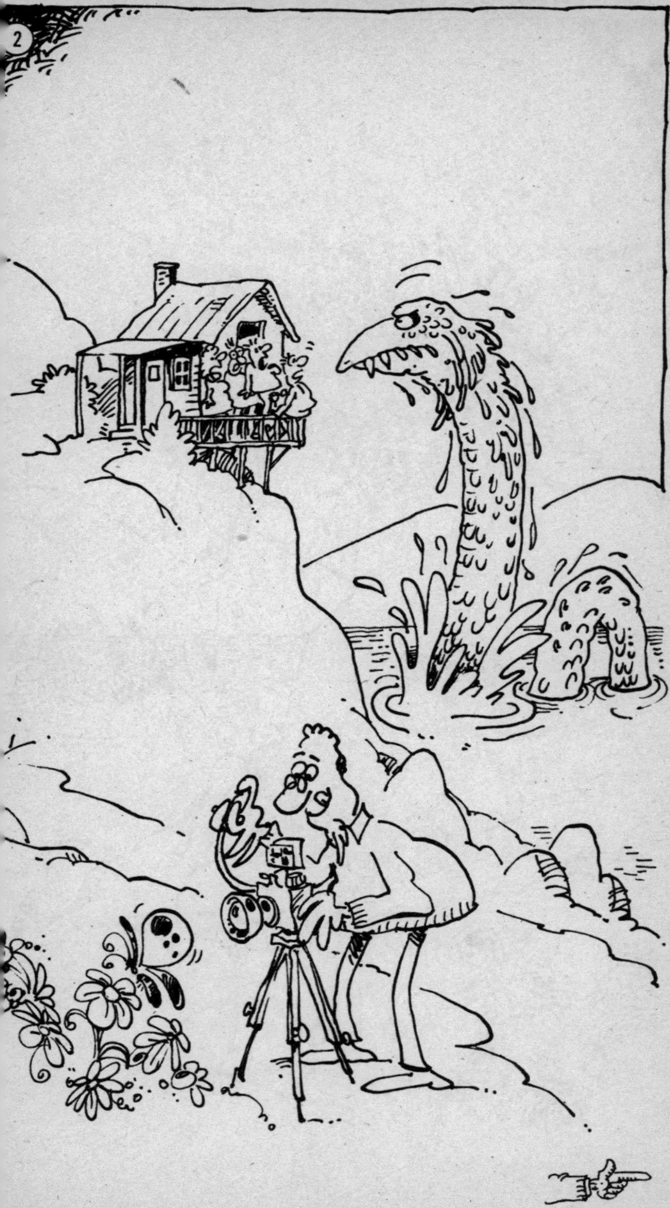

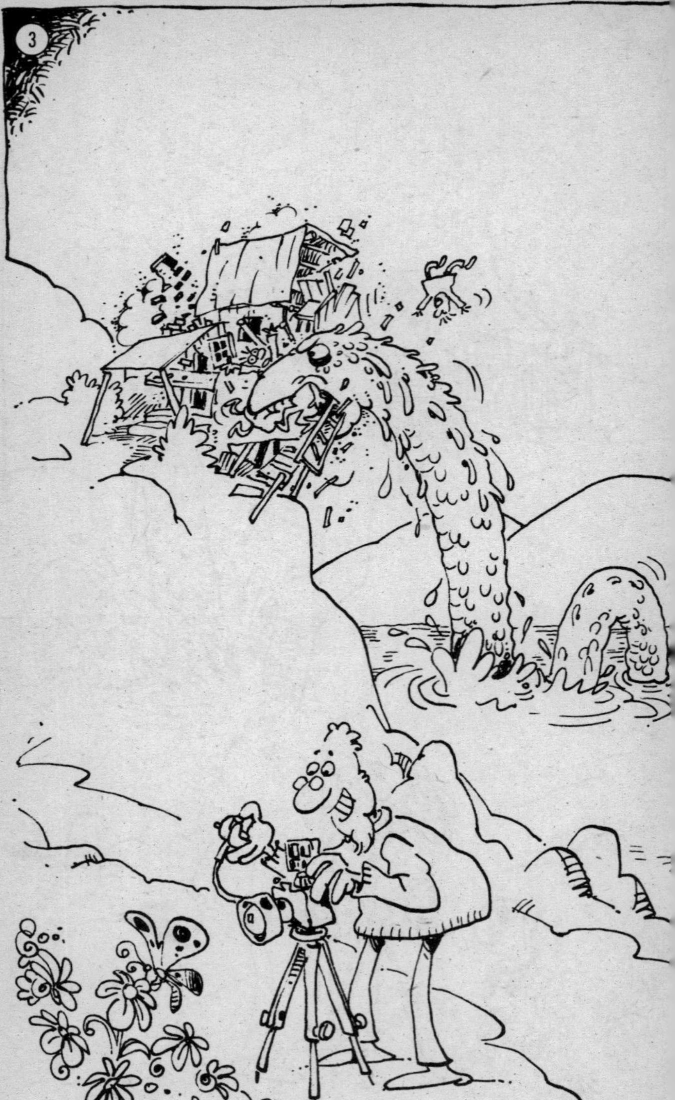
3

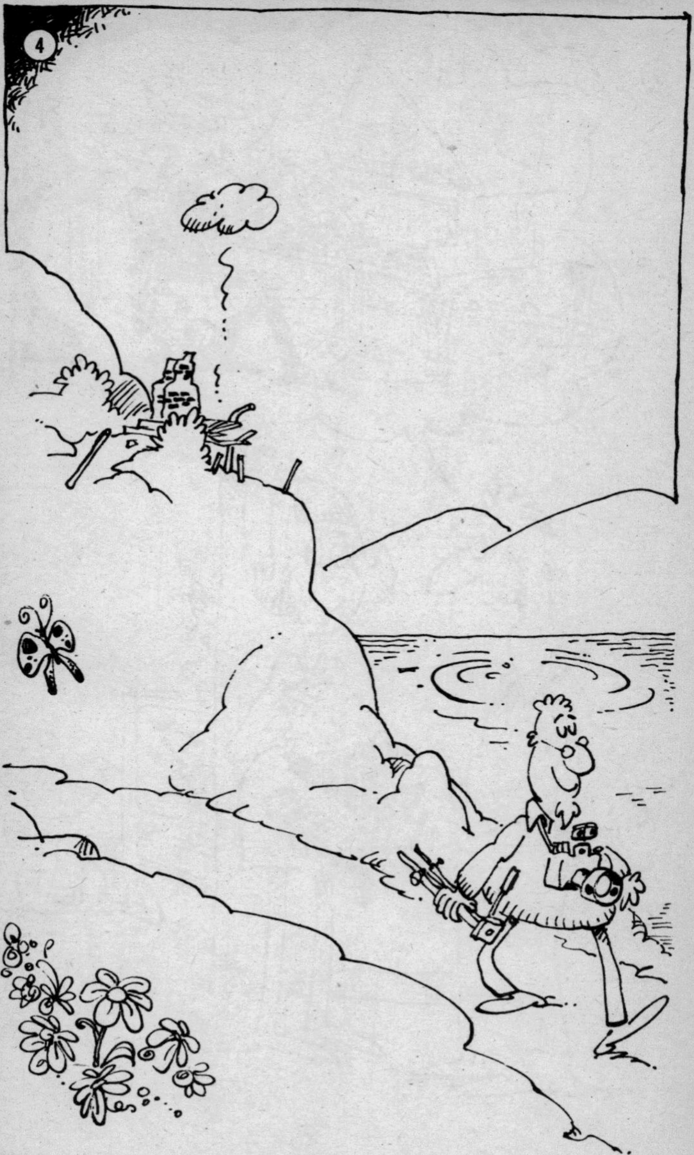
4

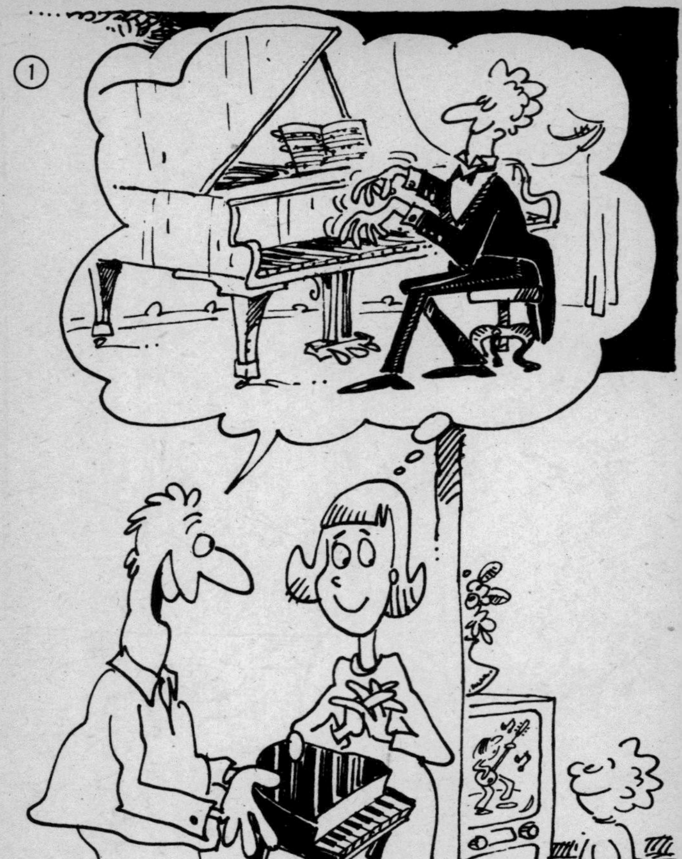
1

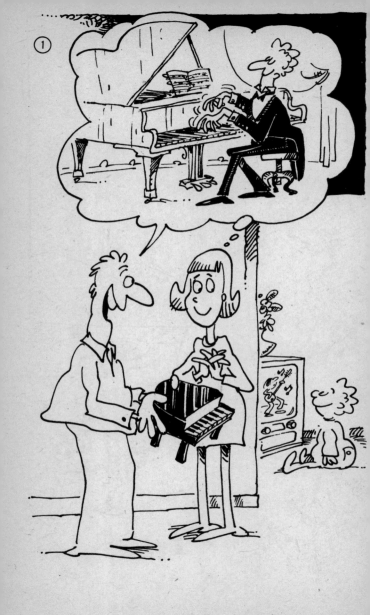

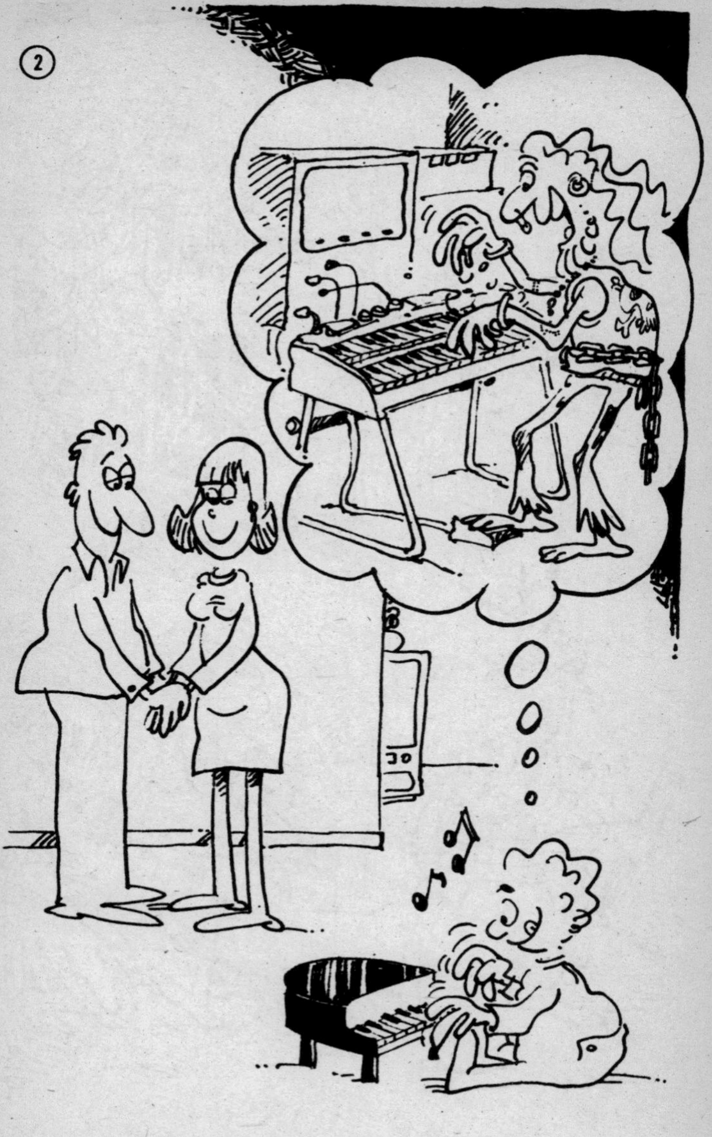
2

1

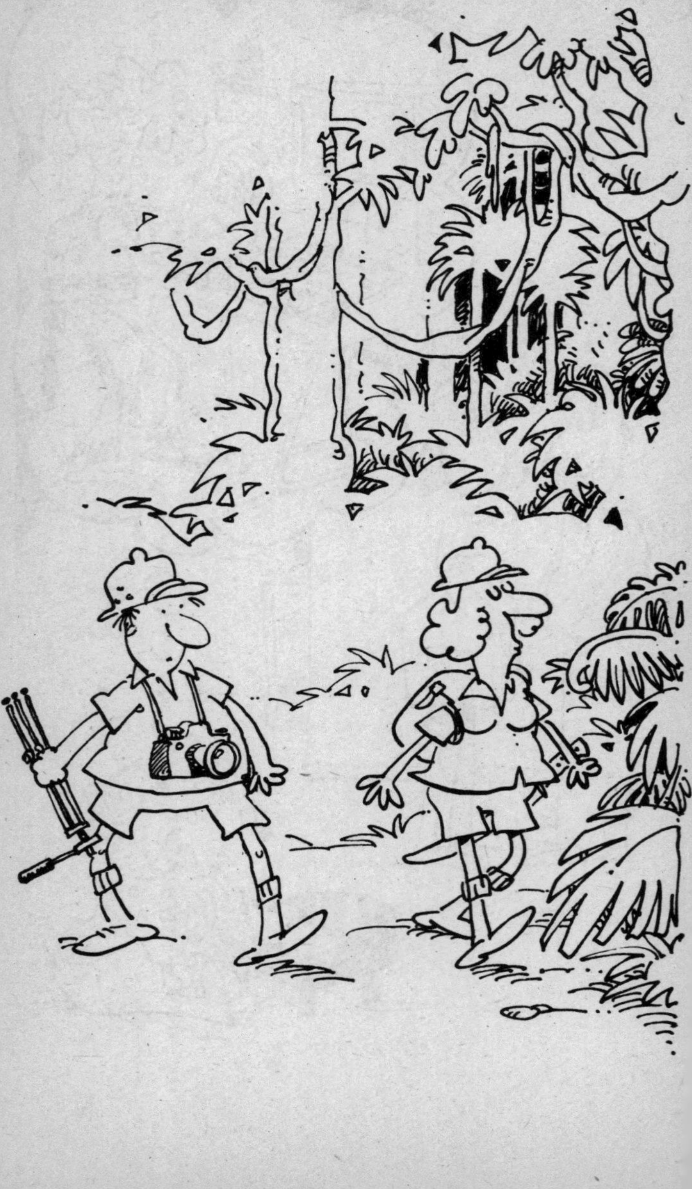

(2)

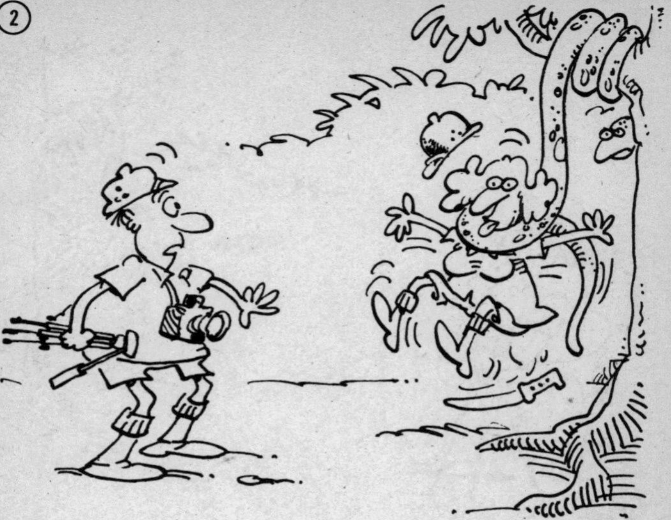

(3)

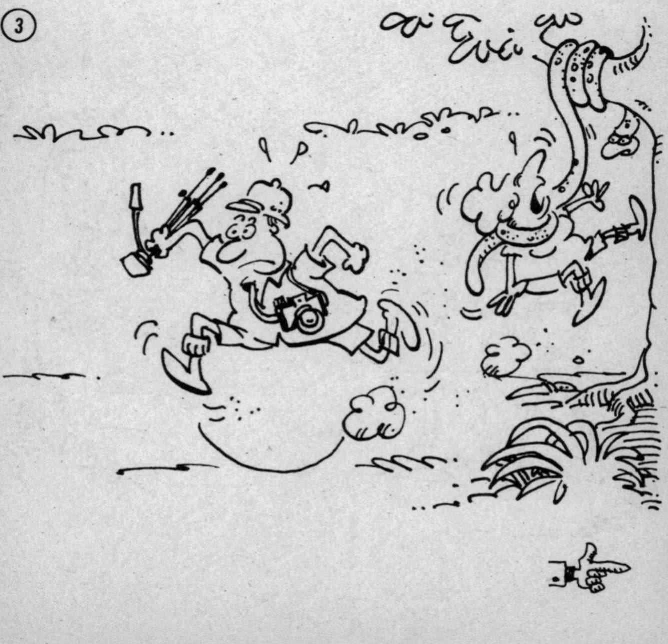

4

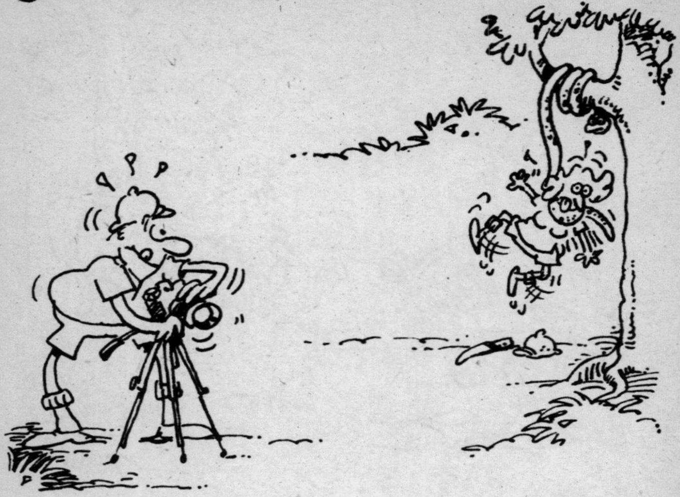

5

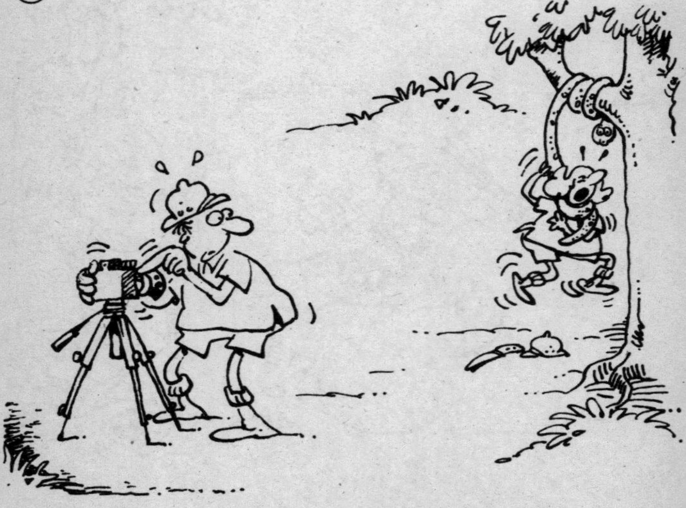

6

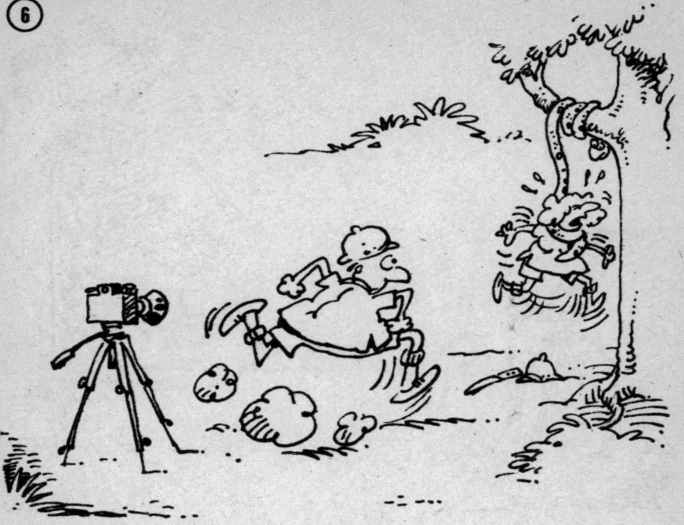

7

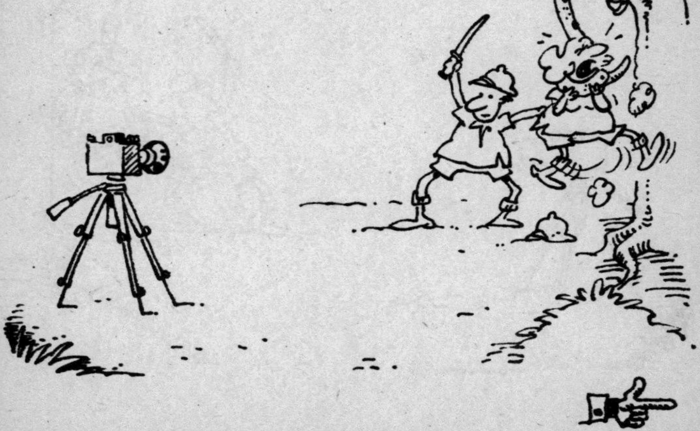

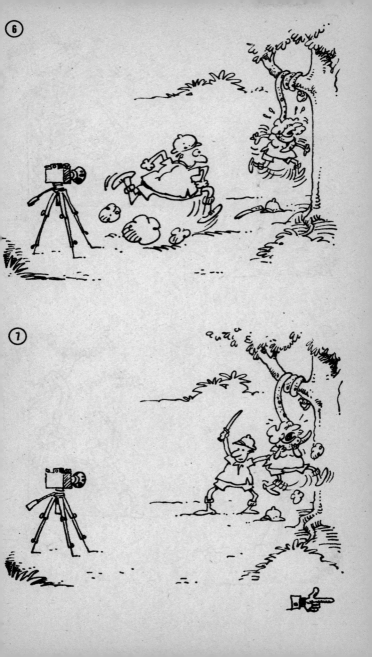

8

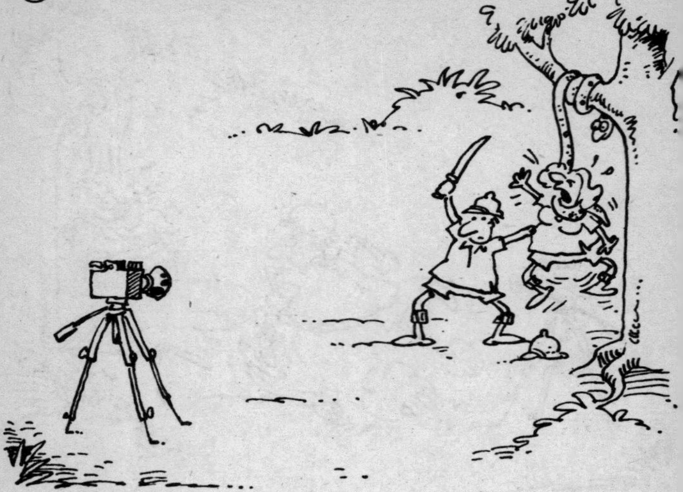

9

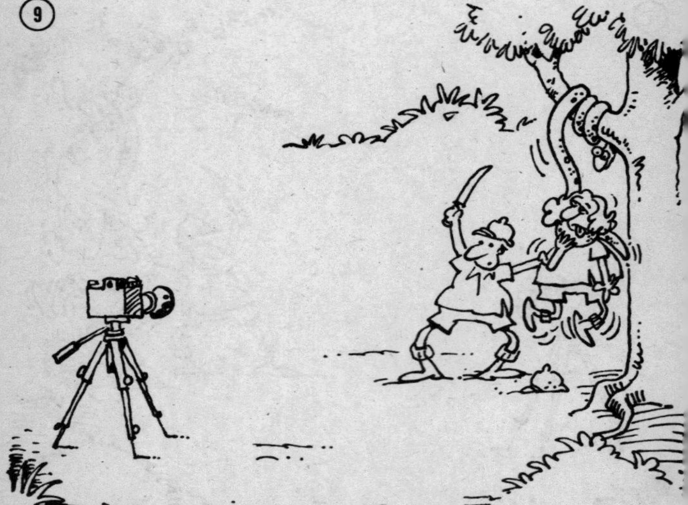

10

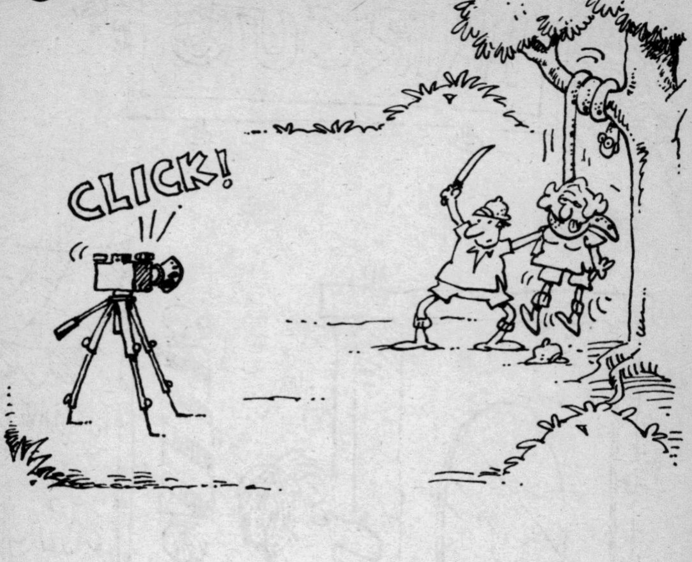
CLICK!

11

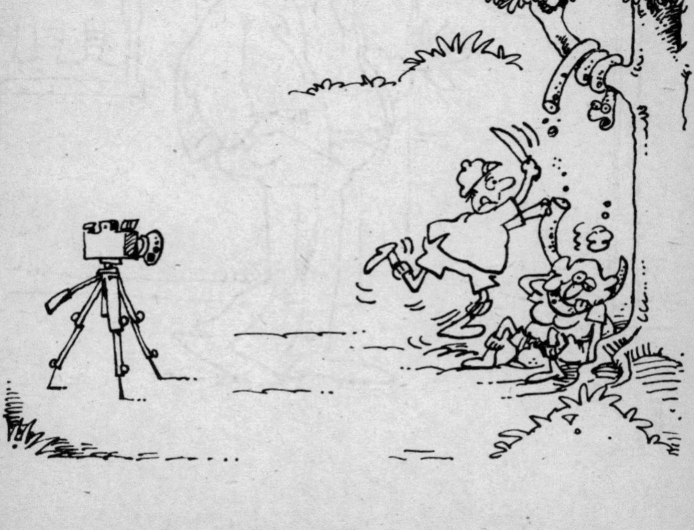

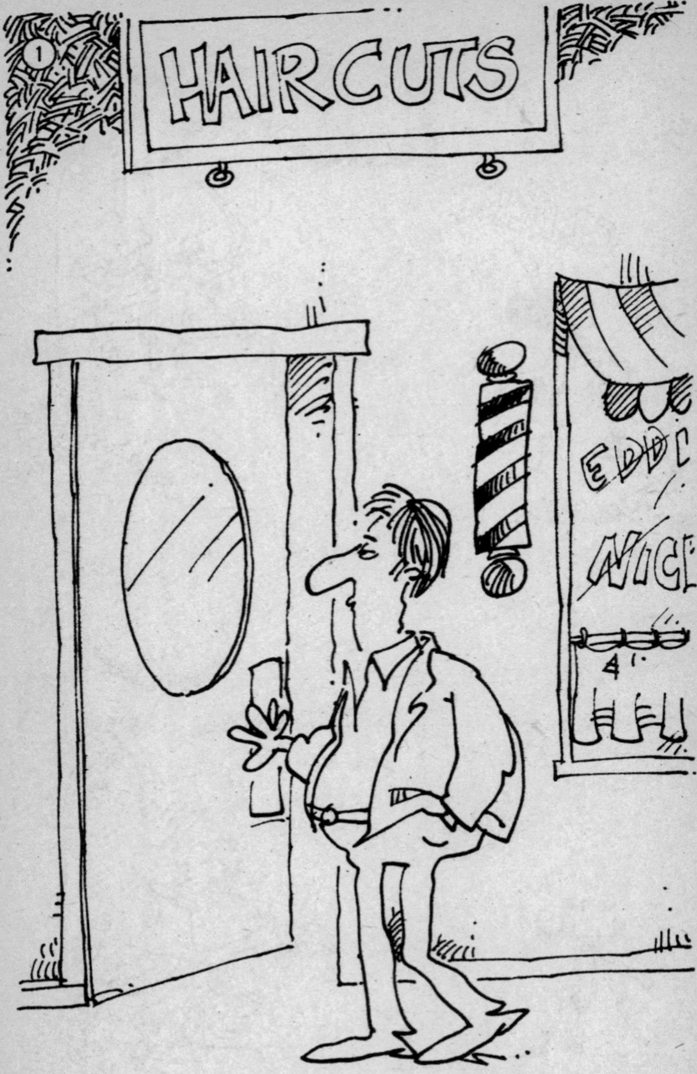
HAIRCUTS

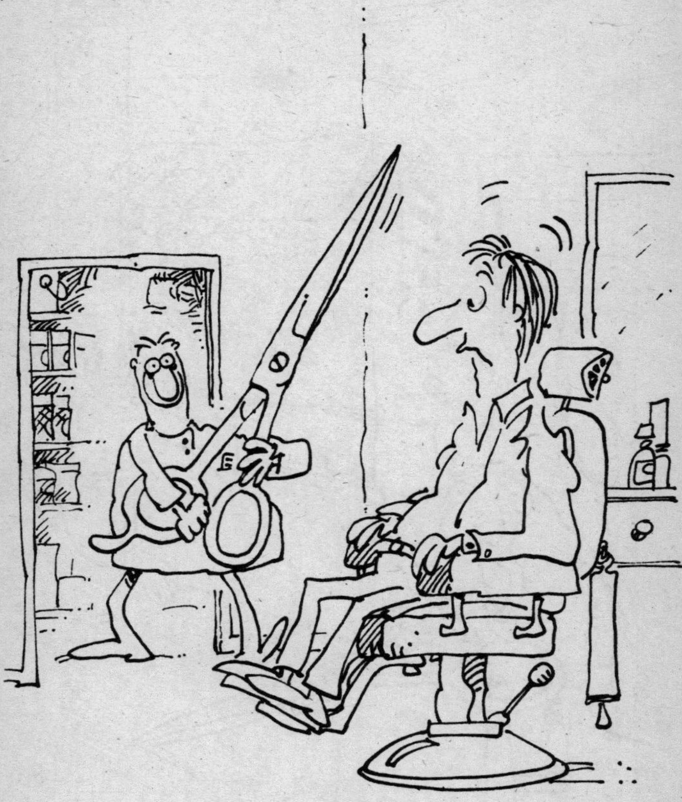

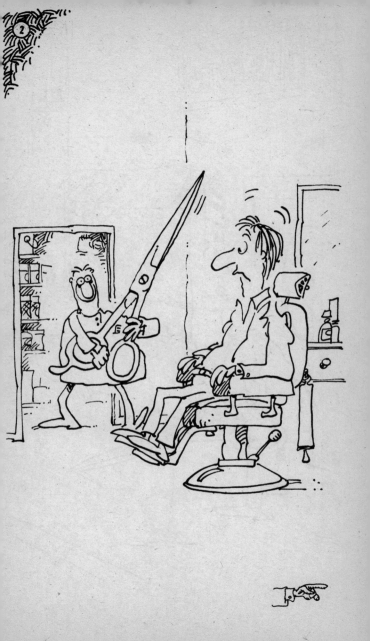

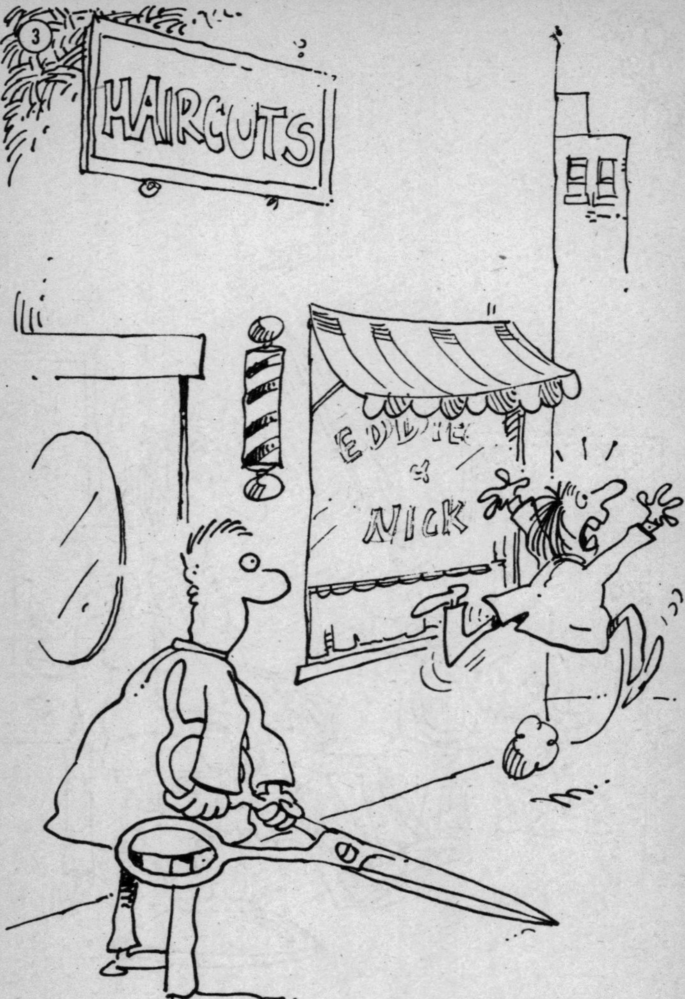
3
HAIRCUTS
EDDIE
&
NICK

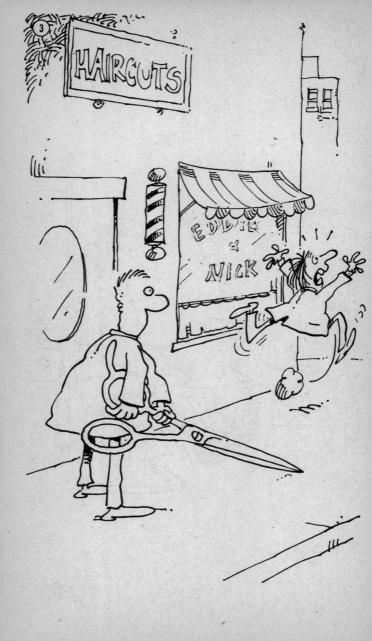

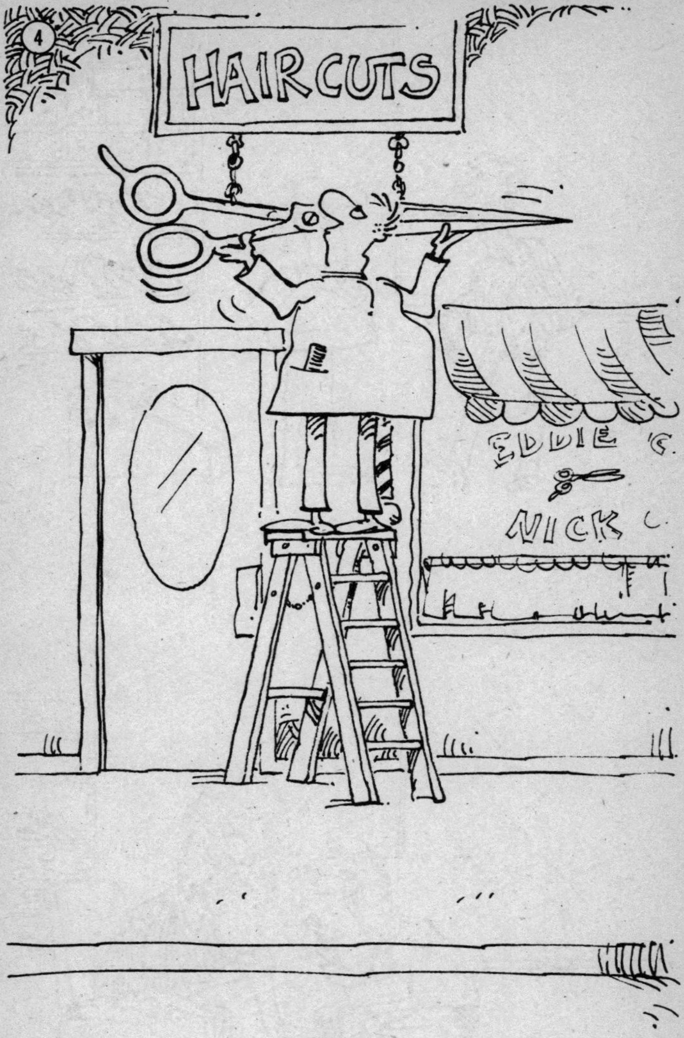
4
HAIR CUTS
EDDIE
NICK

1

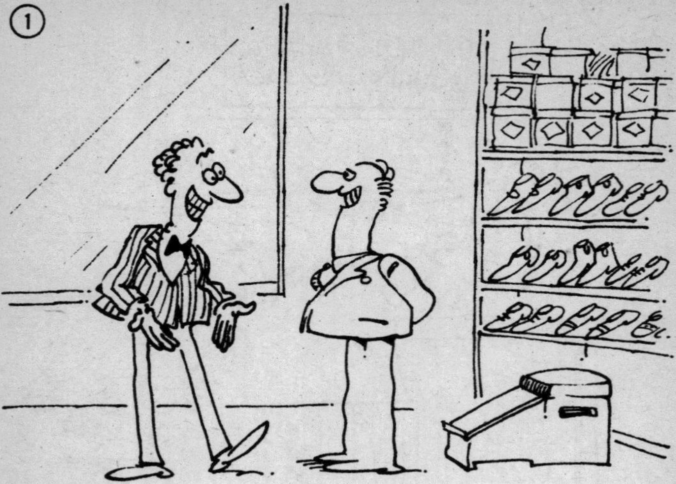

2

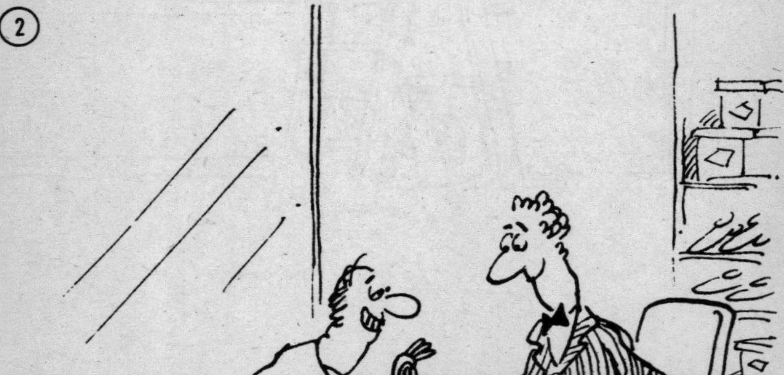

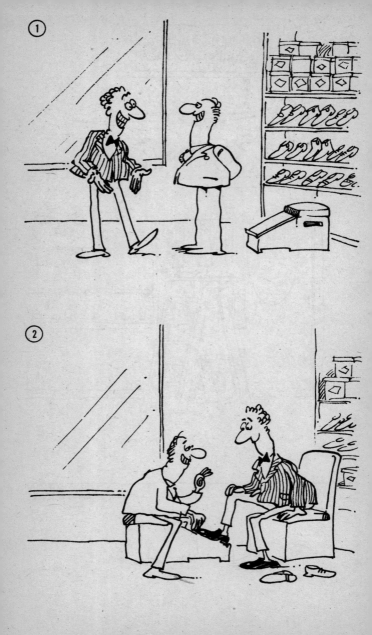

3

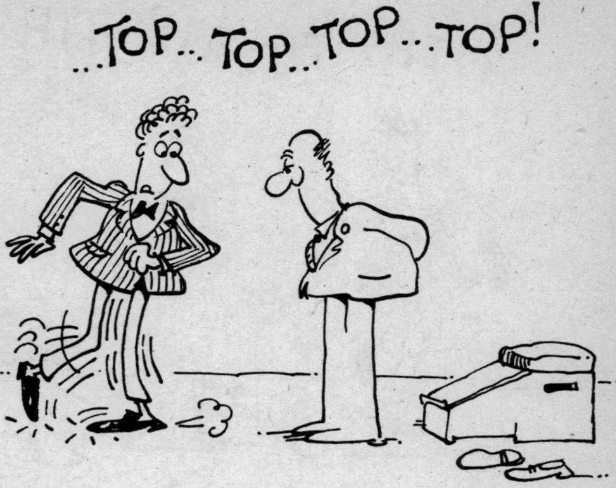
...TOP... TOP... TOP... TOP!

4

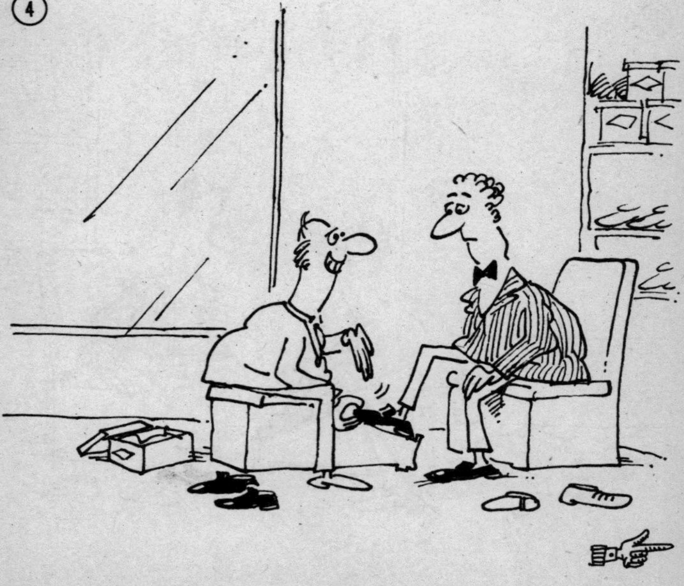

5

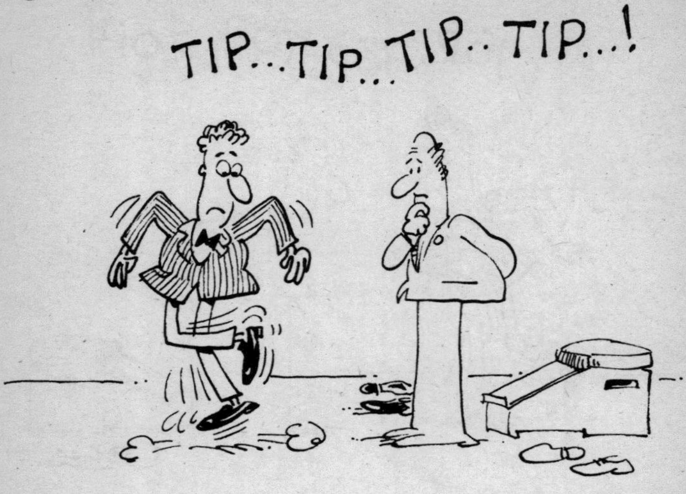
TIP...TIP...TIP...TIP...!

6

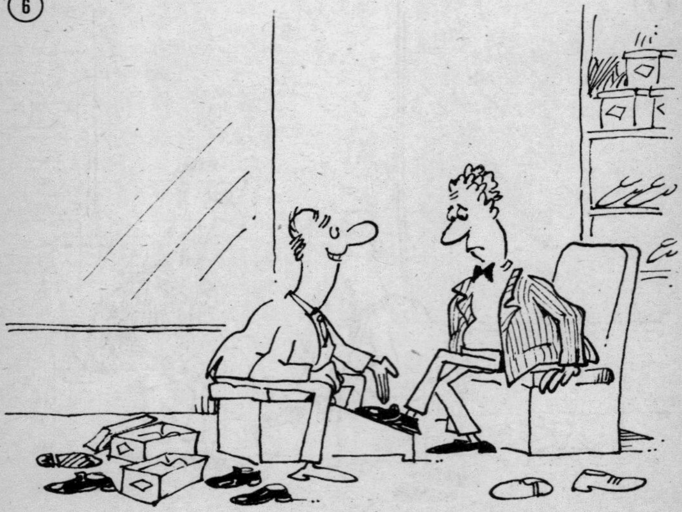

7

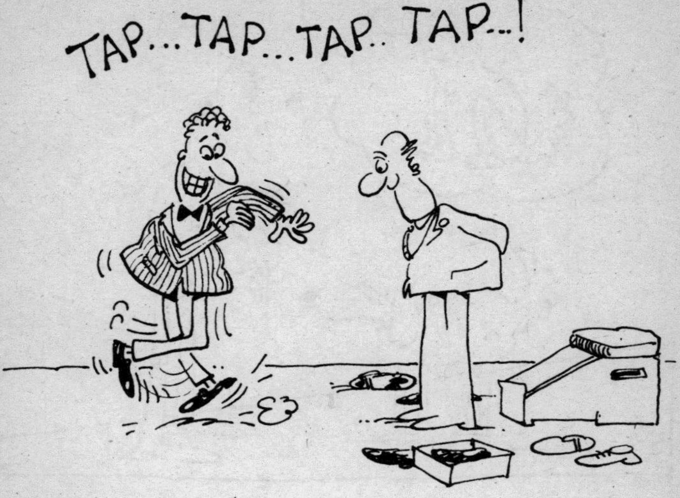
TAP...TAP...TAP.. TAP...!

8

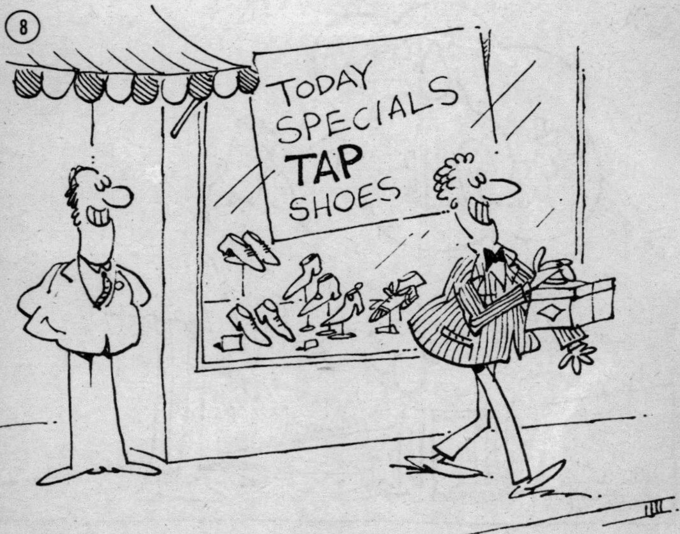
TODAY
SPECIALS
TAP
SHOES

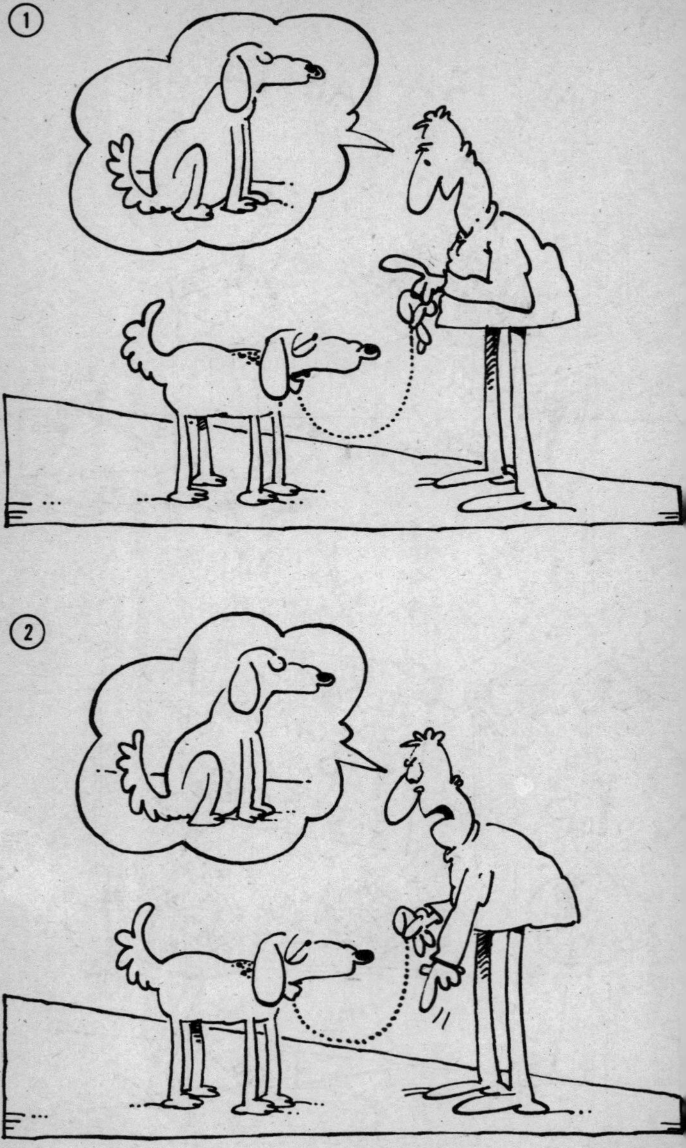
1
2

3

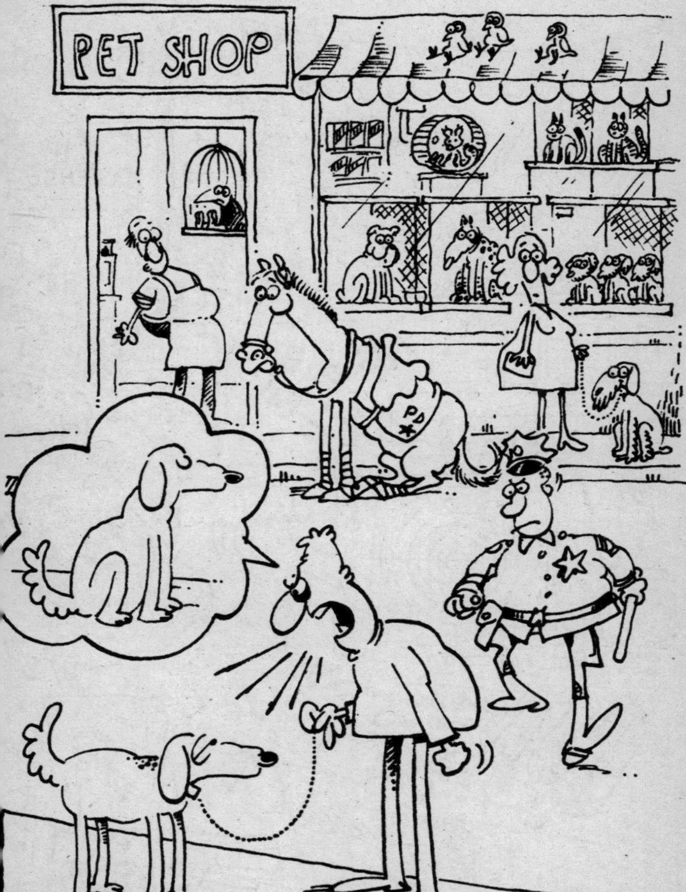
PET SHOP
PD

1

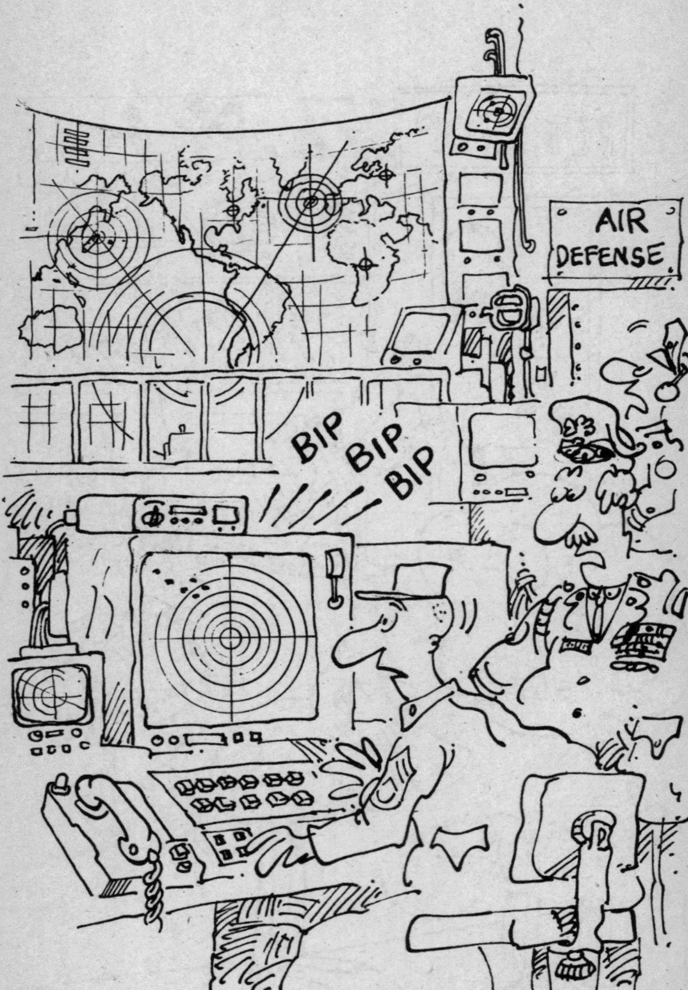
AIR DEFENSE
BIP
BIP
BIP

2

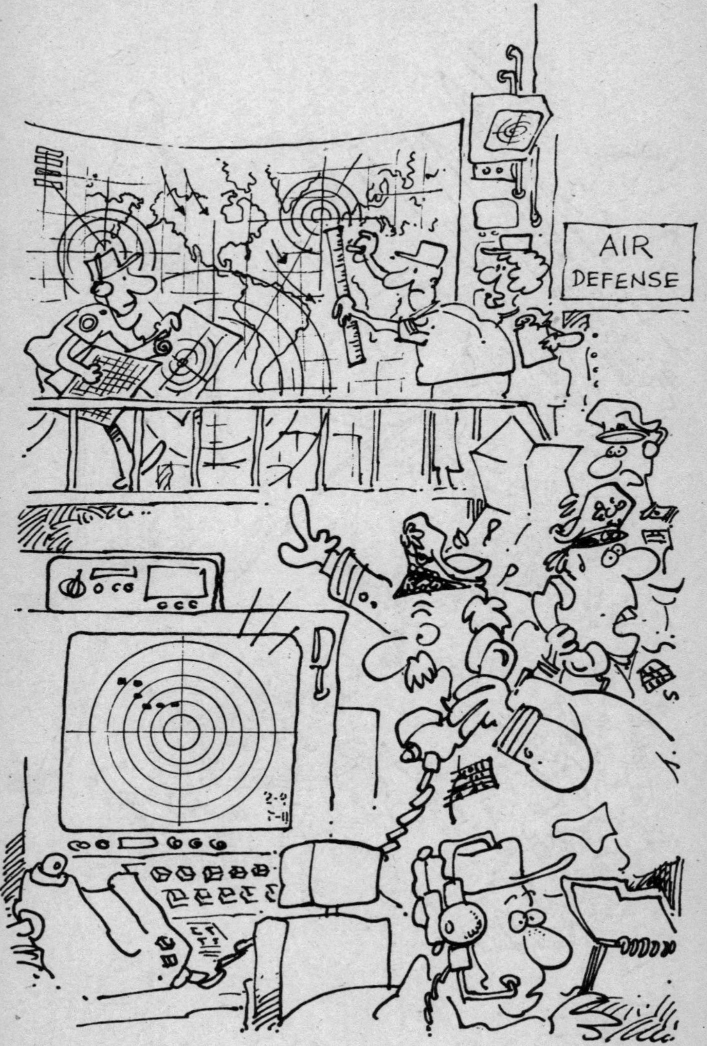
AIR
DEFENSE

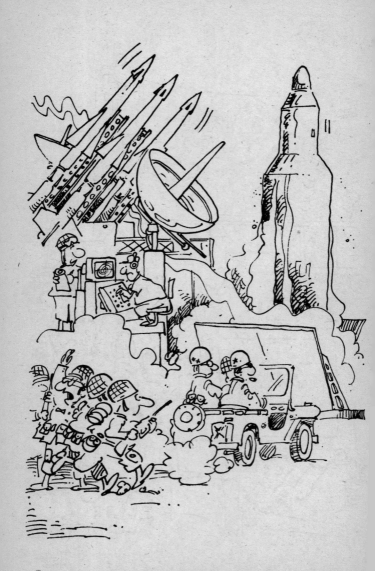

4

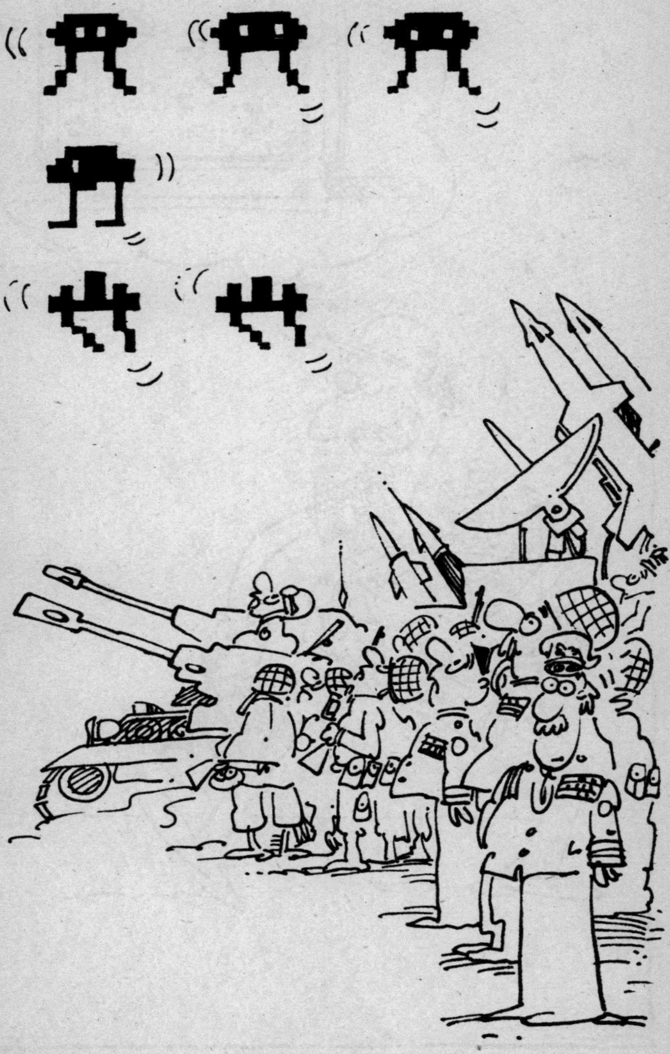

1

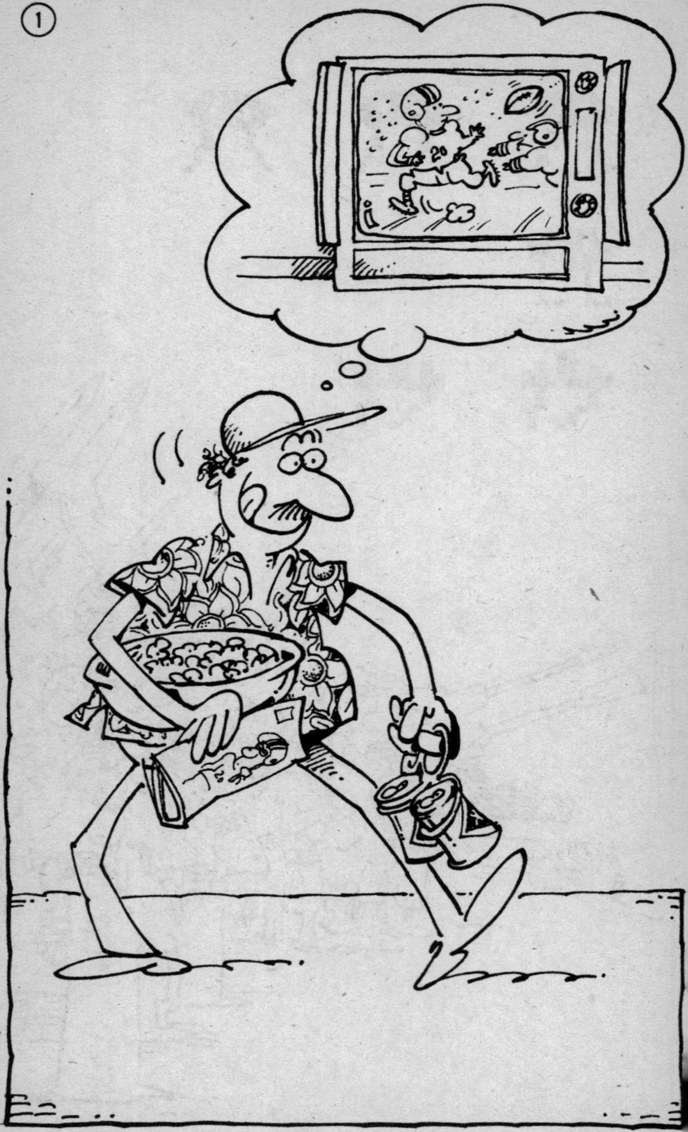

2

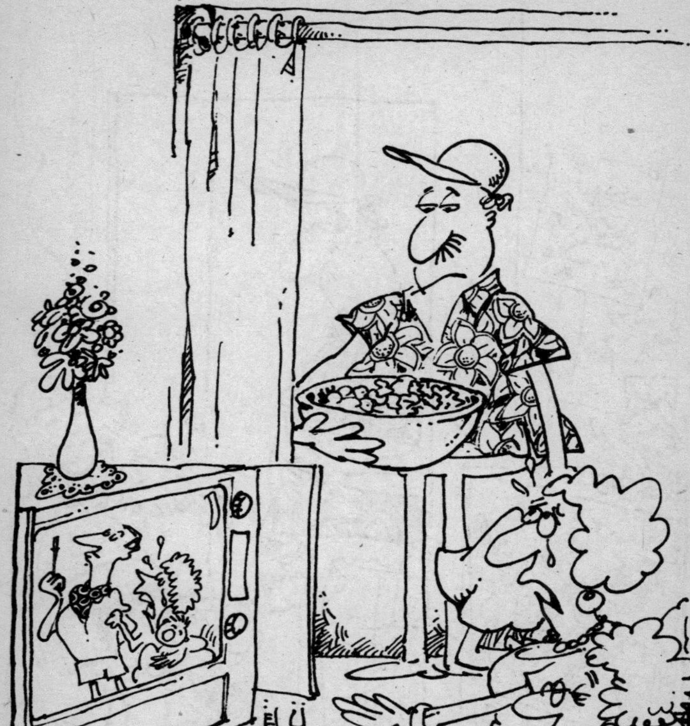

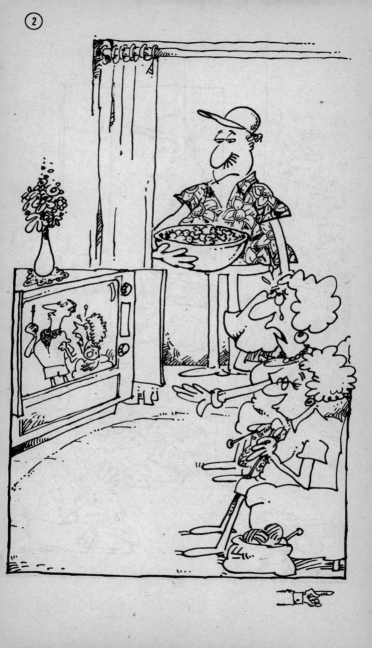

3

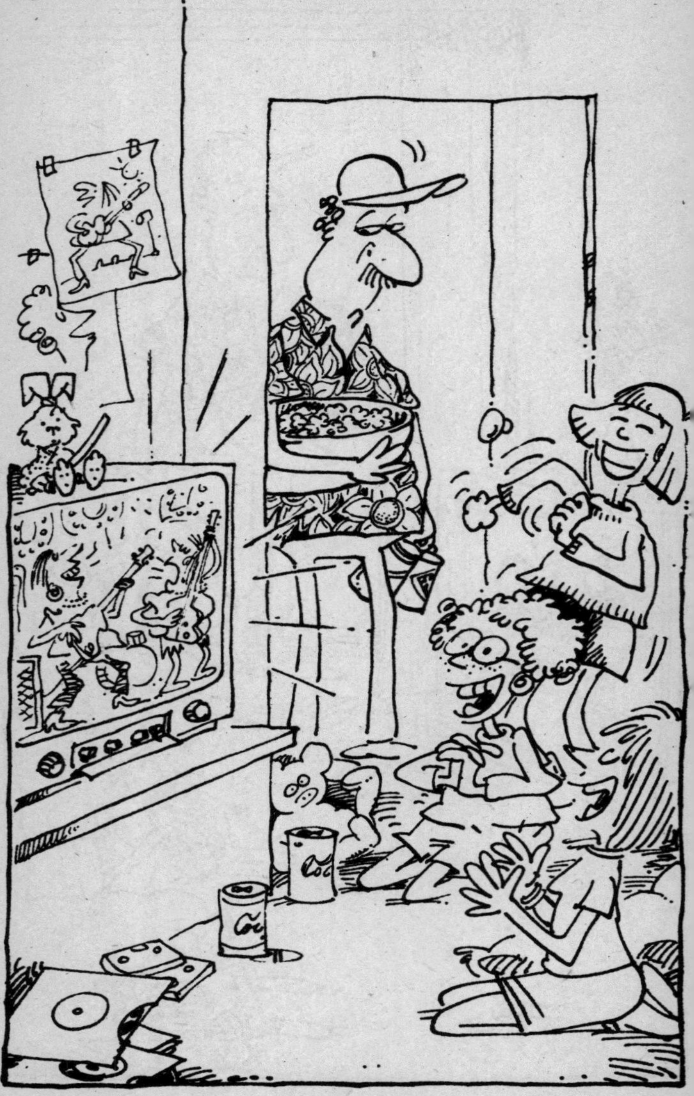

4

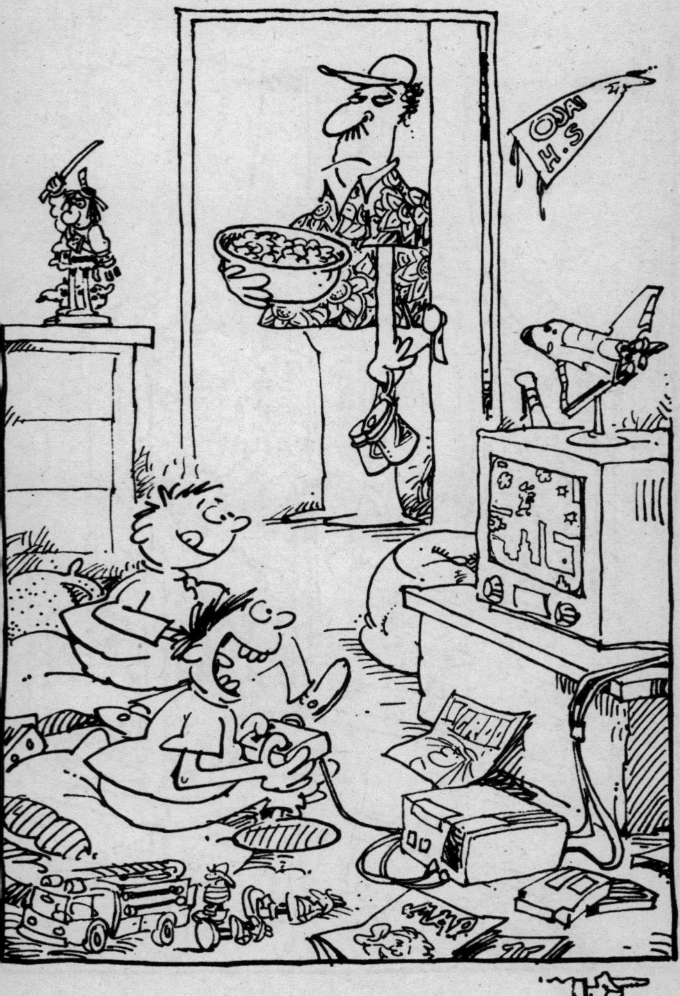
OJAI
H.S

5

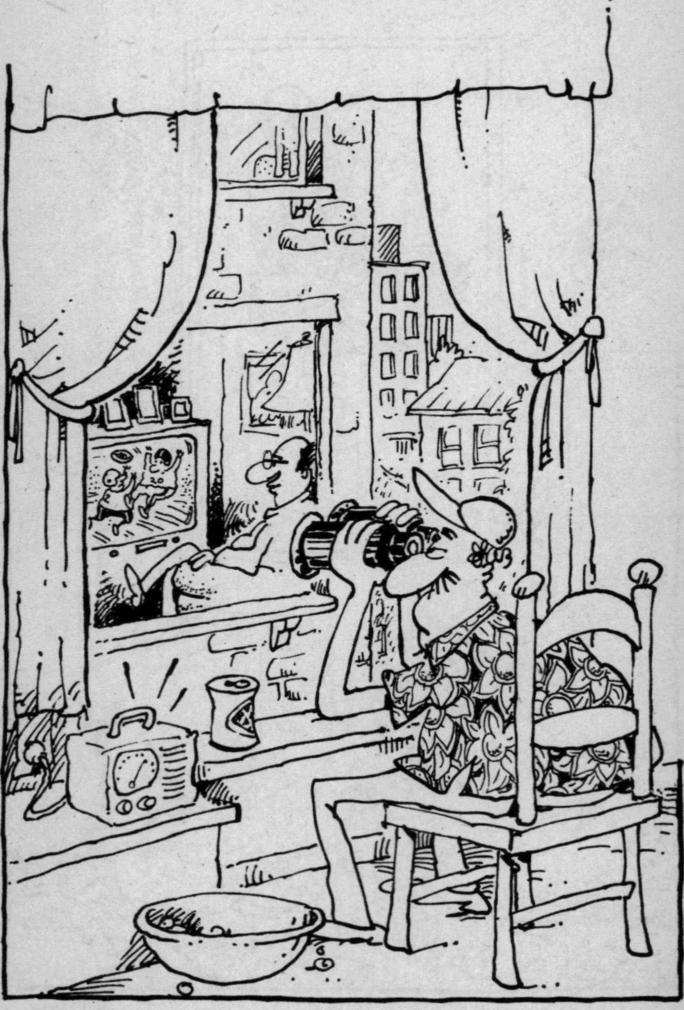

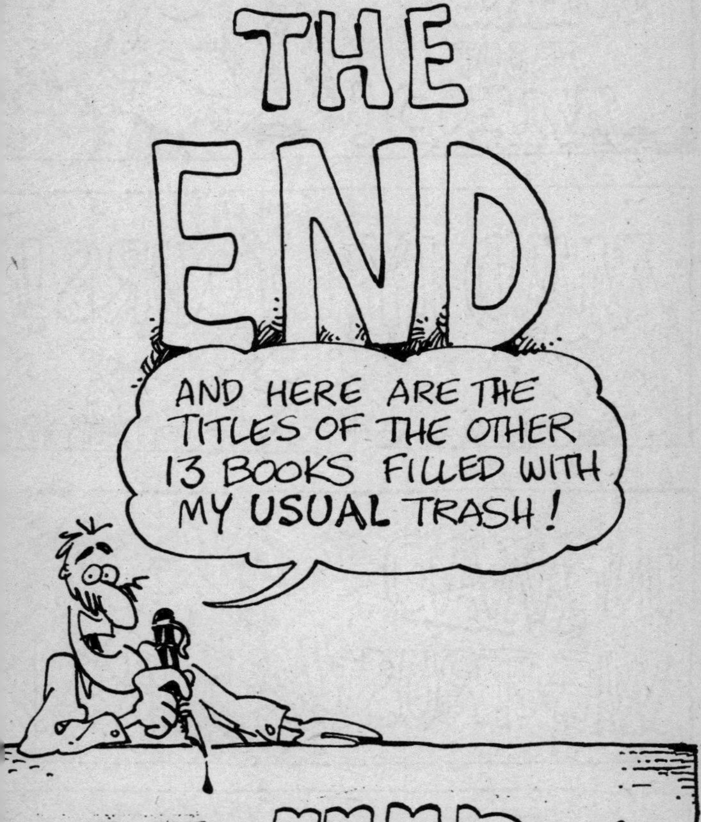
THE END
AND HERE ARE THE TITLES OF THE OTHER 13 BOOKS FILLED WITH MY USUAL TRASH!
VIVA MAD

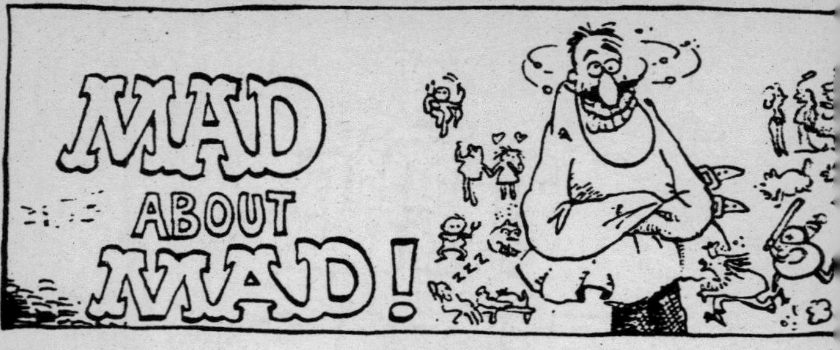
MAD
ABOUT
MAD!

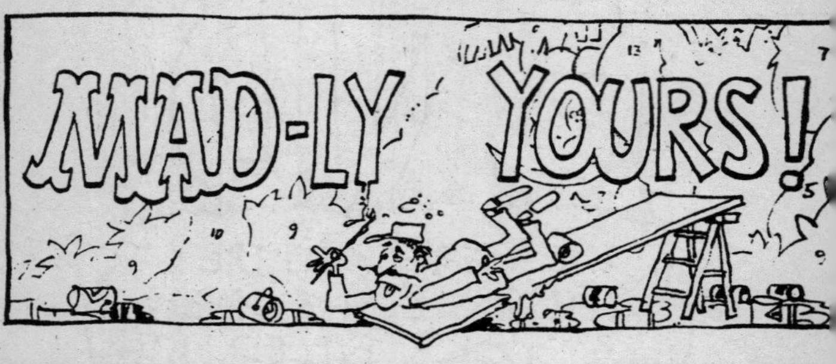
MAD-LY YOURS!

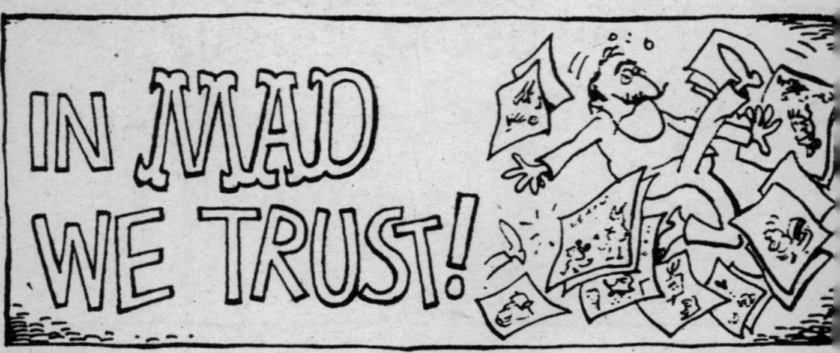
IN MAD
WE TRUST!

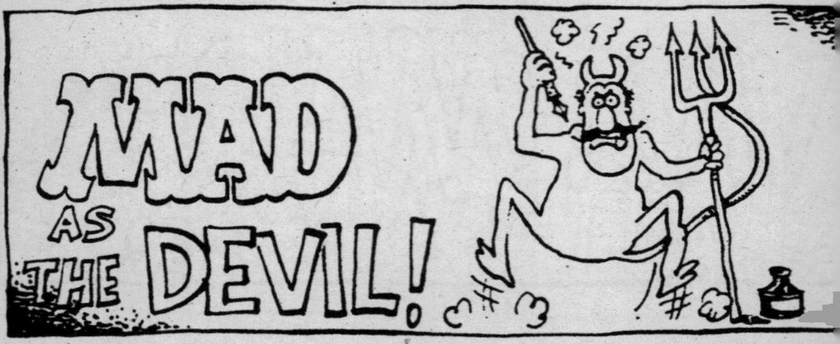
MAD
AS
THE DEVIL!

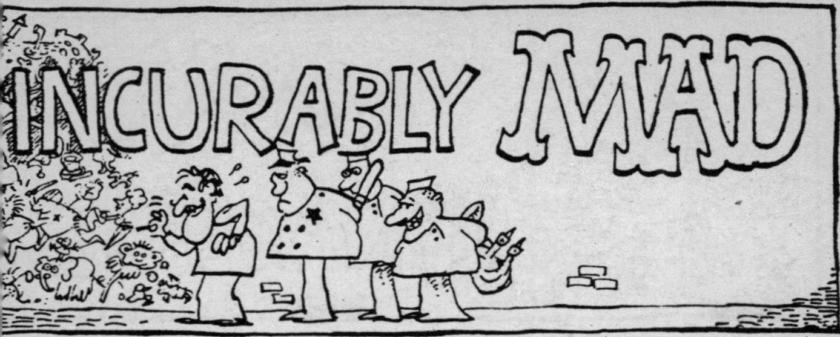
INCURABLY MAD

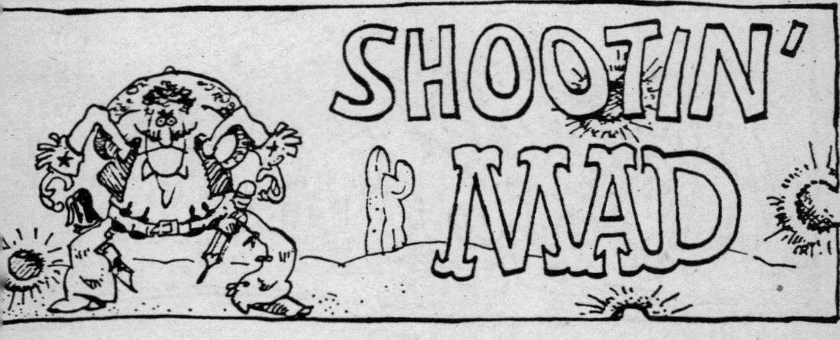
SHOOTIN' MAD

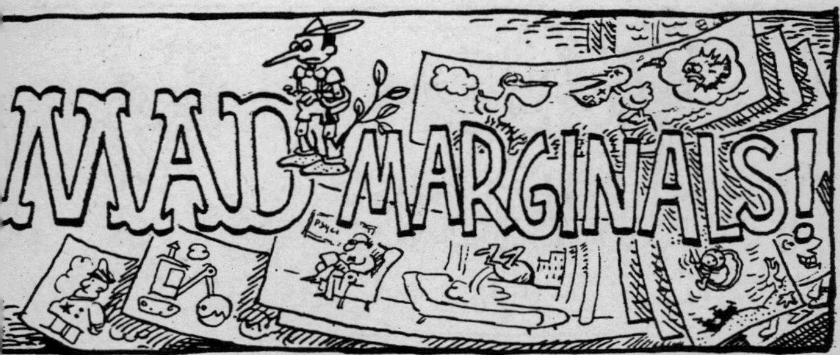
MAD MARGINALS!

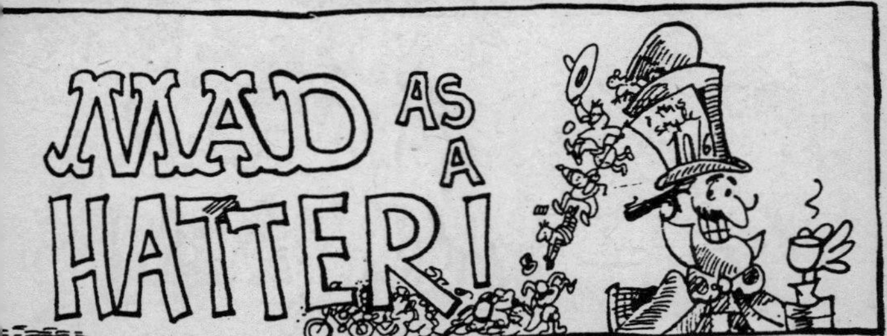
MAD AS A HATTER!

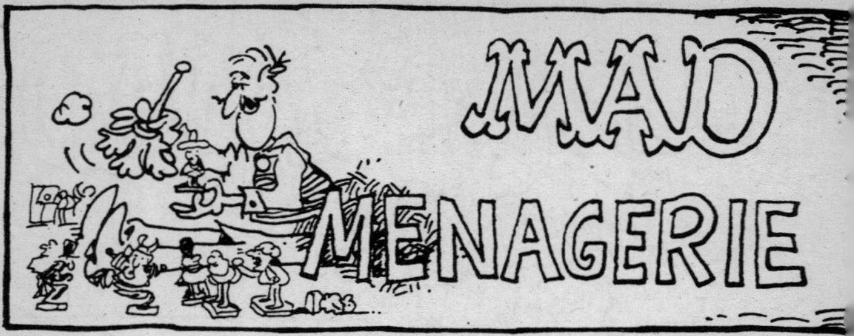
MAD
MENAGERIE

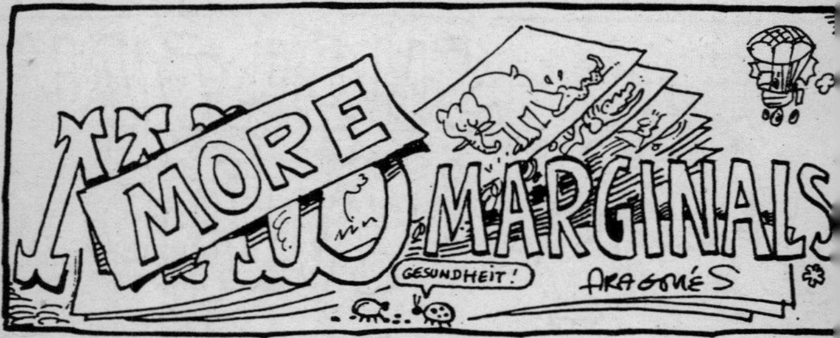
MORE
MAD
MARGINALS
GESUNDHEIT!
ARAGONÉS

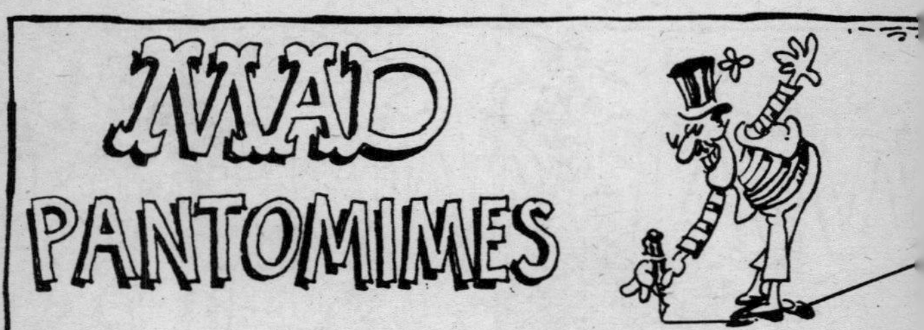
MAD
PANTOMIMES

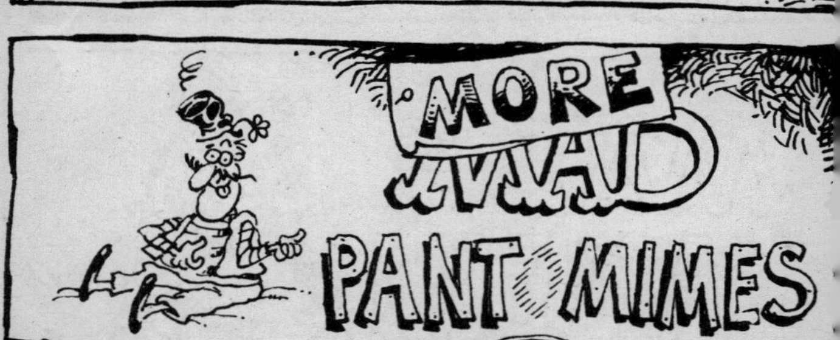
MORE
MAD
PANTOMIMES